ADVANCE PRAISE FOR

After the Pain

"At last, a serious, sophisticated, audacious collection of scholarly essays worthy of the reach and imagination of Gayl Jones's craft. *After the Pain* approaches Jones's career with the fresh eyes of critics willfully unencumbered by the obscurant niceties of traditional African American literary criticism. Mills and Mitchell have done the fields of African American and American literature an incalculable service. Gayl Jones is a literary giant and to continue to pretend not to notice her genius, because we have not yet wholly grasped it, diminishes us more than her. Compellingly, *After the Pain* challenges the black literary orthodoxy by calling into question Jones's exclusion from it. Its unified labor to reclaim Gayl Jones shows a caring for Jones, for black women writers, and for the truth of race, sex, and silenced subjects seldom achieved in critical collections. *After the Pain* is a necessary work. Most necessary."

*Maurice O. Wallace, Associate Professor of English
and Associate Professor of African & African American Studies, Duke University*

"Gayl Jones is one of the most provocative African American writers of the second half of the twentieth century, and she has long deserved the keen and perceptive examination of her work offered here. This landmark collection of illuminating essays covers the full range of Jones's work, from her controversial *Corregidora* and *Eva's Man* to her more recent and remarkable *Mosquito*. This anthology will prove indispensable to students, scholars, and teachers alike—to those who read Jones as well as those who study her sharp, unflinching portrayals of women and men struggling with the complex and contradictory inheritance of North American slavery. Every page flashes with the knife of close insight."

Jennifer Cognard-Black, Assistant Professor of English, St. Mary's College of Maryland

"With the publication of *After the Pain: Critical Essays on Gayl Jones*, Fiona Mills and Keith B. Mitchell take up the long overdue task of retrieving Jones from the margins of African American literary studies. Their work of reclamation is indeed comparable to Alice Walker's artistic 'excavation' in the 1970s of Zora Neale Hurston's œuvre. The conclusions drawn in these sophisticated, theoretically dexterous essays are as startling and imaginative as the subject herself. Undoubtedly, this book will re-map the boundaries of the African American literary landscape and help situate Jones into her deserved place as a major voice within the canon. This pioneering work will fill a critical lacuna in Jones scholarship, introduce and re-introduce an artist whose rich and voluminous writings merit a wider readership, and stimulate further critical interrogation of an iconoclastic, nuanced author whose fiction defies facile literary categorization."

Keith Clark, Associate Professor of English and African American Studies,
George Mason University

After
 the
Pain

AFRICAN AMERICAN LITERATURE AND CULTURE

Expanding and Exploding the Boundaries

Carlyle V. Thompson
General Editor

Vol. 8

PETER LANG
New York • Washington, D.C./Baltimore • Bern
Frankfurt am Main • Berlin • Brussels • Vienna • Oxford

After the Pain

CRITICAL ESSAYS ON GAYL JONES

FIONA MILLS, EDITOR
KEITH MITCHELL, ASSISTANT EDITOR

PETER LANG
New York • Washington, D.C./Baltimore • Bern
Frankfurt am Main • Berlin • Brussels • Vienna • Oxford

Library of Congress Cataloging-in-Publication Data

After the pain : critical essays on Gayl Jones /
Fiona Mills, editor, and Keith B. Mitchell, assistant editor.
p. cm. — (African-American literature and culture; v. 8)
Includes bibliographical references.
1. Jones, Gayl—Criticism and interpretation. 2. Feminism and
Literature—History—20th century. 3. African American women
—Intellectual life. 4. African American women in literature.
5. Caribbean Area—In literature. 6. African Americans in literature.
7. Sex role in literature. 8. Brazil—In literature. I. Mills, Fiona.
II. Mitchell, Keith B. III. Series.
PS3560.O483Z69   813'.54—dc22   2006008938
ISBN 0-8204-7838-5
ISSN 1528-3887

Bibliographic information published by **Die Deutsche Bibliothek**.
Die Deutsche Bibliothek lists this publication in the "Deutsche
Nationalbibliografie"; detailed bibliographic data is available
on the Internet at http://dnb.ddb.de/.

Cover art,"Las Tortugas," by Marta Ayala
Cover design by Lisa Barfield

© 2006 Peter Lang Publishing, Inc., New York
29 Broadway, New York, NY 10006
www.peterlang.com

All rights reserved.
Reprint or reproduction, even partially, in all forms such as microfilm,
xerography, microfiche, microcard, and offset strictly prohibited.

Reflecting back while looking towards the future.

In loving memory of Richard Phillip Mills, Jr.

for Savannah Kelly

Contents

Foreword..ix
    Trudier Harris

Acknowledgments..xv

After the Pain: An Introduction...1
    Fiona Mills and Keith B. Mitchell

1. Identity and Conceptual Limitation in Gayl Jones's
   The Healing: From Turtle to Human Being................................11
       Heather E. Epes

2. Textual Transfigurations and Female Metamorphosis:
   Reading Gayl Jones's *The Healing*..31
       Shubha Venugopal

3. From Mules to Turtle and Unicorn Women: The Gender-Folk
   Revolution and the Legacy of the Obeah in Gayl Jones's
   The Healing..65
       L.H. Stallings

4. Telling the Untold Tale: Afro-Latino/a Identifications
   in the Work of Gayl Jones..91
       Fiona Mills

5. "reads kinda like jazz in they rhythm": Gayl Jones's
   Recent Jazz Conversations...117
       Jill Terry

CONTENTS

6. Interruptions: Tradition, Borders, and Narrative
   in Gayl Jones's *Mosquito*..137
   Sarika Chandra

7. "Trouble in Mind": (Re)visioning Myth, Sexuality and Race
   in Gayl Jones's *Corregidora*...155
   Keith B. Mitchell

8. Prison Narratives, Narrative Prisons: Incarcerated Women
   Reading Gayl Jones's *Eva's Man*..173
   Megan Sweeney

9. Unsilencing Lesbianism in the Early Fiction of Gayl Jones ...203
   Thomas Fahy

10. Things Deserving Echoes: Gayl Jones's Liberating Poetry.....221
    Howard Rambsy II

11. Resistance, Reappropriation, and Reconciliation: The Blues
    and Flying Africans in Gayl Jones's *Song for Anninho*............241
    Lovalerie King

Afterword: Voicing Gayl Jones..259
   Keith Byerman

List of Contributors..263

Foreword

Anomaly. Phenomenon. These two words perhaps describe Gayl Jones and her literary career more than any others that come immediately to mind. Both have inherent connotations of going against the grain, of being outside, above, or beyond established traditions or easily accepted norms. They also have the power to distance or isolate the writer from her contemporaries as well as from those who preceded and followed her, and place her outside traditional critical and scholarly considerations. Writers who write against the grain of an established tradition—even a minority established tradition—pay the price of being less often written about or less often included in scholarly projects that capture that tradition. For Gayl Jones, the quintessential outsider, these two words reflect a history of perception as well as a history of response to her as human being and as literary artist. The peculiar position into which she has been placed, despite the recognized high quality of her work, warrants this volume of new essays that will undoubtedly lead to reevaluation of Jones's anomalous, phenomenal status.

Jones is an anomaly, first of all, because her educational background is much more comparable to that of African American scholars and professors than to that of African American writers. Whereas many of African America's most famous literary figures, such as Richard Wright and James Baldwin, were largely self-taught in their craft, or received some college or master's level training, as Ralph Ellison, Alice Walker, and Toni Morrison did, Jones received her Ph.D. from prestigious Brown University. From the moment she entered the literary profession, therefore, her credentials enabled her to evaluate other writers in scholarly venues just as she was simultaneously being evaluated by critics and scholars. When she published

Liberating Voices: Oral Tradition in African American Literature (1991), in which she explored several forms of African American folk and popular traditions and evaluated their impact on a variety of writers, including Langston Hughes, Sterling Brown, Zora Neale Hurston, Ralph Ellison, and Ernest Gaines, she entered an arena shared by few other writers. Ellison's *Shadow and Act* (1964) and Toni Morrison's *Playing in the Dark* (1992) certainly illustrate African American writers engaged in the act of critical commentary, but their essays do not take the shape of traditional literary scholarship that defines Jones's work.

Jones is an anomaly as well because her imaginative creations do not superficially intersect with the more obvious defining characteristics of African American literature. Rather than portray African American characters in her novels, short fiction, and poetry who are immediately and directly in conflict with the larger white American society, as much African American literature does, Jones elects a more distant geography for conflict in *Corregidora* (1975), her first novel. By locating the site of European/African conflict in Brazil and its consequences on American soil, Jones paints on a larger canvas than many other African American writers do. The same is true with her portrayal of the wars between enslaved African-Brazilians and the Portuguese in her long poem, *Song for Anninho* (1981). For Jones, the world of enslavement and the racial/sexual/psychological consequences of enslavement are much larger than U.S. soil—even when they are played out on that soil. Her recognition and creative enactment of her belief thereby placed her in solitary confinement as far as African American literary expectations were concerned.

Thus writing in bas relief against the perceived African American literary geographical tradition, Jones similarly expands her focus for literary exploration. The white men who considered themselves masters of enslaved people may have been cruel, but their sixteenth-through nineteenth-century atrocities are far removed from the scenes of black people exploiting each other sexually and psychologically in twentieth-century America. Jones dares to imply, therefore, that problems frequently inherent in black communities are as much intraracial as they are interracial. Black people can give each other the racial blues, Jones's works make clear, as easily as white people can effect that condition against blacks. This was not the party line that any Bible-toting Black Aesthetic practitioner might have deemed appropriate for the 1970s, when so many other black writers were celebrating the newly found positive expressions of blackness and beauty that overwhelmingly resulted from the politically transforming 1960s. How could this uppity, young black woman writer enter the literary scene and dare to paint African American men as brutally violent toward and psychologically imprisoning of black women? The answer to the question is implied in the reception as well as in the criticism of Jones's work. Several very staid, conservative African American male critics took swipes at Jones after the publication of her first two books to illustrate where they thought she had strayed from the straight and narrow path of African American literary uplift.

Such critical response was especially intense with *Eva's Man* (1976), Jones's second novel. Not only did Jones locate sexual conflict and physical violence within an African American framework, thus questioning the basic health of male/female relationships in that context, but she painted a picture of an African American male psychologically and literally imprisoning an African American female—or at least creating an environment in which her ability to leave is not matched by her comfort level in attempting to leave. When that female retaliates by poisoning the black man and biting off his penis, the African American literary critical house almost came tumbling down around Jones's head. She was already considered anomalous enough for having ventured onto Brazilian soil (sane black writers who focused on foreign soil, so this logic would go, chose equally sane places such as Scandinavia and France on which to locate their black characters) and suggesting that, as a consequence of their ancestors' experiences there, black people in America enslave themselves and each other. Now she added insult to injury by positing that murder and castration could occur just as easily *within* black communities, with black folks as perpetrators, as they could occur with European Americans perpetrating such acts against people of African descent.

Perhaps more than this insult, however, is the perception that Jones seems to legitimize mental institutionalization as an option for an African American female character and, as a result of that institutionalization, the same-sex relationship that ensues from it. There is perhaps no taboo more assiduously avoided in African American literature than lesbianism. Ann Allen Shockley's *Loving Her* (1974) and *Say Jesus and Come to Me* (1982), for example, are far less palatable to African American readers and scholars than James Baldwin's *Giovanni's Room* (1953). For Jones to portray a character who embraces such an alternative sexuality at the end of *Eva's Man* was a bit more than most readers and scholars could take. Jones thus entered into a set-aside literary critical space, where shock value for discussion earned more accolades than serious critical engagement. Indeed, some male readers found Jones's representation of Eva to be a direct affront to them. Because Eva did not resonate with any canonical African American literary experience to which readers and scholars could point, she and her story have thus received less critical commentary than might otherwise have been the case.

To be an anomaly in African American literature—as a writer or as a literary work—has a direct impact upon perception, study, and research. After all, African American college teachers are not appreciably unlike their non-African American counterparts; they teach the familiar, the already-taught, the traditional, and the readily available. Consequently, Gayl Jones, with her slightly askew slant on African American experience, has earned far less sustained critical attention than black writers whose literary outputs are comparable to hers. Scholars were not quite sure what to do with the work, how to get a hold on it for the focus of lengthy articles or book-length studies.

While critical attention to her works may have lagged, the gossip mill about Jones's life has not. In this arena, Gayl Jones is a phenomenon. The lives of few literary artists become the subjects of media, mail, email, and critical focus as has that of Gayl Jones. Her legendary shyness has perhaps attained a level comparable to her outlandish writings, as some would label them. Her disappearance from the University of Michigan, along with her male partner, under mysterious circumstances in 1985 made her into a legend. Her whereabouts over the next ten years enhanced her legendary status, as there were ambiguous communications from her from various locations in Europe, offering sometimes incoherent defenses of the person with whom she left Michigan (there were apparently some legal implications). Interest in her life was renewed when it was discovered, in the late 1990s, that she was back in the United States, in Kentucky, living with the man with whom she disappeared in 1985. That voyeuristic interest reached a crescendo of curiosity and titillation when, as newspapers reported the incident, her partner committed suicide rather than be taken into custody by local police. The nature of his wrongdoing was not clear. Nor was Jones's status, for she was reputed to have been hospitalized after the incident.

Phenomenon. Anomaly. Legend. Fact. Reality. With Gayl Jones, it is difficult to know at times where one leaves off and another begins. What *is* clear is that Jones was amazingly productive during her so-called disappearance. She furthered her adeptness for languages by studying several and by publishing in German. She produced two additional novels that are as unusual as her first two. They continue the pattern she established of being her own best influence, following her own voice, indeed establishing her own tradition. *The Healing* (1998) focuses on a black woman spiritualist/healer who is also a gambler and engages in rather questionable sexual practices. As with *Corregidora* and *Eva's Man,* Jones is not concerned about fitting into any pre-existing mold of representation of black female character. Her major concern for accuracy in representation is in capturing the vernacular voice of her characters. The same is true of *Mosquito* (1999), which not only challenges/expands representation of black female characters by portraying a black woman on the Texas/Mexican border who drives an eighteen-wheeler for a living, but meanders its way in doing so. Jones seems to feel little obligation to respect a traditional sense of novelistic narration even as she meticulously respects African American orality and voice.

It is also clear that Jones is not surrounded by a nurturing community of black writers or scholars. She is in the precarious position of being the anomaly about whom others seek information through roundabout means. Hearsay and rumor take the place of dissertations and books. Such practices merely perpetuate the legendary status that continues to surround Jones, to set her apart. She is out there, somewhere, one of our better known African American writers, and yet she remains, to a large extent, unclaimed.

This volume, then, is a part of that reclamation process. These young scholars have recognized the quality of Jones's work, have met her at a moment separated from historical anomalization and legend-making, and have decided to close the clear lack of critical attention to her works by focusing exclusively on them in these essays. For their centering of Jones as a writer whose works deserve more critical commentary than her life, these young editors and writers have done yeoman service. Fiona Mills and Keith B. Mitchell, who have edited this volume, have joined their contributors in learning about Jones in contexts less clouded with the surrounding circumstances of Jones's life or the staid expectations of African American literary conventions and conventional scholarship. They have met the works where they live and breathe, and they are thereby offering to many in the larger scholarly community the opportunity to reacquaint themselves with what Jones offers the African American literary tradition and with what she offers the enterprise of scholarly inquiry.

Designed to focus primarily on Jones's works, this collection of essays will undoubtedly become a mainstay in African American literary scholarship. These new eyes, new voices, and new critical insights promise to encourage older scholars to re-engage Jones's contributions to African American literature and what less-blinded commentary on her work can offer to that scholarly tradition. The editors and contributors are to be commended for initiating and bringing this project to fruition. It will be invaluable to readers, teachers, and scholars who seek truth over rumor and legend, who prefer reality to distant phenomenon, and who desire to become seriously engaged with African American literature in its multiplicity of manifestations.

Trudier Harris
J. Carlyle Sitterson Professor of English
The University of North Carolina at Chapel Hill

Acknowledgments

As I near completion of this long, long-awaited project, I find that I have much to be thankful for and many to whom I owe deep gratitude. First and foremost, I am grateful to my treasured friends Thomas Fahy and Keith B. Mitchell, also my Assistant Editor. I recall fondly a day many years ago when the three of us sat in the warm North Carolina sun and came up with the idea for this project given our mutual interest in Gayl Jones. Since then, both Tom and Keith have provided much-needed insight, helpful advice, and worked hard in the development of this manuscript. I am grateful to the contributors of this book for their insights into the work of the enigmatic Jones as well as for their incredible patience over the many years that have passed since they first agreed to participate in this project. An especial thanks to Keith Byerman and Trudier Harris, both noted scholars in the field of African American literature, for lending their support and their voices to what initially was a graduate student's dream. I am also grateful for the support of my colleagues and the administration at Curry College—in particular, David Fedo, who generously provided a research stipend to fund various costs associated with this project as well as granting me release time in the fall of 2004 during which I was able to substantially revise this manuscript. Melissa Bostrom, a dear friend, proved to be a lifesaver when she willingly agreed to format this manuscript despite her already over-committed schedule. I am also especially grateful to my editor at Peter Lang Publishing, Phyllis Korper, whose immediate enthusiasm for this project proved to be a light at the end of what seemed to be a never-ending tunnel. Bernadette Shade, another exceedingly capable member of Peter Lang Publishing, has been incredibly patient throughout this process and dutifully fielded my numerous questions. Although she did not participate in this project,

Chotsani Elaine Dean has proven to be a friend for life and our numerous conversations have kept me grounded in the maelstrom of academia. Lastly, immeasurable love to A.M., A.S., M.H., M.M., S.K., and J. & P.

—*Fiona Mills*

I would like to acknowledge my mother, Mrs. Virgina Brown, who always believed in me and who supported me, in every sense of the world, throughout my life's journey. In addition, I want the world to know that this project could never have come into fruition without the tireless work and boundless drive of my co-editor, Dr. Fiona Mills. Finally, I would also like to acknowledge all of the wonderful friends, teachers, and mentors, especially Mr. Terry Bird, who proved to me time and time again that it is always possible to make a way out of no way. I love you all.
—*Keith B. Mitchell*

Grateful acknowledgment is hereby made to copyright holders for permission to use the following copyrighted material:

Ayala, Marta. "Las Tortugas." Mixed Media. San Francisco, CA: 2000. Reprinted on the cover by permission of the artist. All rights reserved.

Lovalerie King, "Resistance, Reappropriation, and Reconciliation: The Blues and Flying Africans in Gayl Jones's *Song for Anninho*." *Callaloo* 27:3(2004), 755-767. © Charles H. Rowell. Reprinted with permission of The Johns Hopkins University Press.

Megan Sweeney, "Prison Narratives, Narrative Prisons: Incarcerated Women Reading Gayl Jones's *Eva's Man*," was originally published in *Feminist Studies*, Volume 30, Number 2 (Summer 2004): 456-482, by permission of the publisher, *Feminist Studies*, Inc.

After the Pain: An Introduction

Fiona Mills
Keith B. Mitchell

Sometimes it is the hurt that heals.

—*Song of Anninho*

Since the publication of her first novel, *Corregidora* (1976), Gayl Jones has been praised for her complex, thought-provoking depictions of black women who struggle against various forms of oppression. Her unconventional writings not only challenge readers to interrogate the ways race, class, and gender often intersect to limit, if not destroy, black women, but they also frustrate scholars who try to classify her work and place it in clearly defined categories and traditions. For decades, critics have compared Jones with canonical African American writers such as Toni Morrison, Alice Walker, and Gloria Naylor. Yet with the exception of *Corregidora* and *Eva's Man*, Jones's writing has failed to receive significant critical attention. In fact, no collection of essays exploring her work has been published. This neglect can be attributed, in part, to the fact that Jones's writing does not fit neatly into any of the established schools of African American literary aesthetics. In *The Signifying Monkey* (1988), for example, Henry Louis Gates ostensibly divides the African American literary canon into two camps—texts that follow along the lines of Richard Wright's neo-realism (The Wrightsian School) and those that follow the metaphysical aesthetics of Ralph Ellison (The

Ellisonian School). Jones's writing resists this somewhat rigid, totalizing dichotomy by straddling the line between these aesthetic methodologies. More specifically, her poetry illustrates what critic Alejo Carpentier calls "lo real maravilloso" or magic realism; whereas Jones's early fiction plunges the reader deep into the heart of gritty realism. Yet "lo real maravilloso" is not absent from such "realistic" works, nor is realism missing from her poetry collections *Xarque* and *The Hermit Woman*. Jones manages to fuse the two, but this "straddling" of the African American literary canonical border has made it difficult for scholars and critics to categorize her, which, in turn, has made it easier for them to either ignore or dismiss her work.

Another possible reason for the lack of critical attention to Jones's oeuvre might be its tenuous relationship with black feminist criticism. During the mid-1970s, the publication of *Corregidora* and *Eva's Man* set off a firestorm of controversy among black feminist scholars. The novels' protagonists, Ursa Corregidora and Eva Medina, did not fit the image of the strong, black, independent woman that black feminist scholars, such as Barbara Smith, desperately sought in literature at the height of the Black Women's Movement. As a result, they dismissed Jones's work as less important than others more ideologically in tune with black women writers of the time including Alice Walker, Toni Cade Bambara, and Toni Morrison. Not coincidentally, Jones herself has decried the monolithic representations of blackness espoused by adherents of the Black Arts Movement and has deliberately sought to avoid such simplifications of the African American experience in her work. Jones expressed this desire early in her writing career during a 1982 interview with Charles Rowell, in which she stated that she would "like to be able to deal with the whole American continent in my fiction—the whole Americas—and to write imaginatively of blacks anywhere/everywhere."[1]

In truth, Jones defies being ideologically confined by the African American literary tradition and even strives to create characters who, in the words of critic George Kent, possess "contradictory selves." Considering all of her work, it becomes evident that part of Jones's project as an artist is to move beyond the strictures of totalizing ideologies. Much of her writing centers on issues of border crossing—

be it racial, national, or sexual. From her earliest publications, Jones has been concerned with both the histories of African American people and the shared histories and experiences of African, Latin American, and American peoples. Her interrogation of complex issues of race and nationality continues in her latest novel, *Mosquito*, which centers on relationships between persons of African American, Latino/a, and Native American descent living in the southwestern United States. Tied to this exploration is Jones's desire to recover and reveal the untold histories of marginalized peoples that have so often been erased by official historical narratives. In doing so, she seeks to counter essentialist depictions of ethnic persons around the globe. In her "Introduction" to her 1994 book-length essay "The Quest for Wholeness Re-Imagining the African-American Novel: An Essay on Third World Aesthetics," for example, Jones asserts her desire to resist simplistic, dichotomous definitions of race by stating that:

> There are not just Africans and Europeans in the New World, but Asians and Mexican-Americans and the Original People. And of these there are many kinds of peoples within peoples.[...] I am a multicultural, multilinguistic, multi-vernacular novel and at the same time, I am a self-defined African American novel, that is la verdadera historia, an African novel born in the New World.[2]

Instead, she privileges multiplicitous conceptions of race and foregrounds heterogeneity in her work. Unfortunately, little scholarship has engaged these elements of her work. However, a number of essays in this collection explore Jones's complex depiction of the histories and relationships of persons of varied ethnic backgrounds, in particular, those of Afro-Latino/a descent.

Arguably, the most important trait that ties Jones's literary aesthetic to that of other great writers is her understanding of oral literature and her commitment to writing oral forms. Jones asserts in *Liberating Voices* that "to write in the oral tradition, yet to be taken seriously, like Twain, such writers are often led to some form of the composite novel or the composite poem, multilinguistic writings that admix both vernacular and literary styles" (13). Like her literary influences, Zora Neale Hurston, Carlos Fuentes, and Gabriel Garcia Marquez, Jones places vernacular on the same level of complexity and importance as standard language usage. As a black author, Jones is fully aware of the hazards of being an African American writer, trapped between using African American vernacular speech and "proving [s]he can write traditionally and meeting the inventive demands of modernity" (13).

As a poet, playwright, novelist, short-story writer, and critic, Gayl Jones has always resisted labels in her quest to find a liberating voice for black women and herself. With a poet's lyricism and a musician's ear for rhythm, she continually seeks new ways to confront the barriers, traumas, insecurities, and prejudices oppressing black women, and, by extension, all women. Her importance in African American letters and the more recent developments in black feminist criticism cannot be overstated. Her recent publications *The Healing* and *Mosquito* firmly reestablish her place as a preeminent novelist in the twentieth century, but a number of things have changed for Gayl Jones. A new type of character has emerged from the ashes of the past—a character who has achieved a degree of healing, a sense of self that moves beyond personal pain and suffering. This collection, *After the Pain*, considers her most recent works as a starting point for understanding her oeuvre. It views recovery as a process that requires looking back in order to understand the present.

Overview

One of the ways that Gayl Jones crosses borders to resist oversimplified understandings of the past and present, of race and gender, and of the world more broadly is by complicating notions of identity. Characters with mixed ethnic backgrounds and conflicting sexual desires permeate her works. Wandering around like ghosts, they often seem more aware of their own traumatic histories and anguished loves than the present. This process of discovery—and the forces that shape it—remains at the core of Jones's writing, and all of the essays in this collection wrestle, to some extent, with the ways that Jones presents identity formation as a long, labored process. Ultimately, however, it is a journey that brings about a greater awareness of self and the world.

The first three essays examine questions of identity in *The Healing*. Heather Epes's "Identity and Conceptual Limitation in Gayl Jones's

The Healing: From Turtle to Human Being" considers this novel as a study in the constant dilemmas of identity and perception. Using the construct of a "language of exception," Epes explores Jones's concerns with the complexities and contradictions of identity, prejudice, perception, and the limitations of language. She examines how the narrative functions to elucidate the conceptual limitations of language for expressing identity and reality. Ultimately, the "language of exception" opens the door for multiple perceptions of reality, addresses the leaky boundaries around any category constructed for the sake of identity, and honors both ambivalence and contingency as important aspects of reality and humanity.

Shubha Venugopal and LaMonda Horton-Stallings take up this problem of identity as it relates to notions of black womanhood. In "Textual Transfigurations and Female Metamorphosis: Reading Gayl Jones's *The Healing*," Venugopal notes that Jones continues to explore the theme of violence in *The Healing*, but she reconstructs this violence as an implicit aspect of a relationship between women that heals as much as it harms. No longer the enactment of male-generated negative stereotypes about black women, and no longer subject to the loss of her sexual organs and/or her homeland, the protagonist of *The Healing*, Harlan, is free in ways Jones's other protagonists are not to investigate her desires and define her womanhood. Through the discourse of remembered voices and the blues, this text explores the shifting and elusive nature of black womanhood, motherhood, community, identity, and sexuality. The novel's presentation of alternate possibilities for healing through a laying on of hands not only echoes tales of black folklore, but also recalls the metaphors for healing and conjuring frequently adopted by black feminist criticism. In this way, *The Healing*, Venugopal argues, is both a product and a shaper of black literary criticism written in the 1980s and 90s.

LaMonda Horton-Stallings's essay, "Constructing a Discourse for Black Women's Subjectivity through Turtle Woman Lessons and Black Unicorn Philosophies," examines how Gayl Jones's depiction of faith healing creates a folkloric discourse to help revise the subject position of black females. As post-modernist discourse has created the destabilization of subject format, African American women writers and critics have worked to define their literature and literary theory using subject moments transfixed between moments of deconstruction and strategic essentialism. Horton-Stallings suggests that Jones adeptly deconstructs and questions the edifice of gender in Western discourse, specifically the construction of the black woman. *The Healing*, therefore, asks readers to reconsider how they conceive of gender for the black female. Using the oral stories of the turtle woman and the unicorn woman, Jones explores how black women can heal themselves by articulating their subjectivity through mythical discourse and metaphors rather than traditional discourse on gender.

With a particular emphasis on her most recent novel, *Mosquito*, the next three essays examine the different ways that Gayl Jones complicates notions of ethnic and racial identity. Fiona Mills explores the intersection among African, African American, and Latin American peoples and experiences throughout Jones's work. In "Telling the Untold Tale: Afro-Latino/a Identifications in the Work of Gayl Jones," Mills considers Jones from an "Afro-Latino/a" perspective, arguing that her cumulative body of work reveals an ongoing commitment to representing exchanges between African American and Latino/a cultures. According to Mills, Jones re-maps the experience of Afro-Latino/a peoples in the Americas. While several scholars have analyzed Jones's interest in the Africanist presence in Brazil, as depicted in her prose poem *Song for Anninho*, most have failed to pay adequate attention to her interest in making connections between African American and Latino/a cultures in her work. Examining Jones as an Afro-Latino/a writer facilitates a new understanding of her cumulative body of work and provides a more relevant theoretical approach to *Mosquito*, which centers on the experiences of persons of color living in the southwestern United States and Mexico.

Through an examination of music, Jill Terry's "'reads kinda like jazz in they rhythm': *Mosquito*'s Jazz Conversations" examines the ways that Jones rejects a unitary view of black identity and instead embraces the multicultural and multinational reality and fluidity of cultural exchange in Black American society. Seeing jazz as a metaphor for the polyphonic qualities of black cultural expression, Terry argues that Jones uses improvisatory voices to destabilize axiomatic versions of "authenticity," challenging her readers to consider a more complex understanding of black identity. Like the exploration of multiethnic identity in the essays by Mills and Terry, Sarika Chandra reads *Mosquito* as a neo-slave narrative that engages in a cross-ethnic project. As "Interruptions: Borders and Narrative in Gayl Jones's *Mosquito*" points out, the narrator's intimate connection with the Sanctuary movement—which helps Latin American refugees with legal affairs, obtaining documentation, work, and housing—seems to be outside her own culture and identity. Yet the novel compares the condition of modern-day Latin American refugees to colonial or New World slavery in general. Specifically, *Mosquito* likens the situation of the Latin American refugees crossing borders to that of the African-American slaves attempting to flee slavery in the late 1800s. By linking antebellum slave narratives with present debates on race and ethnicity, Jones questions dominant conceptions of race and ethnicity.

With Keith B. Mitchell's "'Trouble in Mind': (Re)visioning Myth, Sexuality, and Race in Gayl Jones's *Corregidora*," this collection revisits the traumas and violence that led up to and influenced Jones's most recent exploration of identity formation and border crossings. Considering the trend in current scholarship[1] to prioritize psychoanalysis over folklore and myth in the study of African American literature, Mitchell specifically argues that the study of mythology and psychoanalysis in an African American literary context need not be mutually exclusive. In many ways, Gayl Jones's interest in both psychoanalysis and mythology throughout her oeuvre coalesces in her novel *Corregidora* (1975)—making for a complex, richer, and more meaningful close reading of the novel. Mitchell shows both Jones's use and critique of Freudian psychoanalysis in *Corregidora*. Using Lacanian and Jungian psychoanalytic hermeneutics and a re-reading of the Demeter/Kore-Persephone myth as an allegorical frame for the novel, Mitchell underscores Jones's attempt to bridge the gap between myth and psychoanalysis as a way to (re)present white and black male patriarchal oppression of black women as presented in *Corregidora*. More specifically, this essay explores the impact of patriarchal oppression on the emotional and psychological identity of Ursa.

Megan Sweeney and Thomas Fahy consider the literal and metaphoric oppression of black women in Jones's early fiction. In "Prison Narratives, Narrative Prisons: Incarcerated Women Reading Gayl Jones's *Eva's Man*," Sweeney outlines some of the knowledge and insight that emerges from eleven incarcerated women's readings of *Eva's Man*. This essay highlights how various readers use Jones's novel as a tool for understanding more fully the relationship between sexual violence, race, class, gender, and crime; for coming to terms with the many roles that silence has played in their lives; and for situating themselves in relation to discourses about victimization and resistance. Sweeney concludes that Jones's ambivalent portrait of Eva, and the incarcerated women's critical readings of the text, help to illuminate spaces of occlusion—of narrative imprisonment—in existing discourses about women, crime, and violence. In particular, the novel and the featured readers highlight the need for, and contribute to, more complex theorizations of African-American women's varied experiences of sexual violence and their equally varied attempts to exercise agency and resistance.

In "Unsilencing Lesbianism and Bisexuality in the Early Fiction of Gayl Jones," Thomas Fahy begins by noting a rupture between black feminism's desire to examine multiple levels of oppression—sexuality, race, and gender—and the critical application of this model. He uses the early fiction of Gayl Jones as a way to reevaluate the scholarship that has "interpreted" her texts. Jones's first publications coincided with the foundation of black feminist criticism, and, in many respects, her work was caught in a crossfire of anxieties about the image and place of lesbianism in this early critical discourse. Because of Jones's identity as a heterosexual and her complex portraits of same-sex desire in works about black women struggling to achieve intellectual, social, and sexual independence, much criticism has "silenced" and overlooked her portrayal of bisexual and lesbian identities. This essay reclaims lesbian readings of her early fiction by examining the crucial tensions among bisexuality, heterosexuality, and lesbianism within the black communities of her texts. It also looks at the ways her characters attempt to form a discourse that communicates same-sex desire. As Fahy explores the linguistic expressions available to silenced black lesbians—

storytelling, sexualized talk, the blues, and fiction like Jones's works—he argues that Jones effectively contributes to a black lesbian political project by giving voice to sexual identities that have been stifled by heterosexism.

The final essays of the collection examine the intersection of history and black women's identity in Gayl Jones's poetry. In "Things Deserving Echoes: Gayl Jones's Liberating Poetry," Howard Rambsy examines the theme of exploration as well as the idea of ordinary yet extraordinary black women throughout Jones's poetry. By producing histories of impossibility—stories of seemingly unbelievable women—in her poetry, Jones re/presents a wide range of possibilities in her narratives. Even more possibilities are revealed when considering the fact that much of Jones's poetry is published in black forums (i.e. African American presses and literary magazines). In short, taking black forums into account gives readers/listeners a greater appreciation of Jones as a writer/storyteller *for* "the" African American community or communities of African Americans where her works are located or published. The forms, forums, and functions of Jones's liberating poetry, he argues, are things deserving echoes (resoundings, responses, and repetition).

Finally, Lovalerie King's "Singing the Blues and Reappropriating the Story of Palmares" examines Jones's use of the Myth of the Flying Africans to reinterpret and revise a specific aspect of the final assault (1694 or 1697, depending on the source) on Palmares, a seventeenth-century African state located in the Barriga Mountains between Alagôas and Pernambuco in Brazil. Palmares predated Haiti and has thus been designated by some as the first independent African nation established in the New World. Gayl Jones uses African and African American folklore in the long narrative poem *Song for Anninho* (1981) to resist traditional linear histories about Palmares that were compiled from colonial archives and to reinterpret available facts. Like the *maroons* in the Caribbean and the *outlyers* in the United States, the original Palmareans were escaping New World slavery. At its zenith in the mid-1670s, Palmares boasted between twenty and thirty thousand inhabitants of varying ethnic backgrounds. With the exception of about two decades' time during its almost one-hundred-year existence, the nation was under perpetual assault from Dutch or

Portuguese colonial forces. The legacy of Palmarean resistance to these forces, which is intricately connected to and interwoven into the historical record, becomes explicit in Jones's poem. As the poem opens, Almeyda, the quintessential blues singer, awakens to find that her home has been destroyed, her man Anninho is missing, and her breasts have been severed. Jones imagines a version of the history of Palmares, especially its final destruction, as it might have been told through the eyes of such a woman, who survived the final assault.

All of these essays explore the impact of various forces on black women's identity—racial, sexual, patriarchal, cultural, and psychological. In Jones's early works, trauma prevents her characters from removing the shackles of the past and achieving an identity of their own. Yet, as her most recent novels suggest, healing starts with the ability to shape one's identity. For decades, her characters, and women of color more broadly, have resisted the social and cultural mores restricting them. This resistance is the focal point of the collection. These essays examine both the forces limiting Jones's characters and their struggles to achieve personal freedom. As a novelist, poet, dramatist, and critic, Gayl Jones takes us on a journey from trauma to healing, pain to recovery, and silence to speech.

Notes

[1] See Charles Rowell's "An Interview with Gayl Jones" in *Callaloo* 5 (1982): 38.
[2] See "The Quest for Wholeness Re-Imagining the African-American Novel: An Essay on Third World Aesthetics" by Gayl Jones in *Callaloo* 17.2 (1994): 509.

CHAPTER ONE

Identity and Conceptual Limitation in Gayl Jones's *The Healing*: From Turtle to Human Being

Heather E. Epes

> I know that for a fact, though like the poet says sometimes the facts about a people obscures the truth about 'em.
> —Josephine Wisdom, *The Healing*

Near the end of Gayl Jones's novel *The Healing*, Harlan Jane Truth Eagleton briefly remembers her husband Norvelle explaining African "dilemma tales" to her. Norvelle tells her that the tales are "a different way of learning" (277). These folk tales present a variety of dilemmas but refrain from providing culminating or defining answers to them. Endings are left open to possibility and to interpretation by the listener. As the result of an intense use of narrative language, which I will call the "language of exception," Jones's own tale may be perceived as a series of dilemmas with no "true" answers. *The Healing* serves as a study in the constant dilemmas of identity and perception, leaving final interpretations to the reader.

By using a "language of exception" in *The Healing*, Jones offers us a "different way of learning" about the complexities and contradictions of identity, prejudice, perception, and the related limitations of language. Harlan Eagleton's narrative flushes out into the open various conceptual limitations of language used to express identity and reality. She very deliberately introduces exceptions for every possible reality she may perceive. For every reality or identifying category Harlan asserts, she foils it with multiple possibilities, contemplates as many exceptions to her potentially essentialist statement as she can articulate. Jones's use of a "language of exception" for Harlan's narrative points out, as often with humor as with a certain sharpness, the leaky boundaries around any category constructed for the sake of identity.

Language and its use elucidate the conceptual categories of a culture, categories that are used, among other things, to create and recognize identity. Harlan's narration functions as a commentary on language and conceptual limitation, raising questions about both the limits of language to express concepts accurately and about the limits of human conceptualization of reality in general. As Jones points out the slipperiness of language, she points to a questionable epistemology. We as human beings have agreed upon the use of a language that provides us with but an impoverished vocabulary for discussing and expressing the ways in which we "know" things and acknowledge identity. But the limits of that very language *also* reflect the ways in which our conceptual limits impact our ability to perceive and know the world around us.

The epistemological questions raised in *The Healing* are concerns we have seen Jones address in previous works. Her investment in examining the conceptual power of essentialism is evident in two of her earlier novels, *Eva's Man* and *Corregidora*. Both of these novels address issues of developing voice and identity in the face of the monolithic tendencies of society and history. In *Eva's Man*, Eva's voice is that of a woman who has been labeled insane for murdering her lover by severing his penis. But her refusal to explain her violent actions and motivations to officials contributes perhaps even more to her psychiatric and legal labels than her original act did.

Eva's combinations of silence, incoherence, and symbolic speech place her in the blind spot of doctors and law workers who cannot conceive of her reality and who attempt to know her through the use of a conventionally limited language. For Eva, however, language functions as a resistance, a bastion against what she perceives as a cold and inhuman systemic intrusion; it is a guerrilla attack on those who would perceive both her and her plight in monolithic terms. She fights tooth and nail with those who would typify her experience away, fit her into standardized conceptual parameters applying to women who commit such a crime, and use her words to normalize and define who she is instead of to acknowledge the fullness and complexity of her life experience. Despite listening to Eva's words, the psychiatrists and lawyers do not really hear her because they do not hear what they expect to hear from her. They cannot come to know her because they believe they already know about her and her circumstances. Essentializing Eva's experiences and identity, they have rendered themselves deaf to her complex voicings.

In *Corregidora*, Jones tackles the monolithic forces of history and politics. "Corregidora's women" develop a narrative to pass along about the realities of South American slavery that were a part of their personal history. Their voices become the only testimony to those events, any official evidence having been destroyed by the political forces in power at the time. "Corregidora's women" bring to light subjugated knowledge[1] that would otherwise remain unuttered and unknown, inconceivable to most. They are preventing their historical reality from being subsumed and forgotten by official historical accounts.

However, Jones also points out how insidiously the monolithic forces of history can affect those who would voice the truth of their experiences. The same historical and political contingencies that supported the burning of official records now exert prescriptive forces on the self-definition, voice, language and perceptions of Corregidora's women. As historical reality forced and limited the experiences of their lives as slaves in South America, so that same historical contingency now forces limitations upon their voices and the experience of their present lives. Although the older women have chosen to give voice to their experiences, their closely-guarded story is told only among themselves, a storytelling that effectively isolates them from men and the rest of the outside world. The women are successful in resisting the often-impenetrable silence with which history seemingly blankets its events. However, they are unable to incorporate their boldly spoken truth into a healthy and interactive existence in the present. The Corregidora women continue to base their present lives and identities on and in their haunting past.

Their legacy oppressively affects the youngest Corregidora woman, Ursa, who has always lived free in the United States. To step outside of the boundaries of their storytelling circle, Ursa must take exception to some of her family's personal and historical traditions. Although she is faithful to her family's storytelling and the reality of Corregidora, more than once Ursa stalwartly denies that she herself is one of Corregidora's women. This move on her part simultaneously denies Corregidora the grip on her present life that he seems to have on her ancestors' lives and attempts to relocate her family's storytelling into the present milieu. Ursa's task, then, is to deny the power of Corregidora to ultimately define her while still honoring the truth of her ancestors' experience and the reality of his existence. Her success requires the development of a voice of her own, the conception of a language that can encompass both what the women in her family have experienced historically and what she experiences in her own present life. We can see her forging both voice and language through singing the blues and through her attempts to share parts of her family's story with the men in her life.

In *The Healing*, these same forces of historical and political contingency are addressed by Harlan's "language of exception." We see Jones's investment in avoiding monolithic and essentializing forces now expressed through the idiom of Harlan's narrative. Harlan's multifarious use of language creates an awareness of the far-reaching influences of personal, historical and political contingencies on conceptual limitation by subtly, and sometimes comically, questioning our epistemological methods and our use of language to express knowledge.

The "Language of Exception" and Conceptual Limitation

Jones has Harlan use language in a way that accounts for the complexity she perceives in the world around her. By introducing exceptions whenever possible, Harlan acknowledges the limitations of her own and everybody else's awareness and of language's capacity to accurately reflect a perceived reality. By partaking of Harlan's thoughts, the reader becomes witness to the failure of a language based on categories of epistemological identification to adequately encompass an identity or to confirm authenticity. Harlan spends a considerable amount of time deconstructing categories by thinking of exceptions to the rule and pointing out blind spots. The issues of category she finds most fertile for her imagination are those related to ethnicity and gender and those related to authenticity and origin. Her considerations of language and conceptual slippage reveal the rarity of individuals who "truly" or "purely" fit into a category. Instead, individuals abound with exceptions and hybridizations.

In her ruminations, Harlan points out discrepancies in our daily definitions for things and examines the way we categorize people. She ultimately questions our methods of knowing and our ability to know anyone or anything completely, truly. Her tacit questioning challenges our typically facile employment of language and its underlying theoretical orientations. For instance, we commonly use language to denote categories like Mexican, Mexican-American, black, white, lesbian, straight, gay, liberal, conservative, and so on, without considering the conceptual theories we animate through this daily use of language. But a theory of reality based on singular definition and categorization turns out to be a conceptually limited one. You may be Mexican, Irish, Greek, and German in ancestry, but if you look Mexican (read: Hispanic) in America, you are Mexican or Mexican-American, few or no questions asked, assumptions made. In cases like these, not only is an entire personal history and reality potentially ignored, but the concept of scripted and immediately recognizable identities is promulgated as well, and the basic building blocks of systemic prejudice and ignorance persist.

Realizing the power of language to create as well as to reflect reality, Harlan seems especially careful not to inadvertently make an essentializing statement. She points out that although individuals may display some of the attributes associated with a category, the category does not encompass who they are. She warns the reader, for instance, "You can't categorize all the scientific-minded as a skeptical people," and goes on to explain, "Ain't all the scientific-minded cynics, though, and ain't all the mystical idealists true believers" (12, 13). Her tone often seems cautionary, as if exhorting the reader to go and consider these kinds of things and what they mean, to keep his or her eyes open for complexity.

Harlan's constant assertion of variation and flexible boundaries results in a narrative that testifies to possibility, open ends, and unknowns. In this way, Harlan's voice combats essentialism in its many forms, bringing it to our attention as a human state of mind, almost a default setting. We automatically think reductively in an attempt to comfortably make sense of new information and experience. The categories "Mexican" or "Mexican-American" label more quickly and easily than if you were to consider all the Central and South American countries an individual may originate from, or to simply find out which one in particular.

The groups of women who greet Harlan at the beginning of the novel do the same kind of thing, using tried and "true" categories to interpret her. Harlan notes, "Zulinda and Josephine don't hide their disappointment. I know they's expecting me to be more impressive, look less like some ordinary, common woman and more like a legend. More like some legendary healer" (22). And one of the women exclaims, "She look like she belong on a submarine or on a motorcycle" (13). Harlan's unconventional appearance alone leads Zulinda to cluck to herself that "She's a regular boogie woogie" from the city (25). Harlan's first impression proves confusing to those trying to establish her identity as a healer.

These women had an *image* of a healer, an image which they had imagined using cultural categories of identification. Very little about Harlan matched their expectations, causing them to feel anxiety, doubt, and a bit of scorn. Jones points out that reductive thinking may be a comfortable way for humans to assess their surroundings, but it may also reduce their ability to conceive of their surroundings with any complexity, to think beyond categories. These women do not pause to ask themselves why a healer couldn't wear a bomber jacket and greased braids (25). They do not ask themselves what exactly about a bomber jacket would make a person unable to heal. Following the wisdom of the theory of categories, they see signifiers they associate with other identities and become confused about which category Harlan fits into. They assume Harlan cannot manage what they consider two separate identities and therefore doubt her authenticity as a healer.

Harlan, on the other hand, makes it her business to imagine all the possibilities and simultaneities of existence. She acknowledges the multivalent qualities of identity, the existence of traits we may find contradictory together in one individual. For the reader, Harlan's narrative introduces a space of ambivalency that eludes any monolithic reading of "the Truth" about an event or a person. A version of truth depends on perspective, which depends on awareness of related historical and day-to-day contingencies. As we have just seen, human awareness varies, and Harlan knows it. Few theories or opinions stated as fact escape her notice and exposé. Even to Josef von Fremd's offhand comment that men can "handle dirty tricks better than a woman," Harlan responds snappily with, "It depends on what kind of dirty tricks. And what kinda woman" (49). She points out that Josef has not considered all of the possibilities, and neither does he know everything there is to know about all women.

Harlan's narrative forces language to take into account reality's contingencies, verbally circling a category of identification until its inaccuracies are laid bare. Even the day-to-day details that escape notice are worth Harlan's time and consideration. Take, for instance, the seemingly innocuous term "tank town." The term "tank town" was coined in America in 1906 for a town where steam engines stopped to fill up their water tanks (Merriam-Webster). As in the case of these "tank towns," we call things what they are because of associative values. However, some associations are stronger than others, and accuracy is often foregone in favor of singular knowable categorization. As Harlan arrives at one of the many "tank towns" she visits as a healer, she digresses thoroughly upon the term, pointing out the imprecision of definition, the differences that are overlooked for the sake of categorization and knowability.

Harlan begins her diatribe with the statement, "And all them little southern and midwestern tank towns, they's all alike," a statement she quickly proceeds to dismantle. First she establishes that there are in reality tank towns that have tanks and tank towns that do *not* have tanks. There are other similarities between these towns that put them in the same category, even without the tank; they are small, dusty, regional. Harlan explains the slippage around the term, "So that tank town is just a metaphor for them little towns" (7). But after her detailed observations, the metaphor seems somehow lacking in expression.

For instance, Harlan tells us that some tank towns are bigger than others. Some may be big enough to advertise their town's industry on the tank, and some may advertise famous people on the tank. Some may not even have the tank; some tanks may still be in use while others are not; some tanks may also collect water for the townsfolk. And beyond that, according to Harlan, these towns are not just in the South and Midwest, "there's little towns up North that's tank towns too. Little towns in Maine and New Jersey and Connecticut and Pennsylvania, and somebody said that all the towns in Rhode Island is tank towns" (7). By the time she is done discussing them, the reader understands that "tank towns" are designated based on a superficial or imposed sameness, when in reality these towns may differ from each other in a number of ways. True to form, Harlan has deconstructed her initial, somewhat essentializing, statement into complete inadequacy.

The Fluidity of Identity and Conceptual Limitation

While Jones points out fundamental limitation of our general conceptual abilities, her main focus remains on issues of identity and perception. Harlan's "language of exception" exposes the facile manner in which we perceive individuals and our world. Her effluent ruminating and listing of possibilities are markedly unwieldy for an essentialist mindset and force the reader to acknowledge the multiple valences of identity. It is one thing to overlook the details of various tank towns and honorary tank towns; it is another to overlook the complexity of details that go into the identity of an individual.

Conventional rules of identity require maintenance of boundaries, a keeping up of appearances so that you may be known, and even so you may know yourself. But to Harlan, this is a troublesome farce, a mere maintenance of leaky levees erected to stave off the complexities of hybridization that actual day-to-day life spawns. The fluidity of identity and its ability to hybridize is testified to in a number of ways.

In the opening pages, as Harlan eyes the magazines of the woman next to her on the bus, she notices one called *Popular Culture*. She notes that the "Americans...with they tattoos and nose rings and sculptured and painted hairdos" closely resemble the "kinda folk you usedta just see in the *National Geographic*-type magazines" (5). In a matter of decades, the adornments of "the so-called primitive peoples" have been reappropriated as cultural fodder for American hipster fashion trends. A look unimaginable for an average American several decades ago, due to its association with people perceived as primitive, has become hybrid, taken on a new identity. Piercings and tattoos no longer make you uncivilized; they make you cool in America. We see that over time the signifiers for a particular identity (the perception of which may be limited to begin with) may shift to encompass other identities as well. Leaky levees indeed.

The fluidity of identity can also be recognized by the anxiety it may provoke. It is important to have stable categories if they are to be used for the purposes of knowing and identifying a thing. Acknowledging any slipperiness in the use of categories to identify is like opening a can of worms; it raises too many questions about how you can know something for sure. Take Josephine Wisdom's comments from a debate with Zulinda and Martha on whether Harlan has healed insane people or just people with "ailment of spirit:" "Though looking crazy don't mean you is. Do looking crazy mean you is? If that looking crazy mean you is, then them psychiatrists and psychologists would have more work than they's got now.... I know insanity don't run in us. Maybe some of the New York Wisdoms is crazy, 'cause that's New York...but the Wisdoms from around here ain't crazy" (21). Her assertive opening statement is followed by self-questioning, an attempt to laugh off her anxiety, and finally a definite assertion of *her* family's sanity, at least. Of that category, she can be sure.

Josephine ends her observations with further redefinition of "crazy": "There might be some ailment of the spirit people amongst the people she heals in her world travels, or even amongst the New York Wisdoms, but around here the crazy peoples that's crazy is crazy. Ain't they Zulinda?" (21) Josephine is forced to acknowledge the slipperiness of the very concept: "crazy." Is crazy about the way you look? Does where you live or your family determine craziness? Can craziness be the same as an "ailment of spirit?" The tendency of the mind to essentialize reality until it is manageable prompts Josephine to reassure herself by declaring the sanity of her local family and the absolute insanity of local "crazy peoples." She asserts that she knows what it means to be crazy, but even after all of this, she asks for more reassurance: "Ain't they Zulinda?"

Joan Savage, the research-chemist-turned-rock-singer Harlan manages, is an interesting and disturbing study in essentialist tendencies. A person who seems bent on occupying the edge of what she sees as intellectual and social revolution, Joan is well-read, well-educated, and well-traveled. She rages about capitalism and discrimination. She's a crusader for the multicultural. But Joan has an ironic blind spot. She is unable to process the multiple realities of a person like Harlan Eagleton.

When Harlan first introduces herself as a cosmetician, Joan cheers, "It's about time I met somebody real" (275). She romantically labels Harlan "a real gal," assumes that her identity is that of some kind of everywoman (275). But Harlan's complexity as a real person with a pied existence eludes Joan and leaves her insecure and resentful. Joan's essentializing perception limits the ways she may know Harlan and, therefore, she makes a series of judgments about her, stemming from her inability to encompass all that Harlan is and is not.

After first practically provoking involvement between her ex-husband, James, and Harlan, she then reacts unpredictably about finding them together. Although she seems to bury this resentment, she periodically lashes out at Harlan in other ways, calling her a "con artist," a "rogue," a "pretender," and an "imposter" (232, 282). She increasingly becomes suspicious of Harlan and refuses to accept aspects of Harlan's complex and varied life. For instance, she refuses to fully believe that Harlan has traveled a significant portion of Africa. By the end of their relationship, Joan regularly questions many of Harlan's realities, erasing the existence of her ex-husband, Norvelle, and her ability to heal.

The reader watches as Joan seems to lose perspective towards the end of the novel. She lashes out at Harlan more frequently, and her resentment transmutes more easily into aggression, leading to her murder attempt. Not only does she resent Harlan and think her deceitful, she literally cannot tolerate the existence of all those possibilities inside the same individual. She sets out to eliminate that which is incomprehensible, unknowable according to her identifying categories. That Joan cannot actually hurt Harlan somehow, in her opinion, validates all the suspicions she had about Harlan's multiplicity of character. As the knife falls uselessly to the floor, Joan says, "I thought you were a real person...you ain't even a real human being" (280). Harlan's apparent ability to heal is the last straw for Joan. The objectification of essentialist thought allows her to disqualify Harlan as human. She fits in no categories; she is inhuman.

The "Language of Exception" and Identity

On the other hand, Harlan makes room for the slippery and hybridized in her consciousness and her daily use of language, whether she remarks on something as minor as tank town semantics or something as globally and culturally significant as national and ethnic identity. When Harlan first meets Josef Ehelich von Fremd at the horse races, she's not sure of his nationality, although something seems foreign about him. After discovering he's from Germany, Harlan exclaims, "But you's African looking. You a real German?" (43) She explains further, perhaps in an attempt to clarify what could be misconstrued as a rather essentializing statement, "I mean, I know the only colored people ain't in America, I mean, I've seen Africans in Germany, but not any German Africans, I mean not any African Germans" (43). Harlan is already wrestling with the idea of who exactly Josef is or could be, trying to use language that addresses that identity accurately. German African, African German...is one more accurate than the other? A German of African descent versus an African of German descent? Once Harlan discovers his African heritage is Hottentot[2], that detail enters the mix as well. Does that specificity make the label more accurate: Hottentot German? German Hottentot? She stretches language to its limits searching for a satisfactory label.

Whether to call a German of African descent German African or African German may seem an issue of nominal importance. However, the same circumstances that create a complexity of identity often also create identity-based prejudice and animosity. Josef explains that in his own country, people mistook him for and treated him like a foreigner. But once he moves to America for that very reason, he receives a variety of threats, also related to his blackness. Americans doing business with him on the phone had assumed he was "Aryan German." When Kentucky's horse racing scene discovered that he was black despite his name and his speech, they were shocked and even angered. Josef did not fit the identity they had assumed was his according to the evidence and the categories they knew to apply.

When Harlan introduces us to the guitar player, Jimmy Cuervo, "one of them African-looking Mexicans from South Texas," we can expect more commentary concerning hybridization (83). Her ruminations on Jimmy again point out various ways nationality, ethnicity, and identity are related. She hears Joan Savage call him Caballero, and she considers Mexican Spanish. "Or maybe Cuervo the way them Mexicans pronounce Caballero, 'cause them Mexicans ain't supposed to pronounce Spanish the same way them Spaniards from Spain pronounce Spanish. Theirs is American Spanish." And later: "Maybe in Spain his true name be Jimmy Caballero, though, that Jimmy Cuervo, but in American Mexico or Mexican America his name Jimmy Cuervo. And that Jimmy ain't his true Spanish name.... What's the Spanish for Jimmy? Jaime? Ain't Jaime the Spanish for Jimmy? Ain't Jaime Mexican for Jimmy?" (82)

Although a number of details about Jimmy are provided, his identity remains elusive. He could be Jimmy Cuervo, Jimmy Caballero, Jaime Cuervo, or Jaime Caballero, in any combination. How is one to know his "true" name? He could speak English or Mexican Spanish or both. He could be Mexican, American, Texan or Mexican American. Mexican Texan? Harlan's exercise in language and possibility does little to pin down who Jimmy Cuervo actually is; it does, however, show that you cannot assume to know Jimmy just because he looks Mexican and is from Texas. Harlan's thought process brings into question the way we try to construct identity. She makes the same point to Josef during their first conversation, "It wouldn't be honest of me to say I know you telling the truth about who you yourself are, 'cause I don't know you" (48). Despite knowing where someone is from and what language they speak, you may have no idea of who that person actually is, how they behave. Categories of ethnicity used for identification do not provide the ability to know an individual completely.

Jones is not blind to an element of the absurd in the project of recognizing and expressing fluid and hybridizing identity. Creating and recognizing identity can take decidedly unexpected turns towards the personal. Even when using categories to identify, our perceptions also are influenced by the personal and idiosyncratic. Jones humorously points out the conceptual divide between using monolithic categories and using personal experience to perceive and express reality.

As Harlan contemplates Josef's bodyguards, she notes one in particular, "I think he a gypsy but Joan say he a Turk. Or maybe he a Turkish Gypsy" (77). Then, in the middle of her habitual contemplative avoidance of monolithic categories, Harlan blithely states, "and to tell the truth that Turkish-looking Gypsy or Gypsy-looking Turk also kinda look like Steven Seagal" (77). A Turkish Gypsy Turk who looks like Steven Seagal! If the reader had been trying to picture Harlan's bodyguard, I doubt seriously that Steven Seagal had come to mind. Given only "Turkish" and "Gypsy," most readers probably read inside the preconceived lines associated with those categories. But Harlan reminds us that essentializing categories can't address the details of identity for either the perceiver or the perceived. While essentializing categories require adherence to definite boundaries, personal and idiosyncratic perception may allow for potentially limitless recombination of information.

Jones also often employs a bitter humor. Harlan compares Josef romancing her in German, which she does not care for, to him romancing her in French. Then her mind takes an abrupt and historical leap. "Least that French sound like the universal language of love. Course if you's Algerian during that war, or a Algerian in France after the war, you wouldn't think of that French as a lover's language" (52). Indeed not. Jones reminds us sharply, but still humorously, of the fact that not everyone sees reality from the same perspective.

Gayl Jones's use of the "language of exception" is thorough, or relentless, depending on how you look at it. She gives the same consideration to identity and gender that she does to identity and ethnicity. I will give two quick examples. Harlan very aptly explains the limiting influence of gender archetypes in the heterosexual romance. As usual, Harlan starts out with a definite statement, this time that all the men she knows have something the same about them. Then she conceives of a more complex understanding of the issue. She suggests: "maybe it's just that women don't know men the same way that men know themselves; maybe we only know us idea of a man, and if we got a certain idea of a man, then we see something of the same man in every man, 'cause it's us own idea of a man us own archetypal man that we think we see in every man, like maybe only all men know is their idea of a woman or they idea of the archetypal woman" (28). Harlan has simultaneously addressed two issues. Firstly, she has pointed out the role that individual perception plays in the identification of others, our constructions of our own archetypes. And by doing so, she has also raised an issue concerning the influence gender archetypes have on personal relationships between men and women.

Harlan also deftly points out the conflation of conceptual categories for the purposes of identification related to gender. She fumes about Josef's closest bodyguard, Nicholas, giving her a look: "one I know. I ain't no whore, I ain't no trollop, if that what he thinking. Mens they's always thinking shit like that about a woman, and especially us womens of color. Don't care what woman of color, Asian, African, Native American, African-American or one of them islanders, the first thing they think of is you's a trollop. Even mens of color thinks that about they own women. And it don't matter what sorta woman you are. I might be a scavenger maybe and a gambler, but I ain't no whore" (56). Harlan asserts that men always will conflate the category of female promiscuity with that of female color, although she is careful not to say *all* men. She does not make it clear whether she means men will conflate these categories in order to scorn a woman, or to advance sexually, or both. Perhaps this remains unclear because the personal motivation behind this sort of treatment often remains unclear.

Harlan *does* make it clear that you cannot assume to fully know the identity of an individual simply because you can fit them into one or two conceptual categories. Harlan fits into the categories of woman and black, but neither one of them, either singly or when considered together, can simply be equated with sexual promiscuity. Harlan further proves her point at the end, when she refers to two other aspects of her life and character, scavenging and gambling. You may expect a woman who scavenges and gambles to also be a whore, but that is due to your limited perception, not to an essential truth.

Identity and Authenticity

Identity is contingent upon authenticity. Only the matter of a stable and consistently identifiable category can be known with surety. When identity is at issue, so are authenticity and origin. Essentializing perception craves a verification of identification. But Harlan's thoughtfulness again begs that issue. Her musings prompt a reader to wonder how you can ever be *sure* that you have gotten or seen the real thing. Her implied questions are complex. Not only should we wonder what qualifies as authentic, but we should also think twice about who is to make the judgment. And when judging, do we consider point of origin, purity in rendition, or historical accuracy? Are variations on an original necessarily *un*authentic or just different and authentic in and of themselves?

When discussing the guitar player Jimmy Cuervo, Harlan points out that Mexicans "got they own music...that mariachi music," just like they have their own kind of Spanish. Immediately she wonders if mariachi is not actually an "Americanization of that flamenco." But determining an authentic flamenco to compare with apparently poses some difficulty. "You got that flamenco they do for them tourists, and then you's got the true flamenco, the flamenco that them Spaniards do for each other." She explains that tourists associate sexuality with flamenco dancing, but "that ain't the same as that true flamenco." But flamenco dancing done by Spaniards for Spaniards can be sensuous as well. If we cannot even tell flamenco from flamenco, is it not therefore suspect to judge close relatives like the mariachi as somehow *unauthentic* because they have altered the generally accepted parameters of "true flamenco," or because they are in a different location from the point of origin? (82)

One could even suggest that flamenco in its Americanized mariachi incarnation is somehow *more* authentic than tourist-grade Spanish flamenco due to its more easily recognizable identity. Whether it descended from flamenco or not, mariachi has taken its undeniable and particular place in Mexican and American cultures. It is authentic in and of itself, as can be seen in comparison to a somehow diminished and commodified tourist form of flamenco. At any rate, such judgments and any like them depend on establishing original standards for authentication; in this case, are we to take Spain, Mexico, or America/s as our point of origin? And determining the importance of the music's point of origin and present location would be the easy part. To judge fairly on mariachi and other phenomena, we would need to evaluate performance, appearance, and effect as well. Until some decisions are made about what constitutes authenticity, we would not be able to define or judge the phenomena for certain. But with so many variables, the chances that all of them would rate one hundred percent authenticity seems slim. This is exactly Harlan's point.

Harlan peels back layers of questions about authenticity. She knows Josephine and Zulinda are thinking that she is a fake. She takes the opportunity to comment on the nature of belief and authenticity. Beyond deciding upon and enforcing the maintenance of definable category parameters for the purpose of identification, there is the question of perception itself. Perceiving that you are meeting the standards of a category doesn't ensure that perception as essential truth. Harlan explains: "If I ain't a faker, then I'm a crazy woman that just believes in her own fakery. There's people like that; they's innocent believers, or gullible believers, but it's they own fakery or somebody else's fakery they believe in. And it might not be fakery, it might just be other people believe it to be fakery. You don't always know fakery from fakery" (5). In other words, you cannot count upon standards of authenticity when it comes to knowing. Merely appearing authentic by no means ensures a definably authentic thing at the core. Neither can it ensure that the thing is a complete fake. It attempts to ensure your inability to know. And often enough, truth doesn't look like you would expect, but it is truth nonetheless.

Later, Harlan discusses the authenticity of the healer's witness. Obtaining the genuine is so important that the authenticity of one individual can impact the authenticity of an associate, regardless of the associate's character. She comments that a lot of fakers hire witnesses.

Then she complicates the seemingly clear-cut statement. "You know, maybe one of them evangelist fakers have a true witness to they healings, but the people don't believe the true witness so's they's got to hire theyselves a fake witness, 'cause the fake witness to the healings is more believable than the true witness. Now I'm wondering whether that would make the healer a faker, if the healings theyselves is real, but the healer got to hire a fake witness, 'cause even the true believers don't believe the true witness" (11). The quandary Harlan describes about the fake witness speaks to the role of perception in establishing and recognizing identity. A truth may not be heard, even by those who want to hear it, and sometimes a liar makes a truth evident. For truths and identities, perception depends heavily upon experience. If you believe, you could be healed even by a faker. If you do not believe, then not even a "true evangelist" could heal you.

Becoming Human

When contemplating Jones's diligent use of the "language of exception" and Harlan's multiplicity of character, it is worth asking *why* Harlan shares her narrative of many possibilities. Perhaps we should begin by asking ourselves the significance of her Grandmother Jaboti's seemingly unrelated but highly entertaining "turtle stories." After all, it is Grandmother Jaboti who most clearly voices the philosophy of exception and contingency behind Harlan's narrative.

Grandmother Jaboti played a Turtle Woman in a carnival sideshow in her youth, and she frequently told her carnival tales to young Harlan. During one storytelling session, her monologue on the authenticity of the Unicorn Woman's horn has filled almost a page of Jones's novel when she follows up her diatribe in a familiar way—by complicating things. "At least I think that horn was real. I can't testify to the reality of that horn, but I believe it to be real. I mean, I know that horn to be real although I can't testify to the reality of it being a real horn. I mean, there wasn't nothing that Unicorn Woman said or did to make me disbelieve the reality of that horn" (136). Harlan's grandmother believes in the authenticity of that horn, but she also is aware of the ways in which authenticity is problematic. In a world of limited language, Grandmother Jaboti creates a way to talk about perception, identity, and truth. She calls her method "Jaboti's logic," a logic that allows for multiple perceptions and realities (137). No wonder Harlan has a knack for seeing the truths in things even when she knows she cannot know "the truth." "Jaboti's logic" clearly functions as a precursor to Harlan's own tricky use of language.

By the same logic, Grandmother Jaboti insisted, to Harlan's mother's annoyance, that she had once been a real turtle. As Harlan's mother would shake her head and wait for a chance to bring the stories back around to conventional reality and carnivals, Grandmother Jaboti would tell Harlan that in those days, she sometimes had to magically transform herself into grass or a rock, so she would not be caught by humans. "She smiled like she knew that her tale was the true one, or that a tale could be true and not be a true tale—that perhaps her Turtle Woman stories were truer than any carnival tale" (136). Grandmother Jaboti understands the dilemmas of knowing, the need for conceptual flexibility in order to perceive our surroundings. In her mind, language must become magical, metaphorical, in order to address some of the realities of experience. For it turns out that her experience as a turtle has far more significance than its role as an entertaining tale for her granddaughter.

Grandmother Jaboti's turtle stories are also linked to the stories about her and Harlan's grandfather. She always said that after she quit following the carnival to follow Harlan's grandfather, she turned into a real human being. Harlan's grandfather recognized her grandmother's reality as a human being, not only as the freak show Turtle Woman the audience preferred to see and maintain as reality (135). Harlan's mother explains, "Them other men just thought of her freakish, as one of them freakish women, whether or not they believed in the reality of that turtle's shell" (135). Whereas the audience is limited by their perception of a carnival show or their perception of the kind of woman who would be in a carnival show, Harlan's grandfather had the ability to conceive of the "genuine woman behind that fake turtle shell" (135). He, too, understood the multiplicity of human reality.

By depicting herself as a turtle who becomes a woman because another human acknowledged her personal reality, Grandmother

Jaboti tries to talk about the way perception can create reality, create identities, create humans. She is addressing an actual transformation in her life. Up to that point, Grandmother Jaboti might as well have been a turtle as far as the carnival audience was concerned, and perhaps herself, too. When her future husband saw her as someone who could love and be loved, when she saw that as well and agreed to join him, she as good as became human. She chose to become human with the same magic she used as a turtle to elude humans. She chose to conceive of herself anew and to change the rhythm of her life. Significantly, her human identity is both as Harlan's grandfather chose to see it and as she chose to make it.

In the end, if Harlan's grandmother was a turtle, Harlan has been a chameleon. From cosmetician to gambler to business manager to closet intellectual to healer to common woman, she has recreated and reintegrated herself again and again, becoming and growing into a complex individual full of possibility. However, when Joan says that Harlan is not human, perhaps there is also some figurative truth in it. Maybe Harlan is not human *yet*. Ironically for Joan, it is when Harlan figures out that she can heal herself that she is on the way to becoming human Grandmother Jaboti-style.

For both granddaughter and grandmother, the transformation of becoming human, the most complex identity of all, requires effort, growth, sacrifice, vision, healing. In that first moment of self-healing, Harlan experiences a moment of self-conception. She recognizes the healing ability within herself, as a possible aspect of her identity. The beginning of her transformation occurs when she changes her perception of herself in this way. In her comment about how long it has been since the last time she's seen Josef, Harlan herself recognizes the eventual extent of the transformation, "I know I ain't the one he met up at Saratoga...I'm the one who touched my own wound. I'm the one who healed my own self first" (35). As her grandmother conceives herself anew from a turtle, so does her granddaughter conceive herself anew, as a healer, encompassing all her other identities. Harlan has become the ultimate foil to essentialist thinking. She has become human.

Notes

[1] For a full explanation of "subjugated knowledge," see Patricia Hill Collins, *Black Feminist Thought: Knowledge, Consciousness and the Politics of Empowerment* (Boston, 1990).

[2] The Khoikhoin (literally, "men of men") tribe of southern Africa, related to the Bushmen and Bantu, live largely in South Africa and Namibia, some on official reserves. The Dutch/Afrikaner name for the tribe, Hottentot, was perjorative in origin and perhaps was a reaction to the click sounds in the language of the Khoikhoin. In recent history, the traditional Khoi clan system of nomadic tribes has given way to settlement and systems of reserve governments, which has affected both their economy and social order. See Colin McEvedy, *The Penguin Atlas of African History* (New York, 1995).

Works Cited

Anzaldua, Gloria. *Borderlands/La Frontera: the New Mestiza.* San Francisco: Spinsters/Aunt Lute, 1987.

Basu, Bima. "Public and Private Discourses and the Black Female Subject: Gayl Jones' Eva's Man." *Callaloo* 19.1 (1996): 193-208.

Byerman, Keith E. *Fingering the Jagged Grain: Tradition and Form in Recent Black Fiction.* Athens: University of Georgia Press, 1985.

Davies, Carole Boyce. *Black Women, Writing and Identity: Migrations of the Subject.* New York: Routledge, 1994.

Dubhey, Madhu. *Black Women Novelists and the Nationalist Aesthetic.* Bloomington: Indiana University Press, 1994.

Empowerment. Boston: Unwin Hyman, 1990.

Jones, Gayl. *Corregidora.* Boston: Beacon Press, 1986.

———. *Eva's Man.* New York: Random House, 1976.

———. *The Healing.* Boston: Beacon Press, 1998.

McEvedy, Colin. *The Penguin Atlas of African History.* Revised edition. New York: Penguin Books, 1995.

Merriam Webster Collegiate Dictionary. Tenth Edition. Ed., Merriam-Webster. Springfield, MA: Merriam-Webster, Inc., 1995.

Minh-Ha, Trinh T. *Woman, Native, Other: Writing Postcoloniality and Feminism.* Bloomington: Indiana University Press, 1989.

CHAPTER TWO

Textual Transfigurations and Female Metamorphosis: Reading Gayl Jones's *The Healing*

Shubha Venugopal

Gayl Jones's works both affect as well as result from black artistic, political, and critical communities at particular historical moments. While members of the 1970s Black Aesthetic movement rallied around the notions of unity and ideal portrayals of black communities, for example, Jones refused to offer only glorified images of black communities and heterosexual relationships. Similarly, when early black feminists claimed the matrilineal metaphor and idealized notions of female bonding as empowering symbols of a black feminist tradition, Jones questioned the solely positive nature of woman-woman and mother-daughter literal and figurative relationships.[1] The criticism of the 1970s and '80s, which often relegated Jones to the margins of black feminist discourse, has metamorphosed in recent years as feminist critics began to challenge essentializing, homogenizing, and often exclusionary notions of black womanhood. This critical turn towards once-marginalized authors like Jones who explore alternative representations of black womanhood and matrilineage has in turn influenced the nature of Jones's work itself. The debilitating violence and physical mutilation which underlie Jones's poem *Song for Anninho* (1981) and her novels, *Corregidora* (1975) and *Eva's Man* (1976), and which force the protagonists of these texts to redefine their womanhood in ways that go beyond limiting historical definitions, become reconfigured in her later novel, *The Healing* (1998). In her new novel Jones continues to explore the thematic of violence, but she reconstructs this violence as an implicit aspect of a relationship between women that heals as much as it harms. No longer the enactment of male-generated negative stereotypes about black women, and no longer subject to the loss of her sexual organs and/or her homeland, the protagonist of *The Healing* is free in ways Jones's other protagonists are not to investigate her desires and define her womanhood.

In this essay, I will examine Jones's recent work, *The Healing*, as both a product and a shaper of black literary criticism written in the 1980s and '90s. In this innovative new novel, Jones continues her interest in the shifting and elusive nature of black womanhood, motherhood, community, identity, and sexuality. In *The Healing*, the voice of protagonist Harlan Jane dominates the text, and indeed the entire story reads as if Harlan is speaking directly to the reader and thus implicating the reader in her story. Jones comments on the importance of this character/reader interaction frequently in her writings and states that, "To me the reader is a listener and the listener is as much a part of the story as the teller" ("The Quest," 1994, 509). By emphasizing the orality of black novels and their call-and-response patterns, Jones illustrates the concept of the Afro-American "speakerly text," as Henry Louis Gates, Jr. has termed such texts whose "rhetorical strategy is designed to represent an oral literary tradition" (1988, 181). Jones describes her novels as "oral storytelling monologues—stories within stories" (Jones, "Interview," 1982, 34), and explains that she learned to write by listening to verbal dialogues, for she best relates to her written texts when they reflect oral speech (*Liberating voices*, 1991). As Jones explains, "One must often balance and counterbalance techniques from oral tradition with those indispensable to writing.... Such literature often reads better than it appears on the page; it must therefore oblige itself to visual as well as auditory magic. Even then, the most effective reading is the reading that 'hears' it, rather than the strictly silent one" (*Liberating Voices*, 1991, 13). Just as in Jones's earlier works, in which "Ursa is telling a story and there are stories within stories. Eva is also telling hers" ("Interview," 1982, 33), Harlan's stories and her "stories within stories" serve as the foundation of this novel. While it is solely Harlan's voice the reader hears, however, the narrative also enables other people's voices to merge in and out of Harlan's memories, her imagination, and her life. The diction and speech mannerisms remain Harlan's regardless of the identity of other speakers—a singular literary technique that enables the stories of the community to become a part of Harlan's psyche and to affect her transformation into a faith healer.

The blues-like nature of the narrative becomes Harlan's song of metamorphosis as differing voices, past and present, fantasy and reality, individual and community, merge and separate in intricate patterns which resemble the melodies of jazz and the blues. The blues structure of repetition-with-variation is replicated in the language and rhythms of the text: a woman transforms into her competitor, a granddaughter relives (but differently) the fairy tale of her grandmother, a daughter rebels against the fate of her mother, a wandering woman learns to reclaim the language of love. The essences of black womanhood are explored through Harlan's desire for movement and traveling—a desire which resembles the lyrics of many blues songs as well as recalls the theme of voyage itself, which reappears throughout black literature. While this theme of voyage occurs with greater frequency in songs by black male singers, however, Jones's text, like some of the songs sung by black female blues singers that I will later discuss, reconfigures the thematic of traveling as it pertains to women's lives. In addition to the prevalence of movement in black music and literature, in Jones's novel alternate possibilities for healing through a laying on of hands echo the tales of black folklore and legend, and recall the metaphors for healing and conjuring frequently adopted by black feminist criticism. Indeed, the story of Harlan's transformation does not occur in isolation, for it reflects as well as transfigures the history and criticism which surround the writings of black women writers like Gayl Jones.

Although Gayl Jones published many of her texts in the 1970s, her works do not conform to the major movements that defined that era, such as the Black Aesthetic and related Black Power movements. Black Aesthetician Larry Neal explains the relationship between Black Power and the Black Aesthetic as such: "these two movements have begun to merge: the political values inherent in the Black Power concept are now finding concrete expression in the aesthetics of Afro-American[s]" ("The Black Arts," 1968/1994, 184). This highly political black art involved the ideals of unity and community, which were integral to both the Black Power and Black Aesthetic movements. Stokely Carmichael and Charles Hamilton, for example, explain that Black Power "is a call for black people in this country to unity, to recognize their heritage, to build a sense of community" (Carmichael and Hamilton, 1967, 44). The production of a unified black community similarly becomes a crucial aspect of defining the Black Aesthetic's imperatives for Black Aesthetician Ron Karenga. In listing the requirements for black art, Karenga insists that it should be "functional, collective and committing" (Karenga, 1971, 34): it should, in other words, praise black culture, support the black community, and forward the black revolution. While Neal, Karenga, and other Black Aesthetic writers implicitly fuse art and politics in defining their movement, Jones feels uneasy about the connection between the two, and explains that "sometimes politics or political strategies...can be useful in the organization and structuring of one's work...but it can also tell you what you cannot do, tell you what you must avoid, tell you that there's a certain territory politics won't allow you to enter, certain questions politics won't allow you to ask—in order to be 'politically correct'" ("About," 1984, 234).

To demonstrate the restrictions of "politically correct" art, Jones raises the question of whether or not black writers should represent morally problematic characters: "Should a Black writer ignore such characters, refuse to enter 'such territory' because of the 'negative image' and because such characters can be misused politically by others, or should one try to reclaim such complex, contradictory characters?" ("About," 1984, 235). Jones here directly diverges from the Black Aesthetic's commitment to presenting positive, moral black characters in order to strengthen the black community and oppose the negative stereotypes put forth by white America. The introduction to the volume, *The Black Aesthetic*, clearly states that a "critical methodology has no relevance to the black community unless it aids men in becoming better than they are," and so therefore the "Black Aesthetic...is a corrective—a means of helping black people out of the polluted mainstream of Americanism" (Gayle, 1971, xxiii). Jones's unapologetic, violent, powerful, and hard-to-decipher character, Eva Canada, in *Eva's Man* certainly does not comply with the Black Aesthetic's commitment to "destroying those images and myths that have crippled and degraded black people," and their institutionalization of "the new images and myths that will liberate them" (Fuller, 1971, 348). Madhu Dubey argues that stereotypes such as the "bitch" and the "whore" "are not merely imposed upon black women by black men; black women characters in [*Eva's Man*] often appropriate the stereotype because it offers them the only means of exercising power" (*Black Women*, 1994, 91). Jones is thus concerned less with liberating the black community as a whole and more with how black women can appropriate negative stereotypes as a possible means of empowerment. Eva's repeated command, "Don't you explain me. Don't you explain me. Don't you explain me," prevents the reader from trying to sympathize with her, recuperate her from any negative stereotypes, or view her as a woman who has achieved a sense of wholeness. Eva does not function as a corrective, nor does she unite with her community. Rather, she exists as a woman outside any mode of femininity previously defined by communities like the writers of the Black Aesthetic.

The concept of unifying the black community around positivist, black nationalist notions and specifying the role of black art in forwarding the black revolution, while empowering the black community on the one hand, also necessarily alienated black writers who did not follow these strict requirements. Black women writers were especially excluded in many ways from black artistic movements, and, as Dubey notes, "in the heydey of the black cultural nationalist movement, their works were greeted with intense hostility from nationalist reviewers and critics" (*Black Women*, 1994, 1). Indeed, the biases of black nationalism spurred a black feminist movement which writer Pauli Murray describes as a "rising movement for women's liberation [which] is challenging the concept of male dominance which the Black Revolution appears to have embraced" (Murray, 1970, 95). The "collective of Black feminists" known as the Combahee River Collective, explains that although "It was our experience of disillusionment within these liberation movements...that led to the need to develop a politics that was antiracist, unlike those of white women, and anti-sexist, unlike those of Black and white men" (Collective, 1981, 211). The notion of a "black female consciousness" rather than just the "black consciousness" talked about in *The Black Aesthetic*, came to be "the basis of an expanding challenge to the postulates of domination in all its forms" (McLaughlin, 1990, xlv). Alice Walker goes even further in defining this black feminist consciousness by replacing the terminology "black feminist" with "womanist"—a term defined as "a black feminist or feminist of color," and thus tries to save it from its misuses in black male or in white texts (1983, xi).

Although admirable, however, black women's attempts to empower themselves and defy the racist and sexist misconceptions that oppressed them also in some ways mirrored the problems of exclusivity found in Black Aesthetic writings. Black women's reclamation of their subjectivity, their traditions, and their history resulted in metaphors and symbols like the matrilineal metaphor and idealized portrayals of black female bonding. While such notions enabled black women to authorize themselves and their stories, however, they also resulted in the exclusion of certain writers like Jones, who do not uniformly celebrate matrilineage and female friendship.

In the mid-to late 1980s especially, Afro-American criticism and theory was noticeably celebratory of the communal links between black women. Consider, for example, what Mary Helen Washington says of the black women's tradition: "women talk to other women in this tradition, and their friendship with other women—mothers, sisters, grandmothers, friends, lovers—are vital to their growth and well-being" (1990, 35). Similarly, Barbara Christian also elucidates the focus on community in the black women's tradition: "Afro-American women could lay claim to a viable tradition in which they had been strong central persons in their families and communities, not solely because of their relationship to men, but because they themselves had bonded together to ensure the survival of their children, their communities, the race" (quoted in Gates, *Reading Black*, 1990, 14). Christian had earlier visualized this type of tight women's community in the introduction to her book, *Black Feminist Criticism: Perspectives on Black Women Writers*, in which she, while thinking of Paule Marshall's essay "Poets in the Kitchen," reminisces about her own memories of women talking in kitchens, where "communities revolve around food or warmth" (1985, xii). This image is so prominent that it finds various echoes in literature, such as the scene in Toni Morrison's *Song of Solomon* (1977), in which Pilate, Hagar, and Reba sing together in warmth and light, and also in criticism, such as in Marjorie Pryse's discussions of a black woman's "community of kissing" (Pryse, 1985, 13). Indeed, there are many such texts that commemorate the sense of companionship between black women and their kitchen and kissing communities, like some of the essays in *Conjuring: Black Women, Fiction, and Literary Tradition* (1985), *Changing Our Own Words* (1989), *Reading Black, Reading Feminist*, and Michael Awkward's *Inspiriting Influences* (1989), to name but a few.

One of these types of women-women bonds—the mother-daughter bond—has moved beyond the literal and into the figurative. The concept of motherhood and daughterhood has frequently been represented in terms of a matrilineal metaphor that characterizes black feminist criticism and theory itself. Alice Walker's foundational text *In Search of Our Mother's Gardens*, in which her realization that "so many of the stories that I write, that we all write, are my mother's stories" (1983, 240), shaped the idea of a black matrilineal women's tradition while linking actual women's communities with the creations of fictional ones. Awkward terms this "harmonious" system of women writers "inspiriting influences," and thus radically diverges from the "anxiety of influence" model, as Harold Bloom terms it, which characterizes the male literary tradition (Awkward, 1989). Like Walker and others, Awkward also connects the positive influences between women writers with the 'inspiriting' atmosphere between fictional women characters like Zora Neale Hurston's Janie and Pheoby in her famous novel *Their Eyes Were Watching God* (1937).

In thinking of a nurturing matrilineal system, black feminist criticism recuperates the notion of motherhood from the negative biological reality that trapped women most often through ceaseless rapes during and after slavery and that continues to bind them in the racist and sexist society following Emancipation. Instead, motherhood transforms into the symbol of women's textual (versus biological) production.[2] The emphasis on woman-woman bonds and the always-positive matrilineal model, while providing a means to rewrite an oppressive history that wrote women out, also results in alienating black women writers who do not present such positive models of black female communities. Dubey, in a provocative essay about Gayl Jones's work, argues that "The matrilineal model has implicitly relegated some compelling black women novelists to the margins of its familial circle." Dubey finds that the matrilineal model bestows "an imaginary unity on a previously diffused body of texts" which results in the identification of "a cluster of values as essential, defining features of the black woman's fictional tradition" ("Gayl Jones," 1995, 245, 248). This proscriptive model then sets parameters that will not permit those who fall outside to enter within its boundaries.

It is telling that although Jones also explores relationships between black women friends and between daughters, mothers, and grandmothers, she has not been given much attention in many critical anthologies about black women writers.[3] However, the attention that Jones is now beginning to receive reflects a shift in the nature of black criticism itself. A prevalent topic of debate in current black literary criticism revolves around the same notions surrounding the construction of black communities and their desires for unity and coherence that structured early movements like The Black Aesthetic. While earlier texts were strong proponents of unity in black communities, however, Barbara Johnson has recently warned that this notion of unity, encapsulated in the frequent use of the pronoun "we" in communal discourses, can lead to "discourses of false universality," for "the pronoun 'we' has historically proven to be the most empowering and shiftiest shifter of all" (1989, 43). As my discussions of the novels will illustrate, it is precisely these false or slippery notions of unity within communities that are being challenged by various black women writers as they write about communal development and its pitfalls.

This concern surrounding essentialist ideas about community and about black femininity occurs frequently in black feminist criticism. Deborah McDowell, for example, posits that the categories of "'black womanhood,' 'black female identity,' [and] 'black experience,' can no longer be viewed as unchanging essences" for the "critical tendency to homogenize and essentialize black women" causes critics to "dissociate the category 'black woman' from a varied set of complex social and material realities" (1989, 53). Indeed, I argue that Jones's works avoid representing essentialist, unchanging, and unitary concepts of black womanhood by creating female characters whose sole function is not to simply defy negative stereotypes, but who rather flaunt and embody those very stereotypes. Her characters have conflicted, often painful relationships with their mothers, and certainly do not always view their mothers as a source of nurturing and growth. In fact, the daughters often defy the expectations of grandmothers and mothers in Jones's fiction. Ursa Corregidora, for example, struggles against her foremothers' dictum that a woman's role is to produce generations and keep alive a legacy of pain, power, and fury. Similarly, female friendships in Jones's works are not necessarily intimate and idealized, but are instead full of discord, hostility, and mistrust, as my essay will reveal.

Jones's work addresses the concerns in recent literary criticism that black texts often tend to portray only positive images of black unity/communities. While Houston Baker, Jr., in an essay about black women's writing, seeks to examine "selected [and "felicitous"] *imagistic fields* that occur within the 'poetics of Afro-American women's writing'" (original emphasis) (1989, 150). Mae Henderson, in response to Baker, argues against focusing on only positive images in black women's texts. Henderson states that "the real status of black women and their relationship to the rest of society. . . cannot be captured in 'felicitous images' [for] such a representation would suggest that black women inscribe themselves in nonadversarial relationships with both the community and the society at large."

Henderson finds the strength of black women's writing to be in "precisely its ability to disrupt and break with conventional imagery" (1989, 161). My arguments in this essay will center on how Jones's textual images disrupt conventional, communal notions about black women's bodies, desires, sexuality, and social roles through her creation of images of independent, empowered, desiring female subjects and also through her depictions of these same subjects' conflicts, anger, debilitation, and confusion.

Jones's novel *The Healing* continues to explore some of the major interests of the black artistic community in general and the black feminist community in particular—the relationship between an individual and her community, between a daughter and her mother, between a granddaughter and her grandmother, between women friends, and finally, between a woman and her lovers. Rather than idealizing these relationships, however, *The Healing* exquisitely balances between the harmonious and the discordant, the injurious and the healing. In each type of relationship, protagonist Harlan Jane Eagleton experiences difficulties and conflicts but somehow the very problems that confound her also enable her personal development as well as her transformation into a faith healer.

The opening chapter of the novel depicts Harlan traveling on a bus and surveying a fellow passenger. In response to the woman's single query, "You teach Sunday school?" Harlan, after telling the woman she is a faith healer, begins to imagine what the woman might think of her: "She didn't say anything about that faith healing, though, that woman with the Gypsy earrings, but I know what she is thinking: that I'm some kinda charlatan and mercenary, or some kinda crazy woman. All that. If I ain't a faker, then I'm a crazy woman that just beliefs in her own fakery" (5). While Harlan merely imagines a few words about what this particular woman thinks of her, she later begins to imagine, in the form of a conversation complete with intricate dialogues, what the community she is going to visit thinks of her. This conversation is so detailed that the narrative actually switches into the voices of the community and the reader is no longer sure if the speakers are actually talking or if the whole discussion is merely a figment of Harlan's mind.

The narrative, written in Harlan's stream-of-consciousness, states: "I can already hear 'em talking about me, those flibbertigibbets. She ain't no preacher woman or a teacher woman neither, she a faith healer, one of them be saying. What's the difference? She look like she belong on a submarine or a motorcycle. They don't allow womens on no submarine. On the modern submarine they do, 'cause this is the age of feminism..." (13). The narrative rambles on in an informal talk session between random townswomen, and as it continues, the reader becomes aware that he/she is no longer within Harlan's imagination but is actually witnessing the conversation of the community women who are awaiting Harlan's arrival. At one point the townswomen's discussion is interrupted and the scene returns to Harlan on the bus: "I take off my bomber jacket in the heat, roll it up into a pillow and place it in the crevice near the window. The mustard and sardines still gives off its pungent odor" (15). The next line reads, "She really do do some powerful healing, though. And she ain't a root doctor either. She don't need no root to heal..." The details of Harlan's passage thus become a part of the community's conversation about Harlan even though she is miles away. In this manner, Harlan's psyche becomes constantly and intimately intertwined with her community, whether or not she is actually with them. While this merging of voices does fuse Harlan with this community on the one hand, on the other it also makes her distinct from this "tank town" community, as Harlan calls it, for the narrative suggests that this community is so general and generic that they say the same things that Harlan has heard many times before in many different places. In fact, Harlan even remarks, "I don't have to describe them little tank towns to you, 'cause they're all alike" (6). This image of a generic community serves to situate Harlan within a larger world setting, for it is as if she has been everywhere, made comparisons, and seen everything already, and understands both how she relates to the world and how the world relates to her.

While Harlan's voice dominates the narrative as a first person speaker, she also doubles as an omniscient narrator who can read the minds and hear the voices of other characters in the text. Harlan's miraculous mind-reading ability specifically occurs in the beginning pages of the novel, when Harlan has already become a faith healer rather than in the flashback events of the rest of the novel. Harlan's intense communion with other community members thus occurs only when she gains the power to heal. Harlan knows, for example, that townswoman Zulinda is afraid of cats and remarks that Zulinda "is thinking that if I'm a real healing woman I'd know what she's thinking and heal her right then and there. How do you know who to cure first? I just know" (24). Zulinda's unspoken query is mentally answered by Harlan in a conversation within Harlan's mind. Later, as the townswomen drive Harlan to the place where she will perform the healing, Harlan apprehends their mistrust: "The women in the backseat are still thinking how common I am, how full of chitchat, and my vocabulary sounds elementary" (25). When Harlan is out of the women's earshot she perceives their gossip as she stands "listening to those voices downstairs. It ain't a auditory hearing, I should tell y'all" (26). Jones's technique of providing Harlan with this extraordinary ability allows her to function as an even more powerful healer, for she knows just what will impress the community and quell their doubts about her. Because Harlan can hear others' voices within her mind she can be unified with her community on a level far deeper than surface consciousness, even as they criticize or praise her.

Harlan's unification with the community becomes even more apparent if we become aware of how she creates the community by narrating them. Harlan's ability to read minds points to her role as the master storyteller. She creates the dialogue within her own story. In this way, she is both the protagonist of her own tale as well as the narrator. With this phenomenon Jones fuses several genres of literature—the oral storytelling tradition, the autobiography (for Harlan appears to be telling the story of her life), and the novel. The manner in which Harlan functions as both a first-person and omniscient narrator speaks to the process of reading itself and to the role of the reader. While the story begins with Harlan as a typical first-person narrator, when Harlan states in the quotations I cited above, "I don't have to describe them little tank towns to you," and "It ain't an auditory reading, I should tell y'all," we suddenly becomes aware that we, as the reader/audience, are being directly addressed. The reader thus becomes directly implicated in the story and becomes part of Harlan's larger community, and a witness to her entire transformation.

Ashraf Rushdy claims that the narrative style of Jones's previous works constitutes "an act of intersubjective communion, the creating of a sensibility that the hearer is an equal sharer in the story to the degree of being as involved in its events as the teller, of believing oneself to have lived out what another experiences," and I believe that *The Healing* demonstrates a prime example of this type of "intersubjective communion." While Rushdy is referring to the way Jones's characters listen to each other within the novels "so attentively as to feel that they are living out the experiences they describe, hearing them with such intensity that they assume an intersubjective communion with their narrators" (2000, 273), I posit that in this particular novel the reader functions as one of those characters and listens just as intently to Harlan's story as any of her audiences within the text. The reader thus becomes just as involved in the text as Harlan does with her grandmother's stories, for example, specifically because Harlan talks to the reader as she would to any other character. Just as Harlan's original witness, Nicholas, frequently repeats events with certain variations in his testimony of Harlan's first healing, Harlan repeats certain phrases and events with variation to the reader, almost as if she is healing the reader as well by telling her story/sermon. We realize that the entire story is, in a sense, Harlan's testimony during her healing performance, and we are listening to her in order to be healed ourselves.

This repetition-with-variation structure of the text resembles the rhythmical structures often found in black blues and jazz. Indeed, as Keith Byerman posits, "Patterns of repetition...and use of the audience as confidant [are] all characteristics of the blues." Byerman explains that the pattern of repetition in novels "reflects the idea of the 'cut,' a technique in black music" (1985, 172, 7), which James Snead thus describes: "The 'cut' overly insists on the repetitive nature of music, by abruptly skipping it back to another beginning which we have already heard (quoted in Byerman, 1981, 7)." Jones indicates the similarity of her novel with black music when Harlan talks about singer Billie Holiday. She says of the movie and the book about Billie Holiday, *Lady Sings the Blues*: "It's based on her autobiography. The book moves back and forth in time, though, more than the movie. You think you're in one time and the next chapter you're in another.

Joan says it's kinda like jazz. That that's what she's trying to do in that autobiography, kinda suggest the improvisations of jazz" (127). Jones here playfully signifies upon her own work which also flashes back and forth in time and makes sudden switches from chapter to chapter, and which also purposely resembles jazz. As Harlan tells the reader in order to explain the flashback sequences of her narrative, "If you listen to jazz, seem like you'd understand them flashback scene" (68).

Harlan's grandmother, another major storyteller in the novel, also uses a jazz-like structure in her tale-telling. Harlan says of her grandmother, "she never exactly told the story the same way each time. Sometimes she'd add new details, other times she'd tell the same details, but in a different order, in a different syntax" (221). Indeed, the narrative seems to suggest that this technique of repeating the same story again and again but with differences is an act common to all black storytelling, for Nicholas, Harlan's witness to her first healing, performs in the same way during his testifying sessions and unexpectedly adds new details to his story (33).

Another repetition-with-variation technique Jones uses in her novel is to make all the characters speak like Harlan. Indeed, if Harlan were actually telling the story to an audience, then the voices of others would naturally be spoken in Harlan's voice. The novel's structure thus suggests that Harlan describes other people speaking by making the other characters use the same mannerisms, accent, and speech methods of Harlan herself. Again, Jones signifies upon her own narrative technique when Harlan describes a dream she has about her lover, Josef: "In my dream he start talking kinda like me" (81). The dream-narrative that follows this statement supposedly shows Josef speaking, but the voice is Harlan's. In her entire dream/tale/sermon/text all the characters also "talk kinda like" Harlan. Not only does this technique suggest that the tale is spoken, rather than written, but it also enables the voices, stories, and histories of other people to move in and out of Harlan's memories, life, and imagination. The community directly becomes a part of Harlan's history and affects her transformation as she speaks/sings her song of metamorphosis.

Through the gossiping voices of this community that speaks like Harlan speaks, Harlan's story is previewed for the reader before it is actually told. Just as Nicholas testifies for Harlan before she begins her healing, the townswomen testify for Harlan before the reader hears her story. In this way, from the beginning of the novel Harlan is already defined both by the community, as well as by Harlan's own imagination. One of the community members says about Harlan:

> I first seen her picture in the *Louisville Defender* before she started printing up them brochures. It talked about all the travels she'd done over there in Africa, and somebody asked her whether she had learned her healing powers from one them Africans, whether she were apprentice to one of them African healers, but she said she had never been an apprentice to one of them African healers, but did say that she knew of a African healing woman, but they didn't heal exactly the same way. And the woman who were interviewing her said that maybe that African healing woman had transferred some healing powers to her without her knowing it. (18)

This passage, in the most casual way, hints at what will be a major part of Harlan's story—her travels to Africa, her meeting of the Masai healing woman, her refusal to follow that woman, her jealousy towards that woman who so fascinated Harlan's husband, and finally, Harlan's transformation into her Masai competitor as she becomes the very same type of healing, wandering woman she had once envied. In the same way, a townswoman casually mentions Harlan's healing of her grandmother:

> I witnessed it when she healed her own grandmother. Straightened out her shoulders. Say she have a hump in her shoulders just like a turtle's. In fact, there's people usedta refer to her as a turtle woman on account of them shoulders. Others say it ain't on account of them shoulders, that she usedta be a real turtle, which is nonsense, ain't no real turtle turn into no human being, not in the natural world, but I know them shoulders kinda look like that turtle shell. (18)

Again, this gossipy passage relates what will be a major story in Harlan's narrative—the tale of a grandmother who was once a turtle but who transformed into a human. The legend of the turtle woman and the disbelief about that legend thus spreads beyond Harlan's life and into the folklore of the community itself. Not only is Harlan's history part of the community's, but her grandmother's life story is as well.

When the narrative shifts from Harlan's voice into the community's conversation, the different community members all speak together in passages without any quotation marks, names, or separations. These extensive narratives compiled of diverse voices present contrary opinions of Harlan to the reader. While some voices question whether Harlan is a true healer or not, one voice vouches for Harlan: "Then she just looked at me and know my trouble. She said the trouble would end, and touched me, and it did. That's what I mean by she heal by healing. Now I moves easy as wind through trees....Sometimes she speak a word and it's done. Other times she got to lay on hands" (16). Another voice picks up immediately after this one and confides, "Well, I heard other vile things and notions about her. Say she was a gambler. Say she was loose-virtued before she become a celibate. You don't always begin on the right road" (16). Later, after Harlan performs her miracles, one townswoman remarks, "and this ordinary woman, she got herself a mighty appetite to be so holy, ain't she? A mighty devilish appetite to be so holy. They say you's supposed to hunger and thirst after righteousness," while a supporter of Harlan retorts, "Well, she the boss, if you ast me. Eat what she want. Us supposed to invite her here to heal and then let her go hungry?" (36). One townswoman believes Harlan does not deserve credit for her gift because it is just lent to her, and the actual healing is done by "the Lord," as "no gifts of the spirit to be given to ordinary women" (36). The community thus becomes Harlan's worst criticizers and strongest supporters and together tell Harlan's tale while themselves being a part of her narrative. As she tells of them, they in turn tell of her.

The townswomen struggle most with the idea that Harlan, the faith healer extraordinare, is also a simple, ordinary woman with a questionable gambling past and with earthly desires. The term "ordinary woman" appears several times in the novel and shifts its meaning until it comes to mean its opposite. While certain community members insist that Harlan is merely "ordinary," the term itself comes to refer to the most extraordinary women. Harlan says of herself, "Y'all thinks that spirit gifts supposed to be given to extraordinary people, to extraordinary men and women, the kings and queens of the world, the princes and princesses. But that the point of them spirit gifts, the point of them spirit gifts, is that I am just an ordinary woman. I am just an ordinary woman, that is the point of the healing. The spirit gift extraordinary, but as for me, I'm just a ordinary woman" (34). Harlan comments here that the very point of the healing is that this gift comes from an ordinary woman, for Harlan, as one critic puts it, is "ordinary in the way that every black woman is—that is, not ordinary at all, but a compelling testament to the human ability to transcend loss and to heal old wounds in the self and in others" (Jenkins, 2000, 366).

To emphasize those extraordinary qualities found in ordinary black women, Harlan states, "I've always been kinda ambivalent about that feminism. Them women that don't wanna be on no pedestal or say that they don't want to be on no pedestal, 'cause seem like to me a lot of them wants to keep the perks of womanhood, is kinda different from the women that ain't never been on no pedestal" (53). It's the woman who has never been on a pedestal, the woman who does not fit into the "ideals of true womanhood,"[4] whom Jones focuses on in her novel. The notion of "feminism" itself is questioned in the novel, as it has been by other black women such as Alice Walker. The Italian woman who befriends Joan during a performance confides in Joan, "I am not a *feminista*. I only think a woman should be true to who she believes herself to be. Or who she wants herself to be. Or who she imagines herself to be" (238). This definition of what a woman is could be applied to Harlan, who is at various times a beautician, gambler, rock-star manager, and a faith healer. It can refer to the Masai medicine woman, who heals her community and captivates Norvelle, Harlan's anthropologist husband. Joan is also such a woman, for she becomes a singer rather than the scientist her ex-husband desires her to be. This definition of what a woman is can apply to Harlan's grandmother, who insists she was once a turtle that transformed into a genuine woman. It can refer to Harlan's mother, who responds to her husband's desertion by teaching her daughter, "Learn to manage yourself. That is the key to freedom," (209), and who diligently cares for the people that have been neglected and forgotten by society. Indeed, Jones clearly portrays women who are all extraordinary, and who have all redefined feminism as simply meaning a woman who is true to herself. Thus, despite the opinion of critic Bernard Bell, who finds this novel "less radically black feminist than [Jones's] earlier fiction," which was more "raw, sexually explicit and violent" (1999, 247-248), I would argue that *The Healing* is indeed a profoundly feminist novel, even as it questions the nature of the term "feminism" itself, precisely because of its exploration of extraordinary/ordinary women.

Harlan's grandmother, Jaboti, provides an example of a truly extraordinary woman, and acts as a folkloric trickster figure in the novel. Even her name, which was given to her by a Brazilian during her travels, refers to "a turtle trickster in Brazilian folklore" (203). A beautician by trade, and thus a part of one of the centers of black female communal life, Jaboti spins her tales of transformation to her offspring and becomes one of the community's most legendary figures. Jaboti functions as a major character in the text, for she provides Harlan with questions about what makes and defines a woman, what a woman can do, and about how far a woman should go to be with a man. Jaboti tells Harlan about how she met Harlan's grandfather: "I saw this handsomest young man and took a liking to him, she said....Do you want to know how far I followed him? She chuckled. I followed him until I turned into a human being. Is that far enough for you?" (135). This idea of a woman following a man haunts Harlan throughout her life and serves as an example of something Harlan decides to never do. When Harlan tells Joan about how she refused to follow her husband all over Africa, she asserts, "I ain't the kind of woman who'd follow a man anywhere. I decided that a long time ago. I'll follow a man just so far and then. . . . Well, you ain't heard my grandmother Jaboti's story yet. She claimed that she followed a man so far that she turned into a human being. Me, if I wasn't a human being yet, I wouldn't follow a man so far even if his intention was to turn me into one" (119). Harlan directly attributes her decision to not follow a man to her grandmother's story and to the fate of her mother who was deserted by her husband. Harlan wonders, "How come a woman can't follow her ownself to turn human?" (137), and it is the need to provide an answer to this question that fuels most of her actions in the text.

The idea of a woman being able to transform into something else in order to adapt to her surroundings is another one of Jaboti's magical tales that Harlan does not entirely accept. Harlan states that she does not believe in

> the tale of metamorphosis, of how when human beings chased [Jaboti], like every turtle, she ran so slowly that in order to avoid getting caught she had to transform. Once they chased her into grass and she became grass. Another time they chased her into a valley, and she became a running stream. (164)

And yet Harlan herself undergoes many transformations in her life. Indeed, though she may not believe all her grandmother's stories, Harlan enacts these very tales of transformation by proving in her own life that she can come out of the shell of her mistrust, her jealousy, and her loneliness to become a healer of others. At the end of the novel as Harlan goes to heal in another community, Harlan sees a man in the audience who is, as she describes, "the last man in the world I expected to find. Or maybe the first man I'd hoped for" (283). One of her listeners asks her, "Do you think he'll follow you till you become human?" (283), and thus suggests that Harlan has, in a sense, reversed the turtle story. While Harlan may not follow a man to become human, it might take a man (whom I assume to be Norvelle) or an entire community to follow *her* in order to bring her out of her shell and into the realm of love and healing. In this way, not only does Harlan's grandmother act as a negative catalyst for her life, but she also proves her influence on Harlan by drawing her back into the story of the lonely Turtle Woman who transforms into a human being.

Harlan's tale illustrates other instances of Harlan being transformed by the very people she opposes or who oppose her. The Masai woman who inspired Norvelle's admiration and fueled Harlan's decision to leave him, serves as such an example. Harlan explains, "It was only the Masai woman who disoriented me because he wanted to stay with her, because he wanted to keep following her. ...And I guess I envied her independent nomadic life, traveling about, curing folks. I guess the only way she could express her wanderlust...was by being a medicine woman" (228). Norvelle had said of the Masai woman, "She's a treasure chest of medical folklore....Why, I could write a whole book about her" (230). And yet, when his own wife transforms into just such a wandering, healing woman, Norvelle returns to follow her and to discover the treasure within his own wife. Thus, Harlan transforms into the very woman she so envied—the woman who travels, who heals, who could captivate Norvelle—the ordinary woman with extraordinary powers.

The notion of traveling or wandering figures significantly in this novel, and Harlan travels from the moment the novel opens with her sitting on a bus to the closing of the novel when she goes to another town to practice her healing. Harlan travels all over Europe, Africa, South America and the United States in the novel and thus expands upon her knowledge of the world. In this way Harlan follows the example of her grandmother, who, though claiming that she "ain't by nature no wandering woman," relates, "when I was with the carnival, we wandered all through the States and up in Canada too and in Mexico and I told you about Brazil where they renamed me after that trickster" (222). Carol Boyce Davies, in discussing this phenomenon of migration that so often occurs in black women's texts, astutely comments that, "If we see Black women's subjectivity as a migratory subjectivity existing in multiple locations, then we can see how their work, their presences traverse all of the geographical/national boundaries instituted to keep our dislocations in place" (1994, 4). It is no coincidence that Harlan must travel in order to spread her healing, for movement is necessary to a woman's ability to heal herself and others, and to escape the boundaries that contain and dislocate her. Susan Willis notes the importance of the journey in texts about black women's spiritual development: "The voyage over geographic space is an expanded metaphor for the process of one person's coming to know who she is—not as an individual, but as a subject who…gives shape and substance to the self in history" (1995, 220).

Traveling also figures as a prominent trope in blues lyrics, and thus enhances the affinity of the novel with black musical traditions. Angela Davis points out that while "the traveling blues man is a familiar image . . . the traveling blues woman is not so familiar" (1998, 71), and indeed Jones follows the tradition of blues women who redefined mobility as a female and not just male prerogative. Morrison has similarly commented on black men's love of traveling, and notes that in works by black male authors "the big scene is the traveling…scene, for black men. They are moving…going from town to town or place to place or looking out and over and beyond and changing and so on—that...is one of the monumental themes in black literature about men." Morrison reveals her fascination with traveling by remarking that "the fact that [black men] would split in a minute just delights me" ("Intimate things," 1994, 25-26).

Morrison shares her attraction to the mobility of male life with other women authors like Jones as well as with female blues singers. Davis notes that the travels of women in blues lyrics "back and forth, away from and toward home, are frequently associated with the exercise of autonomy in their sexual lives. The subjects of [these] songs...make decisions to embark on various journeys because they have been hurt deeply by their sexual partners but refuse, even in their pain, to relinquish their own agency" (1998, 66-67). Harlan's movements from place to place as well as the novel's structural movements back and forth in time, in and out of Harlan's narratives, her maternal relatives' narratives, and the community women's narratives, echoes Davis's statement by illustrating Harlan's independence and sexual autonomy. Harlan refuses to wallow in her hurt by staying with her husband and instead leaves him as soon as she feels herself to be compromised. Unlike some married women, who have the additional responsibilities of children, Harlan does not allow herself to be "territorially confined by the domestic requirements of family building" (Davis, 1998, 68). Morrison astutely notes that the characteristics of contemporary women "encourage in themselves are more male characteristics, not because [the contemporary woman] has a fundamental identity crisis, but because she wants to be truly free. Part of that is perceived as having the desirable characteristic of maleness, which includes self-sufficiency and adventurousness" ("Toni Morrison," 1981, 105). Harlan's life recalls that of the man who unabashedly "splits" in the face of an emotional crisis, who has no ties to prevent him from leaving, who relishes adventure, and who is fully self-sufficient. By redefining these traditionally male characteristics as female traits, Harlan embodies a new mode of femininity that breaks free from past restrictive notions of female submissiveness and domesticity.

When Harlan decides to leave Norvelle she could easily be singing the words of Ma Rainey in "Traveling Blues," one of Rainey's favorite songs: "I'm dangerous and blue, can't stay here no more/ I'm dangerous and blue, can't stay here no more/ Here come my train, folks, and I've got to go," or the words of Rainey in "Farewell Daddy Blues": "I'm wild about my daddy, I want him all the time/ Wild about my daddy, I want him all the time/ But I don't want you, daddy, if I can't call you mine/ Got the farewell blues, see, and my trunk is packed/ Got the farewell blues, see, and my trunk is packed/ But I don't want no daddy because'n I ain't comin' back" (quoted in Davis, 1998, 251, 216). Indeed Harlan's decision to acknowledge her sexual desires (like Rainey's protagonist who claims to be "wild about my daddy") but to refuse to be trapped by them into passivity and submission, speaks to Rainey's songs like "Gone Daddy Blues," "Goodbye Daddy Blues," "Leavin' This Morning," and "Lost Wandering Blues," in addition to many others. Rainey's song, "Walking Blues," which laments: "Walked and walked 'til I, walked and walked 'til I almost lost my mind, hey, hey, hey/ Walked and walked 'til I almost lost my mind/ I'm afraid to stop walking, 'cause I might lose some time" (quoted in Davis, 1998, 75) has been called "the finest expression of the wandering woman theme," by Sandra Lieb (1981/1998, 75), and the similarity between the song's sentiment and Harlan's actions arguably makes Jones's text an equally renowned narrative of a perpetually wandering woman. In this aspect Jones's latest novel continues the black woman's literary tradition of portraying traveling, mobile women such as Janie in Hurston's *Their Eyes Were Watching God*, Pilate in Morrison's *Song of Solomon*, Avey in Paule Marshall's *Praisesong for the Widow* (1983), and the sisters in Ntozake Shange's *Sassafrass, Cypress & Indigo* (1982), to name but a few.

Harlan's position as the business manager of rock star Joan Savage allows her to indulge her love of traveling, and indeed Joan accuses Harlan of using her position solely to satisfy her wanderlust:

> You've dragged me all over the fucking globe, she said. All over the fucking globe.... Me, I've worked hard. I worked my butt off. I hardly knew what fucking country I was in most of the fucking time. It was all for you, not me. Places you never would have got to go to in a million fucking years, if it wasn't for me. Your husband took you over there to Africa, but you got to travel all over the world because of me. That's the only reason you stay with me. (211)

The fact that Harlan's relationship with Joan enables her to travel, but that Joan insults Harlan for being in this very position, symbolizes Harlan's relationship with Joan in general. Although Harlan and Joan talk constantly in the text and discuss everything from feminism to books, to gambling, to ex-lovers, the two women have an extremely caustic relationship and hardly resemble the close friendships between black women often portrayed in black women's fiction. Harlan states definitively, "I ain't never imagined that me and Joan anything alike, I don't even think of her as my alter ego. She ain't even the sorta woman I imagine myself to be anything like" (88) and thus clearly negates any idea of the two women mirroring each other in any way. Joan trusts Harlan so little that she does not even believe Harlan's story: "I think you're a con artist or some shit. A con woman. I think you just conned me.... I bet you've just been conning my ass. Telling me all of your tales" (232).

Harlan's and Joan's statements about each other directly contrasts with the relationship between two famous fictional black women friends who have inspired much of the positive metaphors in black feminist criticism—Janie and Pheoby in Hurston's *Their Eyes Were Watching God*. Pheoby, who is Janie's "kissing friend," and who is "eager to feel and do through Janie," tells Janie, after listening to her story, "Ah done growed ten feet higher from jus' listenin' tuh you, Janie" (1937/1990, 7,6,182). She certainly does not accuse Janie of "conning" her with lies. Carla Kaplan, in an essay on Hurston's novel, argues that Pheoby functions as an "exaggerated idealization," and that Hurston constructs "ideal listening as virtual mirroring" (1995, 133). In light of the friendship between Janie and Pheoby, which is the epitome of idealizations of black women-women bonds, we can see Jones's depiction of Harlan and Joan as a revolutionary portrait of a black female relationship which does not involve an ideal, intimate, and sympathetic listener or a mirroring of two women characters.

Although Joan depends upon Harlan for everything, from business decisions to praising her performances, she distrusts, insults, and abuses her constantly. From accusing Harlan of trying to "sabotage" her (215), to denying Harlan's skill and usefulness to a client—"She can't do a thing for me but my makeup, and the way I tell her to" (174)—Joan puts Harlan down and negates any possibility of real friendship. What angers Joan most about Harlan, though, is Harlan's one-time sexual fling with Joan's ex-husband, for whom Joan professed no feelings, but in actuality, with whom she remains in love. Despite her anger, however, she plays mind-games with Harlan by denying any negative feelings towards her while continuing to insult her: "For Christsakes, girl, you still thinking about that? You still chewing on that old chestnut? How the hell was I to know? I wouldn't have opened the fucking door if I'd known you two were bumping boody like a couple of bonobo monkies or some shit" (111).

While many black women's texts, including Jones's own previous works, focus on the violence between black men and women, in this novel Jones purposely portrays a rarely discussed event—the violence between black women. This violence is configured in ways that both recall heterosexual violence between men and woman, and that markedly differ from such representations of violence. In an insightful discussion of Jones's use of violence in *Corregidora*, Richard Hardack positions male, heterosexual, and "reproductive sexuality" as being "constructed as written, violent, patriarchal, and immutably inscribed. By contrast, Jones posits orality as an alternative to male heterosexual desire and Western writing, which are thematically . . . characterized as abusive." Hardack continues by stating that this alternative to heterosexual and written violence, is "predicated on several kinds of orality, particularly oral narrative and oral sex, that might offer the possibility of nonviolent relationships and noncoercive communication" (1999, 645). Hardack's observations about *Corregidora* provide for an interesting reading of *The Healing*, for the negative repercussions of the written word do not figure so prominently in the later novel as in the former. Harlan does not struggle as Ursa does to speak her ancestors' stories in order to combat false written documentation. Rather, Harlan's spoken voice dominates the story without any written documentation to counter it, and her relationship to Joan is also constituted by verbal dialogues. And yet Harlan's and Joan's relationship can hardly be characterized as "nonviolent" or "noncoercive." In this novel, Jones thus refuses to allow us to slip into any simple binaries of male vs. female, heterosexual vs. homosexual, written vs. oral, and violent vs.

nonviolent. Hardack argues that "for Jones, bearing witness is a passive response to violence, one that leaves Ursa in the role of mere observer and sexual recipient. Ursa must then...create her own present.... [She] must translate mere speech into song, and passive observance into active orality" (1999). Unlike Ursa, however, Harlan actively speaks/sings her story throughout the novel, and she both bears witness to the life of her maternal ancestors, as well as follows her own unique path. And yet she is also the victim of violence and abuse, and even survives a murderous attack.

Joan's abuse of Harlan goes beyond the verbal, and as Harlan narrates, "She plunged her fist into my stomach. I doubled over. I tried to straighten up, but there were spikes in the pit of my stomach. I started toward the bathroom and held on to the door. You fucked him, she said" (233). The violence Joan enacts upon Harlan rhetorically echoes the violence of male penetration, for Joan plunges her fist into Harlan's abdomen, she digs a knife into Harlan's body, and she constantly talks about how Harlan engages in "fucking." By both Joan's language and acts Jones clearly recalls the depictions of male violence upon the passive female body. But Joan's violence generates a response in Harlan that is far from debilitating or passive. At Harlan and Joan's first meeting, Joan had told Harlan, "It's about time I met somebody real for a change.... A real girl" (275). Later, Harlan dramatically narrates what Joan says during her final act of violence:

> It is not intoxication. It is not insanity. It is Joan holding the knife. She has come up to the chair, in the living room, looking as if she is bathed in light, and there is something sparkling. Suddenly the knife is here and casually she drives it in. This is the truth of the story. Not Nicholas' tale, but this one. The knife bends even before Nicholas gets to the chair to grab her arm, and save me. I think it has struck bone and bent. But it's struck not where any bone would be. I thought you were a real person, she says. But you're not even a human woman, you're not even a real human woman. This is the truth of it. The knife fell out. I put my hand to the wound and it healed. Nicholas came to save me, and Joan stood there raising her arms to the ceiling in disbelief. (280)

Joan here denies the thing she had originally most admired about Harlan—her humanity. While Joan's speech and murderous act are the ultimate forms of mistreatment, her words in one sense do ring true, for Harlan, at this point in the story, is still in her shell and has not yet turned into a "genuine" human woman. It takes her transformation into a faith healer, her merging with the community, and her return to love—to a man who follows her until she becomes human—to make her "real."

The diction of the above passage imitates the nature of Joan's and Harlan's relationship, for Joan is described as being "bathed in light" with "something sparkling"—a rather surreal and heavenly description of a soon-to-be murderer. Amy Gottsfried, in a discussion about the trope of violence in women's novels, notes that "these works address the reader's often reluctant role as witness, because they uncover such painful historic moments." Gottsfried explains that, "Strategies for drawing in readers include . . . the association of lyrical language or beautiful images with particularly horrific scenes . . . as if to transform their violence and victimization" (1998, 10). The language of the passage certainly captivates the reader as well as changes the scene from a simple description of murder to something strangely beautiful and transforming. The image of Joan as angelic or prophetic and holding something bright coincides with Harlan's miraculous act of healing. These coinciding images point to a pertinent fact—that without Joan, Harlan could not have become a faith healer and would never have learned to heal herself. Harlan's major transformation in the novel is dependent upon Joan's single act. Joan's act, then, transforms from being purely reminiscent of male penetrative violence and becomes a source of empowerment for Harlan. She enables Harlan to be the healer who first heals herself.

Hardack notes that in *Corregidora*, "Ursa's fall, the wounds scarring her belly and voice—must be transformed into tools for learning, and characters must not simply survive violence, but use the history of that violence to find a means of salvation" (1999, 652). Ursa must thus overcome the brutality of slave owner Corregidora brought upon her maternal ancestors and the pain this has mentally caused her, as well as overcome the loss of her womb due to Mutt's violence. The novel describes Ursa's struggle to regain a sense of identity outside her delegated role as mother and her shock at no longer being able to fulfill this duty—at no longer being what she perceives as a "whole" woman. While it is true that Mutt's violence is transformed into a learning experience that eventually enables Ursa to sing her own song, I argue that Joan's violence has a somewhat different effect upon Harlan—an effect that is especially highlighted in the heavenly language describing Joan's attempt at murder. Harlan does not have a mental conflict due to Joan's act, and she does not have to undergo a long, painful process of redeeming her mutilated body and her scarred soul. Rather, the passage shows how Harlan immediately and naturally heals from Joan's knife wound and then embraces her newfound healing powers. Unlike Mutt's injury of Ursa and the deep emotional distress resulting from her loss, Joan's penetration of Harlan does not cause Harlan to question her womanhood and the wound does not mutilate Harlan's body at all. In fact, Joan's stabbing actually reveals Harlan's supernatural strength and abilities. Although their relationship if full of strife, abuse, and violence, as I have illustrated, Harlan's and Joan's interactions are an implicit part of Harlan's evolution, a natural part of her development which unleashes her power. Thus, while illustrating the conflicts and even abuse between black women, Jones also reveals the interdependence between them and the complexities of their relationships which alternate between love and hatred. For even hatred between women can fuel a woman's strength, as the novel metaphorically reveals.

The dissonant yet dependent relationship between Harlan and Joan recalls another famous fictional female couple in black literature—Nel and Sula in Morrison's *Sula* (1973). Just as Harlan easily sleeps with Joan's ex-husband without a thought of hurting Joan, Sula sleeps with Nel's husband with the confidence that a friendship between women cannot be destroyed because of something as impermanent as a man. Nel cries out in anger to Sula, "You *can't* do it all. You a woman and a colored woman at that. You can't act like a man. You can't be walking around all independent-like, doing whatever you like, taking what you want, leaving what you don't," to which Sula responds, "I know what every colored woman in this county is doing.... Dying. Just like me. But the difference is they dying like a stump. Me, I'm going down like one of those redwoods. I sure did live in this world." Sula's life poignantly illustrates an answer to Harlan's question, "How come a woman can't follow her ownself to turn human?" (137), for following her "ownself" is exactly what Sula always does. Like Sula, Harlan also lives her life fully, is completely independent, and often seems to act "like a man" without any fear of leaving what holds her down. Sula's apparently abusive act towards Nel becomes a way of teaching Nel that, as Sula puts it, "My lonely is *mine*. Now your lonely is somebody else's. Made by somebody else and handed to you…. A secondhand lonely." As Sula lays dying she delightedly imagines her pleasure in confiding her experience of dying to Nel. Nel also returns her thoughts to Sula and eventually realizes their inseparable ties that no amount of pain can break. Her cry, "Oh Lord, Sula…girl, girl, girlgirlgirl" (142, 143, 174), becomes her most true or "real" utterance in the novel. Like Harlan and Joan, Nel and Sula form two halves of a complete unit—although they are opposite to each other in nearly every way, and although Sula takes something precious from Nel, she eventually allows Nel to heal and to reclaim her womanhood. While Nel consciously returns to the friendship that Sula had always upheld at the end of that novel, however, in *The Healing* Harlan and Joan's interdependence is more metaphorically depicted, for Harlan never verbally acknowledges her debt to Joan, and Joan refuses to speak to Harlan or believe in her powers.

The reaction of critics to Jones's novel and their easy dismissal of the antagonism between Harlan and Joan reveals a tendency to still idealize relationships between black women characters. One review of the novel cites Jones as stating, "The previous novels were meant to be 'blues novels'…but they emphasized the narrowest range of subject matter—the man-done-her-wrong-type of blues—and even the blues itself has more possibility and range. *The Healing* is meant to be a rejection of those earlier novels." The review seems to suggest that Jones is moving beyond her previous "tightly woven tales of murder and sexual violence" (Chambers, 1998, 68). While it is true that this novel, unlike Jones's other works, does not focus on men's abuse of women and sexual violence between men and women, there is no mention of the fact that the novel *does* talk about women's abuse of women and violence between women. Another review contrasts *The Healing* with Jones's previous works—her "stark, disturbing stories [which] explored the sometimes degrading sex between black men and women living in a country consumed with racial identity and power," and finds *The Healing* to be "broadly hopeful" unlike the earlier texts (Sayers 1998, 28). A third review states about *The Healing*, "Gone are many of the graphic and violent images that populated the pages of *Corregidora* and *Eva's Man*" (Jenkins, 2000, 365).

It is true that Harlan does not suffer in the way Ursa does from the lack of a womb, nor is she as unrepentant and violent as Eva is (although Joan does remain unrepentant about her act and does not even believe in Harlan's ability to heal). And while Harlan's transformation certainly is hopeful, these reviews do not detail Joan's attempts to degrade Harlan or the rather disturbing fact that Joan tried to kill her. The imagery Jones uses to depicts Joan's murderous act, and the fact that this act started the very faith healing the novel explores, also seems to diminish the abuse between the women. However, if Joan were a man and treated Harlan in the same way, I believe the reaction of critics would be markedly different and this novel would not seem as "hopeful" or unequivocally positive as some critics find it to be. I argue that we must not ignore the text's representation of violence and abuse, but should rather focus precisely on the balance between violence and healing, disharmony and harmony in all of Harlan's relationships to arrive at a true understanding of this complex novel. The force of Joan's brutality and anger as well as the impact of this violence upon Harlan's transformation should both be considered, just as we should interrogate both the negative and positive impacts of the community, Harlan's grandmother and mother, and the Masai woman upon Harlan's life. The women Harlan most fights or rebels against become the ones who most affect her transformation, just as the man she refuses to follow comes back to follow her and make her whole. By viewing both the detrimental and the beneficial aspects of Harlan's relationships, we can thus avoid easy idealizations that can prevent writers like Jones from either being delegated to the peripheries of a black feminist tradition or from having their works overly simplified.

Notes

[1] Madhu Dubey's *Black women novelists and the nationalist aesthetic*, which I will discuss in more detail later, particularly emphasizes the problems with the positive nature of the black matrilineal tradition.

[2] See Venetria Patton, *Women in chains*, Dianne Sadoff, "Black matrilineage: The case of Alice Walker and Zora Neale Hurston," *Signs: Journal of Women in Culture and Society* 11.1 (1985) 4-26. Chikwenye Oguyenmi, writing in the context of Nigerian women writers, posits that if "birth is the core of woman's vernacular tradition, the source of her cruel predicament, [then] perhaps privileging birth...can be a maneuverable moment in the discourse to set her free" (1996, 8).

[3] For example, these anthologies and books either do not discuss Jones at all or only very briefly mention her work: Barbara Christian, *Black feminist criticism, black literature and literary theory*, ed. Henry Louis Gates, Jr. (New York: Methuen, 1984), *Changing our own words*, ed. Cheryl Wall (New Brunswick, NJ: Rutgers University Press, 1989), *Conjuring: Black women, fiction and literary tradition, Reading black, reading feminist, studies in black American literature, Volume 111: Black feminist criticism and critical theory*, eds. Houston Baker, Jr., and Joe Weixelmann (Greenwood, FL: The Penkevill Publishing Company, 1988).

[4] Historian Barbara Welter defines what she calls the "cult of true womanhood" as such: "The attributes of True Womanhood, by which a woman judged herself and was judged by her husband, her neighbors and society, could be divided into four cardinal virtues – piety, purity, submissiveness, and domesticity.... With them she was promised happiness and power." This cult of true womanhood was defined by a white patriarchal society and thus necessarily excluded black women from its parameters. Black women had to redefine womanhood in order to the particularities of black female life in a racist and sexist America (1976, 21).

Works Cited

Awkward, Michael. 1989. *Inspiriting influences: tradition, revision, and Afro-American women's novels*. New York: Columbia University Press.

Baker, Houston A., Jr. 1989. There is no more beautiful way: theory and the poetics of Afro-American women's writing. *Afro-American literary study in the 1990s*. eds. Houston A. Baker, Jr., and Patricia Redmond. Chicago: The University of Chicago Press.

Bell, Bernard. 1999. The liberating literary and African American voices of Gayl Jones. *Comparative Literature Studies* 36, no. 3: 247-258.

Byerman, Keith. 1985. *Fingering the jagged grain: Tradition and form in recent black fiction*. Athens: The University of Georgia Press.

Carmichael, Stokely and Charles V. Hamilton. 1967. *Black power: The politics of liberation in America*. New York: Random House, Inc.

Chambers, Veronica. 1998. The invisible woman reappears – sort of. *Newsweek* 131:68.

Christian, Barbara. 1985. *Black feminist criticism: Perspectives on black women writers*. New York: Pergamon Press.

———. 1990. *Reading black, reading feminist: A critical anthology*. ed. Henry Louis Gates, Jr. New York: Meridian.

Combahee River Collective. 1981. A black feminist statement. *This bridge called my back: writings by radical women of color*. eds. Cherrie Moraga and Gloria Anzaldua. New York: Kitchen Table: Women of Color Press.

Davies, Carole Boyce. 1994. *Black women, writing and identity: Migrations of the subject*. London: Routledge.

Davis, Angela. 1998. *Blues legacies and black feminism: Gertrude 'Ma' Rainey, Bessie Smith, and Billie Holiday*. New York: Vintage Books.

Dubey, Madhu. 1994. *Black women novelists and the nationalist aesthetic*. Bloomington: Indiana University Press.

———. 1995. Gayl Jones and the matrilineal metaphor of tradition. *Signs: Journal of Women in Culture and Society*. 20, no. 21: 245-267.

Fuller, Hoyt. 1971. The new black literature: protest or affirmation. *The black aesthetic*. ed. Addison Gayle, Jr.. New York: Doubleday & Company, Inc..

Gates, Henry Louis, Jr. 1988. *The signifying monkey: A theory of African American literary criticism*. New York: Oxford University Press.

Giddings, Paula. 1984. *When and where I enter: The impact of black women on race and sex in America*. New York: Bantam Books.

Gottfried, Amy. 1998. *Historical nightmares and imaginative violence in American women's writings*. Westport, CT: Greenwood Press.

Hardack, Richard. 1999. Making generations and bearing witness: violence and orality in Gayl Jones's *Corregidora*. *Prospects: An Annual of American Cultural Studies* 24: 645-661.

Henderson, Mae G. 1989. Response to Baker's 'there is no more beautiful way.' *Afro-American literary study in the 1990s*. eds. Houston A. Baker, Jr., and Patricia Redmond. Chicago: The University of Chicago Press.

Hull, Gloria T. 1987. *Color, sex, and poetry: three women writers of the Harlem Renaissance*. Bloomington: Indiana University Press.

Hurston, Zora Neale. 1937. *Their eyes were watching god*. New York: Harper & Row Publishers. Rpt. by Perennial Library, 1990.

Jenkins, Candice. 2000. Review of Gayl Jones' *The Healing*. *African American Review* 34, no. 2: 365-366.

Johnson, Barbara E. 1989. Response to Henry Louis Gates, Jr., 'Canon-formation, literary history, and the Afro-American tradition: from the seen to the told. *Afro-American literary study in the 1990s*. eds. Houston A. Baker, Jr., and Patricia Redmond. Chicago: University of Chicago Press.

Jones, Gayl. 1984. About My Work. *Black women writers (1950-1980)*. ed. Mari Evans. New York: Anchor Press/Doubleday: 233-235.

———. 1975. *Corregidora*. Boston: Beacon.

———. 1998. *The Healing*. Boston: Beacon Press.

———. 1982. Interview With Gayl Jones. Conducted by Charles Rowell. *Callaloo* 5, no. 3: 32-53.

———. 1991. *Liberating voices: Oral tradition in African American literature*. Cambridge: Harvard University Press.

———. 1994. The Quest for Wholeness Re-Imagining the African-American novel: an essay on third world aesthetics. *Callaloo* 17, no. 2: 507-518.

Kaplan, Carla. 1995. The erotics of talk: 'that oldest human longing' in *Their eyes were watching God*. *American Literature* 67, no. 1: 115-142.

Karenga, Ron. 1971. Black cultural nationalism. *The black aesthetic*. ed. Addison Gayle, Jr. New York: Doubleday & Company, Inc.

Lieb, Sandra. 1981. *Mother of the blues: A study of Ma Rainey*. Amherst: University of Massachusetts Press.

McDowell, Deborah. 1989. Boundaries: Or distant relations and close Kin. *Afro American literary study in the 1990s*. eds. Houston A. Baker, Jr., and Patricia Redmond. Chicago: University of Chicago Press.

McLaughlin, Andree Nicola. 1990. A renaissance of spirit: black women remaking the universe. *Wild women in the whirlwind: Afra-American culture and the contemporary literary renaissance*. eds. Joanne M. Braxton and Andree Nicola McLaughlin. New Brunswick, NJ: Rutgers University Press.

Morrison, Toni. 1976. Intimate things in place: a conversation with Toni Morrison. Conducted by Robert Steptoe. *Conversations with Toni Morrison*. 1994. ed. Danielle Taylor-Guthrie. Jackson: University Press of Mississippi.

———. 1973. *Sula*. New York: Plume.

———. 1981. Toni Morrison. Conducted by Charles Ruas. *Conversations with Toni Morrison*. 1994. ed. Danielle Taylor-Guthrie. Jackson: University Press of Mississippi.

Murray, Pauli. 1970. The liberation of black women. *Voices of the new feminism*. ed. Mary Lou Thompson. Boston: Bantam Press.

Neal, Larry. 1968. The black arts movement. *The Drama Review*, Vol. 12:4. Reprinted in *Within the Circle: An Anthology of African American Literary Criticism from the Harlem Renaissance to the Present*. 1994. ed. Angelyn Mitchell. Durham, NC: Duke University Press: 184-198.

Oguyenmi, Chikwenye. 1996. *Africa wo/man palava: The nigerian novel by women*. Chicago: University of Chicago Press.

Patton, Venetria. 2000. *Women in chains: The legacy of slavery in black women's fiction*. Albany: State University of New York Press.

Pryse, Marjorie. 1985. Introduction: Zora Neale Hurston, Alice Walker, and the 'ancient power' of black women. *Conjuring: Black women, fiction, and literary tradition*. eds. Marjorie Pryse and Hortense Spillers. Bloomington: Indiana University Press.

Rushdy, Ashraf. 2000. 'Relate sexual to historical': race, resistance, and desire in Gayl Jones's *Corregidora*. *African American Review* 34, no. 2: 273-297.

Sayers, Valerie. 1998. Faith healer. *The New York Times Book Review*. 103:28.

Snead, James. 1981. On repetition in black culture. *Black American Literature Forum*. 15. Quoted in Keith Byerman. 1985. *Fingering the jagged grain: Tradition and form in recent black fiction*. Athens: The University of Georgia Press.

Walker, Alice. 1983. *In search of our mothers' gardens*. San Diego: Harcourt Brace & Company.

Washington, Mary Helen. 1990. 'The darkened eye restored:' notes toward a literary history of black women. *Reading black, reading feminist: A critical anthology*. ed. Henry Louis Gates, Jr. New York: Meridian.

Welter, Barbara. 1976. The cult of true womanhood, 1820-1860. *Dimity convictions: The American woman in the nineteenth century*. Columbus: University of Ohio Press.

Willis, Susan. 1995. Black women writers: taking a critical perspective. *Making a difference: Feminist literary criticism*. eds. Gayle Green and Coppelia Kahn. London: Methuen.

CHAPTER THREE

From Mules to Turtle and Unicorn Women: The Gender-Folk Revolution and the Legacy of the Obeah in Gayl Jones's *The Healing*

L.H. Stallings

> I was a turtle before I became a human being, said my grandmother. She was taking a new order of beauty products out of the boxes and restocking the shelves....Then I saw this handsomest young man and took a liking to him, she said as she put the superior beauty products on the shelves. Do you want to know how far I followed him? She chuckled. I followed him until I turned into a human being. Is that far enough for you?
> —Grandmother Eagleton, *The Healing*

> The black unicorn is restless
> The black unicorn is unrelenting
> The black unicorn is not free.
> —Audre Lorde, *The Black Unicorn*

Would you recognize the beginning of a revolution if it came with talk of Turtle women, Black Unicorn women, and healing powers? I hope so, because Gayl Jones's *The Healing* contains some of the most interesting revolutionary dogma for black women today. Perhaps as a symbolic answer to Audre Lorde's poem, Grandmother Eagleton also expresses how one black female awaits a revolutionary transformation from turtle to something fully capable of expressing her being. Just as Zora Neale Hurston utilized animal folk metaphors in *Mules and Men* (1935) and *Their Eyes Were Watching God* (1937), specifically the mule, to explore the historical experiences and subjectivity of black women through metaphors of animals, Gayl Jones's *The Healing* (1998) serves as the most recent textual embodiment to recall the influence of animal tales and folklore to discuss black female identity.

For more than twenty-five years, Gayl Jones has explored the pain and problematic identity of black women in her writing. Scholarship and criticism have heralded Jones as a creator of the blues-structured novel for her works concerned with pain and oppression, *Corregidora* (1975) and *Eva's Man* (1976). Yet few critics have assessed her aesthetic ingenuity in demonstrating how to heal that pain and oppression. *The Healing* uses a divergent structure based on liminality and an oral narrative structure and discourse defined by illusiveness of gender that differs from Jones's blues aesthetic narratology. In *The Healing*, aesthetics and metaphors in the text rely on a mythic understanding of faith healing produced by oral traditions and grounded in what cannot be named or defined—divinity. Jones creates a narratology based on divination—the language/discourse of that which is unknown to discuss what is known as the "black woman," a misrepresentation and flawed symbol.

The Healing introduces readers to Harlan Eagleton, a black female jack-of-all-trades who becomes a faith healer. Yet from the very beginning of the novel's immediate meditation on a tin of "Spirit of Scandinavian Sardines, floating in mustard sauce" (3), the reader comes to understand how Gayl Jones has taken your mama's healing protagonist (the conjurer woman and hoodoo priestess from Chestnutt and Hurston) and made it into a character touched by her own voice and ideologies. The novel manages to reject the historical figuration the "black woman" in favor of a more fluid discourse on black female identity. Jones's characterization of Harlan as a healer, essentially like the hoodoo doctor Eulalia in Hurston's *Mules and Men*, acts as a way to speak about individuals that cannot be named or defined because of their boundless identity.

In the canon of African American women's literature, *The Healing* is not the first contemporary novel to make use of conjurers, healers, and magical realism. On the contrary, Bambara's Minnie Ransom and Velma in *The Salt Eaters* (1980), Marshall's Rosalie Parvay and Avery

Johnson in *Praisesong for the Widow* (1983), and Naylor's Mattie Michaels and Sapphire in *The Women of Brewster's Place* and *Mama Day* (1988) are characters who have all been touched by or bestowed with healing gifts in various ways. While Jones, like each of the aforementioned novelists, does explore healers and healing in a similar and traditional way—to document and examine the psychological ills of African American women—*The Healing* modernizes the concepts of healing in black women's fiction in several ways. Critics such as Gay Wilentz, Trudier Harris, and Valerie Lee have examined the literary character of the black female healer in ways that reveal that there are some common variables in the above traditional healing protagonist. As they note, these healers are usually exiled or outcasts, asexual, or non-threatening women who focus more on those coming to be healed as opposed to their own self-healing. Through her characterization of Harlan, Jones revises and reconstructs the healer character type: where Minnie was an outcast in Bambara's *The Salt Eaters*, Harlan's ordinariness and ability to shift her stations in life and community are emphasized time and again; where Minnie and Sapphire may have been asexual or nonsexual, Harlan comes to know her healing gift because of her sexual transgressions; and where laying on of hands usually focuses on the healer laying hands on a body other than her own, Harlan's first experience of laying on of hands puts her in contact with her own body. These divergences from previous healing protagonists exist in Jones's text for a reason—to move the identity of black females outside of traditional discourses of gender, which might make them "other." As we will see, Jones's healing protagonist explodes myths of the super (natural) black woman and Western limitations of gender.

Although not primarily concerned with black female identity, Judith Butler's *Gender Trouble: Feminism and the Subversion of Identity* and its discussion on the intelligible logic of gender provides welcomed insight as to why such strategies would be necessary: "The cultural matrix through which gender identity has become intelligible requires that certain 'identities' cannot 'exist.'...Indeed, precisely because certain kinds of 'gender identities' fail to conform to those norms of cultural intelligibility, they appear only as developmental failures or logical impossibilities from within that domain" (1999, 25). Clearly, we could argue that this has been the case for black female identity. Negative images and representations about black women have long endured. Positive images of black females and historical moments of survival and triumph over adversity due to patriarchy and racism have been distorted or eclipsed by the logic of gender, which defines her as the emasculating matriarch. The problem of finding a discourse for black women's identity has been revealed in the works of several critics who approach the issues of healing and the psychological ills of black women. In Trudier Harris's "This Disease Called Strength: Some Observations on the Compensating Construction of Black Female Characters," Harris is concerned with the prevalent type character of the Strong Black Woman (hereafter referred to as SBW) in literary texts by black women. Harris's text adamantly claims that the repetitive manufacturing of the SBW type exemplifies a psychological disease/illness, "a disease called strength" (1995, 110). Harris asserts that strength is the disease of black female characters. However, Jones's text moves beyond the notion of the SBW so that we no longer imagine strength as a disease. The novel reveals that the ideology of the "strong black woman," a myth, is simply another failed attempt to create a Eurocentric discourse of gender for black females.

Jones often mocks the ascribed elements of womanhood (femininity, weakness, and physical beauty) through a concerned examination about the ideas of beauty for her black female characters. The protagonist, Harlan, is a former beautician, as was her grandmother. *The Healing* cleverly takes on the dialogue of beauty and the bio-logic of gender to explore existing hierarchies of gendered identity for black women through Turtle Woman tales and Unicorn Women stories. In the quotation that opens this essay, Harlan's grandmother implies that through the love of a man she follows, whom we later learn abandons her, she too can be a real human woman. Harlan recalls her grandmother's tale: "She say that he could see the genuine woman behind that fake turtle shell" (135). When Harlan's grandmother—a retailer of beauty products—discusses with Harlan her status as a once-upon-a-time-turtle-woman-not-yet-human, we must metaphorically ascertain whether the discourse on gender is so faulty that black females must struggle to see themselves as women as well as human beings! Coincidentally, Harlan's grandmother learns to

The Gender-Folk Revolution and the Obeah 69

sees herself as a woman primarily because Grandfather Eagleton sees her as such. This introduction to the Turtle Woman demonstrates that womanhood, specifically notions of black womanhood, are illogically defined by persons who are not black females.

As Nicholas, Harlan's confidant and witness, explains the healing of Grandmother Eagleton, we can see the critique of gender begin: "Say she have a hump in her shoulders just like a turtle's. In fact, there's people usedta refer to her as a turtle woman on account of them shoulders. Others say it ain't on account of them shoulders, that she usedta be a real turtle, which is nonsense, ain't no real turtle turn into no human being, not in the natural world" (18). Jones establishes the destruction of boundaries early. Even as Nicholas serves as a witness to Harlan's supernatural acts of healing, his witnessing demonstrates that constructions of normality, natural as opposed to supernatural and even constructions of gender are all some he said, she said witnessing. Grandmother Eagleton's identity, in the mouths or discourses of others, changes from person to person. The truth of each construction lies in an understanding, faith, or belief in the culture constructing the myths or ideas. The turtle woman remains a non-entity but flourishes as a rumor. Recognition of the rumor as fiction, rather than fact, serves as the key to gender-folk revolution.

Grandmother Eagleton's history as a turtle (woman) reveals that there is a secondary reading of gender occurring in the text. She fails to recognize "woman" as the result of fiction. In characterizing Harlan and her grandmother as beauticians, Jones could simply address the internalization of racist values and an inferiority complex over beauty in black women. However, she chooses instead a disruption of gender in the text that stems from Grandmother Eagleton's real subjectivity as a black female, as opposed to her counter-reality as a turtle woman rumor. We must now explore how the internalization of the logic of intelligible gender had, and still has, quite a bit to do with black females finding the discourse to express their identity. The ability of dominant discourse and criticism to distort its subjects has truly lent credence to Audre Lorde's suggestion that "the master's tool will not dismantle the master's house."[1]

When we consider how Sojourner Truth becomes a symbol and a shadow for a movement that was not for her (the early (white) feminist movement), it seems clear that early discourse on black females may not have been able to complete the feat of analyzing the construct of gender. However, the late twentieth-century consistently returns to confront the unresolved issue of gender. As Carole Boyce Davies concedes in *Black Women, Writing and Identity: Migrations of the Subject*, "[I]t is the convergence of multiple places and cultures that renegotiates their identities....[O]nce Black women's experience is accounted for, assumptions about identity, community and theory have to be reconsidered" (1994, 3). Davies understands the liminal identity of black females and chooses to use the term and tool of "migratory subject" primarily because her text is concerned with the impact of nationalisms and nationalist borders in her deconstruction of black females and black feminist thought. Yet Davies's term "migratory subjects," while consistently challenging Western discourses of womanhood, still works within the confines of intelligible gender ideologies and the traditional construction of "woman." Nevertheless, we must complete Davies's assigned task to reconsider the theory of gender once we account for the black female experience. Currently, we should move beyond superficial arguments of womanhood and accept that any relevant attempts to construct black female identity must first tackle the issue of gender, and one way to do so is to interrupt and dismantle the rhetoric of gender with the subjectivity of black females, and then proceed to unname the "black woman." Once black female subjectivity sheds the label of "woman," we leave the door open for a more appropriate and less limited language for black femaleness. For Jones, unnaming through folklore philosophy and divine acts, such as healing, becomes a way to reject the construction of gender and traditional ideologies concerning black females. Jones uses the phenomenon of faith healing to unname her black female protagonist. She posits that we consider Harlan's grandmother's predicament: How far will you go to become human and a woman? She then juxtaposes it with her own question: How far will you go to become your self? Will you, black women, unname yourself?

Juxtaposing quotations from Grandmother Eagleton's story with Audre Lorde's "Black Unicorn" provides another way to observe that Jones's novel metaphorically represents the manifestation of a revolution in which black females rebel against discourses that have been used to shape or define them. Ana Louise Keating's *Women Reading, Women Writing: Self-Invention in Paula Gunn Allen, Gloria Anzaldua, and Audre Lorde* explores Lorde's "use of imagination, language, and mythic conversion principles to invent new individual and collective gendered and ethnic identities" (1996, 146). As Keating points out, in Lorde's collection of poems *Black Unicorn* (1978), the poet uses her work to expressly take on what she had always acknowledged as the lack of language to convey the experiences and subjectivity of black females. The title poem, "Black Unicorn," makes significant comments on black female identity: "The black unicorn is greedy. /The black unicorn is impatient. /The black unicorn was mistaken/ for a shadow/or symbol/and taken..." (1978, 3). In this poem, as with the entire collection, Lorde is concerned with black females being construed as signifiers without meaning, like Sojourner Truth and Grandmother Eagleton. It is no longer the entire being itself that we understand and know, but the distinct characteristics divorced from that being, and this is the sad historical experience that comes with accepting the term "black woman" in society. The uniqueness of the black unicorn's presence becomes a shadow without light and a symbol without a context, but it also possesses the ability to be a floating signifier if it is not "other" in the text. The only way to keep this floating signifier from being "othered" is to find a discourse in which to speak of the black unicorn—the black female. Black females will not be free until, as Lorde has asserted through strategic hermeneutics in her works, they can find new spellings of their name, by which she means new tongues for their historical subject and experiences. However, Jones's texts suggest that we move past new spellings to a process of unnaming. A process of unnaming permits that the unique identity of the black female does not have to be othered, because it already acknowledges that its identity can't be fixed.

Like Lorde's collection of poetry, Jones's text explores how misrepresentations and distortions can sometimes become mythic manipulations in our lives. Jones also completes a mythic conversion by exploring how opposing mythic influences exist in our lives to aid us in the struggle to conquer and destroy the former. Jones replaces mythic models such as the "black woman" or the SBW with her own models of the turtle woman and the unicorn woman to create a discourse for Harlan T. Eagleton. In order to recognize the models, we must first realize that an unnaming occurs in the narrative.

On the surface, naming appears to play a minor role in the theme and goals of the novel. For example, in discussing her long-lost grandfather, James B. Eagleton, Harlan reveals that the B. stands for Booker (as in Booker T. Washington). Grandfather Eagleton's middle name suggests the type of political man that he may have been, since we never really see him but only hear of him through Grandmother Eagleton's turtle woman story. James Booker Eagleton, like his namesake, seems to understand the need for racial empowerment in the way he vocally admires and raises Grandmother Eagleton's esteem by saying he could see the real woman in her. However, much like Booker T. Washington's ideologies about economic empowerment, his own methods of black female empowerment are flawed because they accept the system and its hierarchies, rather than undertake a total destruction of the system that causes the oppression. The Eagleton family utilizes a trend of bestowing upon themselves the names of influential African Americans. Harlan's own middle initial, T., stands for Truth, but Harlan's namesake, Sojourner Truth, acts as a major indicator of the struggle for black female identity.

Upon further examination one realizes that Harlan's full name symbolizes the question of black female identity and a language for that identity:

> So my name's Harlan Eagleton. Harlan T. Eagleton, but I do not tell anyone what the T. stands for, because I don't think it's a name that anyone should be given. Well, I'll tell you. It's Harlan Truth Eagleton, named for Sojourner Truth, not Truth itself. (252)

Harlan's desire to softly reject her middle name is significant because embedded in that desire lays the marker that highlights the necessity to unname the black woman. First, Harlan's rejection of her middle name implies that there is no such thing as an absolute Truth (as posited in Enlightenment ideology and aesthetics) but a multiplicity of truths. Harlan's rejection of her middle name is also an acceptance of the divinity that she will become. Harlan knows the importance of multiplicity in discussing herself. She cannot allow herself to be defined or fixed as one absolute. By rejecting the notion of an absolute Truth, Harlan makes it possible to accept many truths about her own identity as a black female, rather than a detrimental monologic discourse of truth about women.

Harlan's name, like that of the divine, also hints at an unknown being. She is not called God, but her very name itself creates a space of unknowability and liminality for its being. Harlan might traditionally be seen as a male name; Jane, a woman's name; Truth, an ambiguous name (male or female); and Eagleton, her family name. Hence, Harlan might very well be made to acknowledge, "I am that I am," that phrase we attribute to that which we cannot name. She does not fit an either/or dichotomy but a liminal discursive space of multiplicity and polyphonic discourse. Harlan seems apprehensive about the name Truth because of its sacred place in time and history, but she also intuitively appears to understand the logic and discursive baggage that comes with that name. If there is no absolute truth, then Harlan, like Sojourner Truth, after whom she was named, must ask herself: Am I a woman? Harlan must decide whether to reject or embrace this subjectivity in the shaping of her identity. Does she accept the discourse that comes with the question, or does she, unlike her grandmother, go further past the one absolute truth? Harlan goes further because she allows herself to be unnamed, and her first small step in doing so manifests itself in her desire to reject her middle name.

Harlan's rejection of her middle name is hardly enough to maintain the state of liminality that will empower her to become the healer. Harlan needs to find other alternatives and tools in unnaming herself, and she finds them in the communal act of healing, primarily in witnessing and testimony. In this novel, witnessing and testifying replace absolute truths, and they shape the narrative of the novel to explore how the revolution can be achieved. Throughout the novel, Harlan's narration is disjointed, her thoughts never end, and thoughts and testimony by someone else speaking about her gift for healing often interrupt the narrative. The acts of testimony, narration, and oral myths refuse to be structured and bound. There is no continuous or specific connection from one person's consciousness to another, unless a character is actually speaking. Understandably, the need to testify and witness cannot be done in a linear structure; true testifying and true witnessing have to be the result of being moved to speak.

The novel's narration is presented in different narrative voices. Yet the narrative continues, sporadically using quotations, as if the same person were always speaking. Jones's narrative technique acts as a testament to the need for multiple truths in healing the discursive ills that can occur for liminal subjects or subjectivities without a discourse. The deeply developed recursive structure (repeated and circular rather than linear) of the novel may initially make it difficult to recognize how Jones is taking up the maladies of black women. However, when we recall the communality that can be achieved from these oral acts, we understand that the author is focused on communal healing rather than individual healing. Jones has emphasized this belief in her previous novels, but makes notable changes to it in *The Healing*. Harlan often gives up narrative control to those who witness for her because in ritual and spiritual spheres testimony acts as a learning and teaching tool. Subsequently, because the telling of a story/witnessing is never the same, rebirth and life are always possible through community exchanges of oral traditions.

From the testimony of one witness, we learn that:

> Doctors couldn't do nothing or didn't want to. I would go from doctor to doctor and none of them could heal me, or didn't want to... then she looked a me and know my trouble. She said the trouble would end, and touched me, and it did. That's what I mean by she heal by healing.... Sometimes she speaks a word and it's done. Other time she got to lay on hands. She don't prescribe none of them herbs and roots and potions, though. She ain't that sorta healing woman. (16)

This particular testimony emphasizes the tradition of laying on of the hands. In "A Laying On of Hands: Black Women Writers Exploring the Roots of Their Folk and Cultural Tradition," Joanne V. Gabbin defines "laying on of hands":

> The term signifies the ancient practice of using hands in a symbolic act of blessing, healing, and ordination. By its very act, it appears to bestow some gift.... Thus it is associated with the healing powers of Christ as he lays hands on sufferers and they are cured. Others see the practice as central to the African concept that the spirit and body are one. Thus sensuality is essential to the process of healing and rebirth. (1990, 247)

The witness's testimony of Harlan's healing affirms the importance of communal healing: touch, sound, and physical exchanges are emphasized over herbs, roots, and potions. Jones suggests that healing is not a solitary process, but is instead a communal course of action that affects those coming to be healed and the healer herself. In her previous novels, witnessing and testifying may have been enough to alter the path to healing. However, the inclusion of "laying on of hands" suggests that more needs to be done. Gabbin's analysis refers to the concepts of unranked binary opposition in African metaphysics. The spirit and body co-exist in one space, and they need not be split, separate, or ranked as they are in Western Christian religious discourse. Gabbin's definition of healing, through laying on of hands, confirms that Jones opts to implant in her protagonist and story an African concept of body and spirit, rather than the Christian elements of healing so as to move away from the healer as otherworldly or unnatural. Jones's concept of faith healings, as indicated earlier, differs from those of other African American women writers in that Harlan is not the exiled freak. Laying on of hands allows the community to remain linked during what might traditionally be conceived as supernatural acts. Therefore, the healer cannot be othered and outcast because she remains as one with the community, and the healed community can physically embrace what they may not know or understand. Hence, the body and spirit can be one in the construction of Harlan T. Eagleton.

Unnaming in African American females' texts, as Jones demonstrates with *The Healing*, must be about remaining unnamed, rather than finding a name, about sustaining a state of liminality. Harlan's second phase of unnaming, the ability to maintain liminality and unnameability is key to understanding the use of turtle woman and unicorn woman stories. To comprehend the statement that addresses the all-important turtle woman myth, "I was a turtle before I became a human being," we must first grasp the meanings of other myths in the novel. The Nicodemus legend has a minor but important place in the plot and theme of the novel. This myth concerns Nicholas. Jones explores the correlation between Harlan's sidekick's name and Nicodemus:

> And N'Orleans that ain't my true name, that just his sometimes name for me.
>
> Then he whispers, He's free.

> Who's free? Nicholas?
>
> They freed Nicodemus.
>
> Who's Nicodemus? Nicodemus? Oh, yeah, yeah. Nicodemus.
>
> That's good. (35)

Again, there are moments when the reader may be unsure of who is actually speaking, but in this brief passage, Harlan's witness and former bodyguard becomes associated with Nicodemus. The name suggests a number of possibilities for understanding the character, but most importantly for understanding myth and ideas of healing. Nicholas could represent Nicodemus, the righteous Monk of Mt. Athos; Nicodemus, the runaway slave; Nicodemus, the Jewish King; Nicodemus of John 3:11 ("What must I do to be saved?"); or the town settled by nineteenth-century Negro migrants from Kentucky who settled on land in Kansas.[2] All of the images share a common link to the notion of rebirth, new life, and separation from mainstream society, and they have a connection to healers and function as witnesses or legacies to an important moment in a race/nation's history.

Jones's Nicholas becomes all of these representations in some way. He serves as the most significant witness to Harlan's work. Harlan explains, "I thought about hiring me another 'witness' but that would be duplicitous and Nicholas the true one witnessed the first healing, and that ain't the same as a hired witness" (10). Later Harlan expands on the role of the witness: "All I know is Nicholas usedta tell the tale with more fanfare, more flourish, more confabulatoriness. And when he tells about that healing, it don't sound like no confabulatory tale. Least the way he usedta tell the tale of that healing. Now he tends to be kinda dry" (11). Nicholas serves as a witness to Harlan's work. As the first person to see Harlan go through her rites of passage into healing, Nicholas lives up to the legend of the monk, runaway slave, Jew, and exoduster by giving up his own life to witness for Harlan. His task is to help make evidence of healing for those in pain.

Karla F.C. Holloway's *Moorings and Metaphors* provides evidence to suggest that Nicholas's repeated testimony and witnessing construct a myth:

> Myth vitalizes language, giving it a presence outside of the interpretive mode and forcing its significance to a level where the community's shared meanings are the basis of its understanding and interactions with both the spiritual and physical worlds; it is both of them. In its ways of recursive signification, it is the perfect vehicle for signification. (1992, 25)

Healing is a performative art that depends on more than the actual act itself. Healing depends on the witnessing of the act. It can only work if the healer and those who are coming to be healed believe in the existence of such a thing. What good is the gift if no one is there to recognize the act, to call it, to name it, to give it a language for its very existence? By constantly retelling the first healing, the story becomes mythical. Nicholas's tale influences the doctrine of faith, and consequently, the lives of all that come to be healed. Not only does Nicholas's selfless act make it possible for those coming to be healed to have faith in Harlan's gift, but it also provides Harlan with the faith that she needs to believe in herself and sustain her abilities. Harlan, temporarily, becomes the healing woman. Each and every time Nicholas testifies he helps to sustain the process of unnaming Harlan by helping to develop a space that permits her to temporarily misplace or replace the black woman with the healer, but she never has to accept one over the other.

In another pre-healing testimony, Nicholas revises his dry tone and narration as he speaks of Harlan's first healing, and in the process, he describes the space for Harlan's changing subjectivity:

> I thought she were some witch at first, says Nicholas. Even she didn't know. ...Maybe that's who she is. The healing woman healed herself first.... Well I'm here to testify that she healed herself first. I'm here to testify that she healed herself first. I'm here to testify that this healing woman healed herself first. And now she trying to heal everybody that want to be healed. (33)

Unlike Grandfather Eagleton's proclamation of Grandmother Eagleton as a woman, Nicholas repeatedly demonstrates hesitancy and indecision in explaining the existence of Harlan. Nicholas's testimony, rather than a naming definition, records the instability or illusive definability of Harlan. He questions whether she is a witch or something else. Even the subject being does not know, or she does not know what to call herself. Yet Nicholas remains a witness to the construction of a space and language for the black female's subjectivities.

Again, Holloway reminds us that "myths are not discrete units of structure as much as they are features of how a sense of language enables the survival and transference of memory" (94). Nicholas's repetitive testimony helps to create a myth that reveals Harlan and the myths that she carries with her as the "perfect vehicle for methodology" (Holloway 25). The testimony of Nicholas and other witnesses removes Harlan from the static subject position of black woman, and it provides her with a liminal space where we can now begin questioning the discourse of gender and Harlan's identity as a black woman. If Harlan wishes to avoid her grandmother's mistake of accepting what others name her, then she should not accept or become the historical figurations of mythology created by her witnesses. Testimony and witnessing initially launch a process of unnaming for Harlan by providing myths to counter the historical figuration of mythology at the center of the text—the black woman. However, as we saw with Sojourner Truth, such figurations can be costly. Harlan does not need to be unnamed as the black woman only to be named again as some "other." She must not fall into the trap of accommodating traditional discourse. Testimony and witnessing build myths, but it is the remaining historical figurations that Harlan must learn to navigate to achieve an empowering identity. The historical figurations are no good to Harlan if they become a fixed identity. Only in the liminal existence of these remaining historical figurations can Harlan begin the important progression of unnaming through her own familial myths.

Jones uses the turtle woman story as her initial assessment of womanhood and gender. She constantly makes the reader aware of how and who defines womanhood and for what reasons. In a discussion with her turtle-woman grandmother, Harlan learns how these discourses work in the lives of African Americans:

> ...and that them other men just thought of her as freakish, as one of them freakish women, whether or not they believed in the reality of that turtle's shell. She say that he (grandfather Eagleton) could see the genuine woman behind that fake turtle shell. She say he say that she more a genuine woman than any woman he know, a category he say ain't just limited to colored women, which some mens do. You know how some mens do. They'll compare you to other colored women, but not to womanhood itself, and refers every other man's woman to they own. (135)

The above passage focuses on freakish womanhood and carnivalesque atmosphere, and it reminds us of how ideologies of the unnamed subject/black female become freakish in the dominant discourse of womanhood. Black female identity may be antithetical to the rhetoric of womanhood, but it also exposes the failures of the intelligiable logic gender. Jones must find another language to explore the construction of gender, and the folk allows her the best way to do so.

Turtles and terrapins have long been figures of tricksterism in African American folklore and literature. However, a folk-reading reveals a surprising parallel between Jones's turtle woman and the turtle as trickster in African folktales. In *Dahomean Narrative*, Melville Herskovits reveals elements about the tortoise in African oral stories that become essential to fully understanding the importance of the turtle woman in *The Healing* and a connection to divination:

> All the animals and birds go at sunrise to the fields to eat. Tortoise whose skin is like stone, also goes out. There was a bird called Awele. When he saw Tortoise, he called together all the birds. None of them had ever seen an animal like that, an animal with skin like stone. Awele said to the other birds, "and today a stone comes to eat with us.... " Since Tortoise walks slowly, the birds flew down to see what was inside this thing Awele said was a stone. But they saw nothing for the Tortoise stopped still. (1958, 191)

The tale later indicates that the stone that came to eat with them perplexed all the animals, and they took their concerns to Mawu (the most high Goddess), asking why a stone ate with them. Eventually, Mawu reveals turtle as an animal and tells the other animals, "Tortoise is the diviner for birds and animals" (Herskovits 1958, 192). In another story, the tortoise is told, "You will always be a diviner because you have suffered much" (Herskovits 1958, 193). The connection between folk tales and the divine is embodied in the tortoise. In many of these tales, the tortoise is also a genderless trickster who is a diviner. The significance of subjectivity, identity, and indefineability cannot be overlooked in these Dahomean tortoise tales. Tortoise is an outcast amongst other animals and unlike anything they have ever known or seen. Tortoise's distinct identity means that the figure will suffer much, but it will be divine. The elements of trickery with divination in the turtle/tortoise are the basis for Jones's mechanism of unnaming the black woman.

Through the turtle woman myth, Jones makes a case that the representation of the shell, the shell being a metaphor for the "black woman," hides and distorts the actual being that exists. Only through Mawu's divine intervention, does the turtle's real identity become known. While the Eagleton women don't turn to Mawu, their folk beliefs in turtle women act as Mawu's divine intervention—a disruption of the discourse on intelligible gender—to provide a discourse for black female identity. Grandfather Eagleton does not view Grandmother Eagleton as freakish. He sees Harlan's grandmother as a woman, but because he defines womanhood for Grandmother Eagleton, the change is never really a true self-transformation. Throughout the text, readers must recognize that Harlan's grandmother, like Sojourner Truth, moves between troubling constructs of womanhood, from turtle woman to human woman, and she never really dismisses any of the false ideologies. Harlan's name significantly draws us back to the identity of black woman and how to translate it. In a scene in which Harlan has asked her mother if she ever believed in the grandmother's turtle stories, Harlan's mother replies, "Yeah, I suppose I did. I suppose when I was a little girl I did.... I even imagined that I was a turtle woman transforming myself to free myself from the tyranny of others" (277). Harlan's mother may not have had the means to go back to the process of unnaming that the turtle stories represent, but as a healer, Harlan has the means to accomplish such a feat.

Harlan's goal, then, is to believe the confabulatory tales of her grandmother and see their usefulness in her own life. Accepting ideologies of womanhood are problematic for black females because these historical discourses of gender remain unable to understand them. Jones continues to create her own discourse of gender for black females through the oral story of the unicorn woman:

> A lot of people when they would see that sign advertising the Unicorn woman, they'd think she was a white woman, you know, cause all the unicorns in the storybooks is white, cause that's supposed to be a sign of purity, you know, and even the colored people that come to see the Unicorn woman, theys's as surprised as the white people that she ain't a white Unicorn woman, cause even colored people think that white's a sign of

purity, and she is a genuine Unicorn woman, but a colored one.... I heard someone say that even if she's a real Unicorn woman, she still a fake one, just by virtue of being colored. (136)

Grandmother Eagleton repeatedly relays these tales to Harlan as a child, and in their repetitive and recursive orality they become myths for Harlan to process. The unicorn woman is bound by the same ideologies of the turtle woman. People assign hierarchies based on race and gender that attempt to define individual identity. Carnival goers view the unicorn woman as an inferior and fake version of a unicorn woman simply by virtue of her color.

If readers juxtapose the myth of the turtle woman with the unicorn woman, then they can envision the choices of womanhood left to Harlan. These myths document that each woman of color lacks a language for her identity and is inclined to choose an inappropriate language so that she might be useful in society or a part of a community. The fact that these women find themselves working in a carnivalesque environment suggests that they are seeking a place. In asking the critical questions, Harlan draws from her grandmother a wealth of wisdom that the young Harlan cannot yet begin to comprehend, and that the grandmother has yet to admit in her own life. In expanding further on the unicorn woman, Grandmother Eagleton states:

...but it takes a true mythical woman to be the ideal of true womanhood, colored or ain't. Why even the proprietor of the first carnival she was at became obsessed with her, until he found him a woman that he thought the more ideal of womanhood than herself. Then he sold the Unicorn woman to another carnival, cause he didn't want them two competing ideals of womanhood. (138)

It might seem as if Jones is endorsing the use of mythical womanhood as a way of empowerment for black women. However, the mention of competing ideals of womanhood is important because it reveals, once again, that womanhood is not the business of women but that of men. Men created the ideologies and buy and sell these representations of women at will, but never for one moment can there be competing ideals, because that would cancel out profits from exploitation of the women. Furthermore, the irony embedded in the above statement reveals that Jones does not wish to replace one mythical womanhood with another; she simply wishes to corrupt the discourse of gender with her own myths. Only a myth can represent another myth. The "ideal of true womanhood" is just as mythical as turtle and unicorn women. Be it a "lady," "woman," the "Super Black Woman," or turtle and unicorn women, use determines the value of those fictions. If black females wish to believe in any myths, it should be those that might empower them instead of those, like that of the cult of womanhood and the logic of gender, which don't. Harlan must find a way to avoid the false recognitions and mistranslations of her identity.

Harlan recalls another moment when her grandmother ruminated over womanhood by repeating a conversation with a man she'd met after transforming from a turtle woman to a human woman. The man exclaims to her grandmother, "The man to woman you. Who'd have the nerve to woman you. Who'd have the nerve to woman a woman like you?" (253). The implication is that women, especially women of color, can become true women with the help of a strong and courageous man. As man remains the primary signifier, woman can only receive meaning from man. The statement reveals that, yes, men define womanhood, men impose womanhood onto women, and for women of color the imposition often results in black females being unable to define themselves by their own ontological, epistemological, and phenomenological visions. Jones also uses the man's comment to implicitly express, through folk idiom, a distinction between gender (social) and sex (biological) that black females must negotiate. Folk strategies are capable of making such distinctions in ways that mainstream verbosity cannot, and this is why folklore manifests itself so deeply in *The Healing*.

Grandmother Eagleton's misconception about her identity does not have to be passed on to Harlan due in large part to a discourse based on liminality and divination. Harlan acknowledges:

> When I grew older, I didn't believe the Turtle Woman stories, not the magical ones. Not the tales of how when she was a turtle she'd had to play all kinds of tricks to keep from getting caught by humans....I believed the one about the carnival, and even the tales of the confabulatory Unicorn Woman, but not that one. Not the tale of metamorphosis, of how when human beings chased her, like every turtle, she ran so slowly that in order to avoid getting caught she had to transform. (164)

Harlan's statement reveals that she once believed that such stories were real and significant. Her goal, then, is to find a way to believe in the magical turtle stories in order to avoid the mistakes and misrecognition made by her grandmother before her, and she soon does. Initially, Harlan does not recognize the significance of these transformation tales as somewhat representative of what she must achieve in order to heal herself and others.

Even before she acquires her healing gift, we can see that she is different because she defies notions of womanhood with which the world provides her. As Harlan recounts the details leading up to her divorce from her husband, Norvelle the medical anthropologist, she remembers how uncomfortable she felt during a conversation with Norvelle's sister:

> I hope you's a nice girl. I hope you's a nicer girl than you looks like you is.
>
> It depends on what you mean by a nice girl, I said.
>
> I hope you's a nicer girl than you looks like you is what I mean. Cause you don't look like you's a wifeable woman at all to me. (169)

Again, Jones emphasizes social constructs to qualify the biological explanation of "woman." These references to "nice girls," "wifeable women," and "men that can woman a woman" irrefutably deny that standard conceptions of gender contain any empowering moments. Throughout Harlan's life, she constantly confronts the denial of herself in such rhetoric, and this struggle leads her onto a path to finally accept the magical stories of unicorn women and myths of turtles that transform to avoid capture.

Harlan's failed marriage to Norvelle brings her face to face with the necessary non-Western and folk language of gender, healing as ordinary divinity. Harlan asserts, "Even when I went to Africa with Norvelle and heard African transformation tales which sounded very much like that one (the turtle story), I still didn't believe it or I thought it was just folklore" (164). Here, we must go back to the turtle/tortoise connection to divinity. Harlan's denial must be called into question because she implies that she may not have believed them, but now she has reason to. After all, she does leave her husband in Africa because he chases after a medicine woman. Ironically,

Norvelle's research on a Masai medicine woman enables Harlan to choose a myth that will allow her to develop her own identity:

> It was only that Masai medicine woman who disoriented me because he wanted to stay with her, because he wanted to keep following her from Korogwe to Morogoro.... And I guess I envied her independent life, traveling about, curing folks. I guess the only way she could express her wanderlust even though the Masai are traditionally nomadic people was by being a medicine woman. (228)

Harlan's decision to leave Norvelle in Africa and pursue her own self concerns the Masai medicine woman as much as it does the unicorn woman she has heard so much about as a child. Harlan's grandmother claimed of the unicorn woman, "There's plenty of mens crazy about her, like I said, crazy in love or infatuation and even follow her from carnival to carnival, her being a mythical-type ideal woman, but she ain't follow none of them.... if it's possible for a woman to follow her ownself, it's her. Free and independent" (139). Norvelle's academic pursuit and study of the Masai medicine woman sounds very much like those men who came to see the unicorn woman. Harlan's choice to leave Norvelle acts as a critical experiment to see if she can, like the Masai woman and the unicorn woman, follow herself.

In the process of following herself, Harlan becomes manager to a rock star, Joan the Savage Bitch, and she continues to be faced with the importance of her decision to leave her husband to his own dreams and to follow her self. In discussing women with a friend of Joan's who claims not to be a "feminista," Abio tells Harlan, "I only think a woman should be true to who she believes herself to be. Or who she wants herself to be. I don't know what I mean, or whether I'm true myself, to any of that. I don't think there are many of us who are true to our possibilities" (238). Throughout the text, such statements work to address Harlan's courage to accept her identity as a black female, and then as a healer. If Harlan ignores the childhood stories about turtle and unicorn women, she cannot stay true to her own possibilities, which becomes the gift of healing.

Harlan's first act of healing occurs after her client, Joan Savage, stabs her. Joan, still in love with her ex-husband, stabs Harlan when she learns of Harlan's sexual relationship with Joan's ex. Throughout the novel, Jones highlights Harlan's lack of commitment to being "a woman" or honoring the ideology of true womanhood. Harlan divorces her husband because she does not wish to be a dutiful wife and follow him across the African continent. She engages in extramarital sex. Indeed, after she has refused to be a traveler with her husband, she becomes a woman traveling the United States alone to promote musicians. The fact that Harlan is stabbed because she has chosen to pursue her own path and sexual desires suggests that the way she wants to live her life and the way the world perceives that she should live it, as "woman," are at odds with each other. Joan, even as she trashes the rhetoric of womanhood, pursues models of that same womanhood, and her violent act against Harlan symbolizes the reckoning of the world with Harlan's problematic subjectivity. After Joan stabs Harlan, Harlan heals herself and recalls her client's disbelief in that moment: "'I thought you were a real person,' she says. 'But you're not even a human woman, you're not even a real human woman'" (280). As a woman who enjoys engages in the rhetoric of womanhood (79), Joan chooses to believes in that particular fiction by othering the reality of Harlan's identity. Harlan says in response to Joan, "This is the truth of it. The knife fell out. I put my hand to the wound and it healed" (280). After Harlan heals herself, she remains unaware and unprepared for the act of healing in her life. As she agrees with Joan's assessment of her identity, she repeats the mistake made by her grandmother. It is only through the continued use of her gift that she comes to know her true self and full possibilities.

Despite the tragic drama of the stabbing, Jones does not end Harlan's life with tragedy, regret, or death; rather, she resolves to prolong Harlan's life with healing and hope. Her decision suggests that the gift of healing that Harlan acquires after the stabbing helps locate a place for her subjectivity. In the liminal performative space of healing, Harlan can generate a space in which she can invent language for that which the world cannot deal with: her blackness, her sexuality, and her independence. By making Harlan a healer, Jones accepts a proclamation that Toni Cade Bambara made in *The Black Woman*:

> We are involved in a struggle for liberation: liberation from the exploitive and dehumanizing system of racism from the manipulative control of a corporation society; liberation from the constrictive norms of "mainstream"

culture, from the synthetic norms that encourage us to fashion ourselves rashly from without (reaction) rather than from within (creation)...(1970, 7).

Jones creates a foundation for black women's revolutionary subjectivity through turtle women lessons and black unicorn woman philosophies. Jones equips Harlan for the struggle for liberation, and in so doing she returns the healer to its New World setting, for as Cedric Robinson has noted (*Black Marxism* 1998): "Obeah men and women were frequently the source of ideology for the slave rebellion"(136). Just as the obeah could put fear into whites and empowerment into blacks, Jones repositions this legacy to explore how the black female's rebellion depends on the black female healer—Harlan's courage to unname herself through various acts of healing.

Harlan's sexuality contributes to her continued process of unnaming. The presentation of Harlan as a sexual person moves beyond traditional ideals of healers as asexual persons. Since her first healing act happens because of her sexual relationships, we can be sure that Jones wishes to distinguish Harlan from other literary healers. Furthermore, it also reconnects to the African ethos of being able to occupy many spaces at once—to be male and female, or sexual and spiritual at the same time. Harlan's self-healing—a laying on of hands—on her body is possible because she has accepted her flesh with her spirit long ago. She accepts her identity despite not having a discourse for it, and this acceptance is a revolutionary act. Revolutionary acts lead to healing and liberation. When Harlan places her hands over the stab wound, she extends her life through healing, but the act also enables her to conceive of a space for herself as subject where she can exist and have a language to define herself. Harlan admits as much: "And when you discover that you can heal yourself, that you can simply put your hand to a wound and it heals, you soon discover that you can heal others. From a horse suffering from a fractured phalange, and then a Turtle Woman" (281). Furthermore, the gift of healing does not come from external forces but from her own being. Harlan has carried her gift of healing with her the whole time; she simply has not recognized it in herself. Her end goal is to continue healing herself as she did that first time. In order to continue healing others, she must face her own fears, despair, pain, and disbelief about herself. Years after she has healed herself, Harlan recognizes that the words of Joan Savage were incorrect, a failure of language to convey what she is:

> I didn't even ask for the spirit gift, I begin softly. I weren't even prepared for the spirit gift. But it came, it came.... A lot of y'all looking at me and just seeing an ordinary woman, and asking y'allself how come a ordinary woman like me to be given the gift of the spirit, how come a ordinary woman like me to be given a spirit gift? But that the point of them spirit gifts, the point of them spirit gifts, is that *I am just a ordinary woman. I am just a ordinary woman*, that is the point of the healing [italics mine]. (34)

Harlan is not freakish, inhuman, or otherwordly. She is ordinary. She admits the truth of it to herself and those coming to be healed. Healing is simply a space where she can exist and know herself. In the end, Jones adeptly disrupts the construction of gender in Western discourse, specifically the construction of the "black woman" as the primary cause of psychological illness in the lives of black women. Jones utilizes the oral myths of the turtle woman and the unicorn woman to explore how black females can heal themselves by expressing their subjectivity through mythical discourse and metaphors, other than that myth—woman as conceived by Western thought. As noted earlier, testifying and witnessing are only the beginning process of Harlan's unnaming; her acceptance of the healing gift and her ordinary existence defy the attempt to name or define her through traditional discourse. She will not be like her grandmother and allow others (her witnesses) to define her. Harlan decides to exist liminally between the historical figuration and her own self. She will not let the myths define or restrict her. She will use them at her leisure to free her from the prevailing discussions of gender. This liminal state keeps Harlan from being static and unwilling to embrace one identity over another. She does not have to choose to be society's definition or the myth's definition of woman and human.

By making Harlan a healer and a black female, Jones asks us to reconsider how we conceive of gender for the black female, to use the subjectivity of those we name black women as a way to conceptualize or reconceptualize gender ideologies, and she exposes that it can be accomplished without making the subject otherworldly, mystical, or other. Jones's narrative structure and her knowledgeable use of mythic structure skillfully navigates this terrain to discuss black women's identity and empowerment in a way that is not denigrating, dominating, or corrupting. The healer's gift, specifically Harlan's, comes from within the self. These gifts derive from a consciousness of self that has been lost in the translation of language, a subjectivity that exists beyond definition. In assigning to Harlan a transformative identity of healer, Gayl Jones provides a methodology that makes it possible for Harlan and other black female subjects to move away from any essentialist or totalizing telos that seeks to falsely determine black female identity. Finally, Harlan can be like the turtle she claims not to believe in. She can live up to her own possibilities, be whatever she wants, and all the while defy and elude those who seek to catch and name her.

Notes

[1] *Sister Outsider: Essays and Speeches by Audre Lorde.* (Freedom, CA: The Crossing Press, 1984) 53-60.
[2] See "Nicodemus: Negro Haven on the Solomon" *Kansas Historical Quarterly* 34 (1968): 10-31. and "Aquilla the Apostle and Nicodemus the Righteous of Mt. Athos," *Orthodox Calendar Company.* July 14.

Works Cited

Bambara, Toni. *The Black Woman.* New York: Signet Press, 1970.

Butler, Judith. *Gender Trouble: Feminism and the Subversion of Identity.* London and New York: Routledge, 1999.

Davies, Carole Boyce. *Black Women, Writing and Identity: Migrations of the Subject.* London and New York: Routledge, 1994.

Gabbin, Joanne V. "A Laying on of Hands: Black Women Writers Exploring the Roots of their Folk and Cultural Traditions." *Wild Women in the Whirlwind: Afra-American Culture and the Contemporary Literary Renaissance.* Eds. Joanne M. Braxton and Andree Nicola McLaughlin. New Brunswick, NJ: Rutgers University Press, 1990.

Grossinger, Richard. *Planet Medicine: From Stone Age Shamansim to Post-Industrial Healing.* Berkley, CA.: New Atlantic Books, 1980.

Harris, Trudier. "This Disease Called Strength: Some Observations on the Compensating Construction of Black Female Characters," *Literature and Medicine* 14:1. 109-126, 1995.

Herskovits, Melville. *Dahomean Narrative: A Cross-Cultural Analysis.* Evanston, IL:

Northwestern University Press, 1958.

Holloway, Karla F.C. *Moorings and Metaphors: Figures of Culture and Gender in Black Women's Literature.* New Brunswick, NJ: Rutgers University Press, 1992.

Jones, Gayl. *Corregidora.* Boston: Beacon Press, 1975.

———. *Eva's Man.* Boston: Beacon Press, 1976.

———. *The Healing.* Boston: Beacon Press, 1998.

Keating, AnaLouise. *Women Reading, Women Writing: Self-Invention in Paula Gunn Allen, Gloria Anzaldua, and Audre Lorde.* Philadelphia: Temple University Press, 1996.

Lorde, Audre. *Black Unicorn.* New York: Norton, 1978.

———. "The Master's Tools Will Never Dismantle the Master's House." *Sister Outsider: Essays and Speeches by Audre Lorde.* Freedom, CA: The Crossing Press. 53-60, 1984.

Robinson, Cedric. *Black Marxism: The Making of the Black Radical Tradition.* Chapel Hill: University of North Carolina Press, 1998.

CHAPTER FOUR

Telling the Untold Tale: Afro-Latino/a Identifications in the Work of Gayl Jones

Fiona Mills

> Still, the need for a broad-based U.S. women of color movement capable of spanning borders of nation and ethnicity has never been so strong.
> —Cherríe Moraga[1]

An interest in the Africanist presence in Brazil resonates throughout the work of African American writer Gayl Jones, beginning with her first novel, *Corregidora*, published in 1975, and continuing in her latest book, *Mosquito*, published in 1999.[2] Not coincidentally, Jones has discussed her pervasive interest in Brazil, studied Spanish language and literature, and conducted significant research on seventeenth-century Brazilian slave history while in graduate school. Additionally, Jones cites Latin American writers Gabriel García Márquez and Carlos Fuentes as sources of influence in several interviews. Her interest in Brazil first surfaces in *Corregidora* and is explored later in depth in *Song for Anninho* (1981). Several scholars have provided significant analysis of Jones's reconstruction and re-imagining of historical data surrounding Palmares,[3] the most successful and well known maroon community of both freed and formerly enslaved Africans, in her work. However, most scholars, with the exception of Brazilian critic Stelamaris Coser, in his provocative and insightful *Bridging the Americas: The Literature of Toni Morrison, Paule Marshall, and Gayl Jones,* have failed to pay significant attention, beyond analyzing her exploration of Brazil, to Jones's interest in making connections between African American and Latino/a cultures in her work. Although her interest in Brazil is substantial and has been critiqued at length, examining Jones as an Afro-Latino/a writer[4] facilitates a new understanding of her cumulative body of work and provides a more relevant theoretical approach to her most recent work, *Mosquito*, which centers on the experiences of persons of color living in the southwestern United States and Mexico.

In her foreword to the 1983 edition of the groundbreaking anthology *This Bridge Called My Back: Writings by Radical Women of Color*, editor Cherríe Moraga presents her vision of the work yet to be accomplished by U.S.-based female writers of color in breaking down rigid borders between ethnic peoples. Although pleased with the overwhelming response to the book's first edition, she insists that much work remains to be done. She maintains that "Still, the need for a broad-based U.S. women of color movement capable of spanning borders of nation and ethnicity has never been so strong." As such, she implores women writers of color to unite across national and ethnic borders in order to overcome oppression and prejudice. Failure to do so will be to the detriment of all persons of color (Anzaldúa and Moraga). Appropriately enough, in assessing Jones's writing, Stelamaris Coser has used this bridge metaphor to describe the important work Jones has done in aligning herself with Latin American writers such as Gabriel García Márquez and Carlos Fuentes, as well as with the experiences of Latin American people in general. Jones's efforts, he contends, have created "bridges that crisscross and touch, they connect races and cultures and approximate geographies and histories" (Coser, 171). In her latest work, *Mosquito*, Jones has heeded Moraga's call, albeit sixteen years later, by expanding her vision of African American life beyond unyielding cultural borders that insist on rigid separation of ethnic groups through her exploration of the complex relationships between persons of African American and Latino/a descent.

The early work of Gayl Jones reveals her interest in expanding the representation of the "African American" experience in literature. Jones formalizes her aversion to limiting definitions of blackness as an impediment to comprehending African American literature in her

1991 critical work *Liberating Voices: Oral Tradition in African American Literature*. In it, she criticizes Black Aesthetic criticism from the 1970s due to its stringent notions of authentic blackness for "while assaulting racist strictures, these critics often employed new strictures of exclusion and created a new hegemony" (Jones, *Liberating Voices: Oral Tradition in African American Literature*, 191). In her own body of work, Jones has sought to circumvent these delimiting constraints by embracing a larger, more fluid definition of African American life and history. She pushes beyond traditional geographic and cultural borders through her incorporation of Brazilian, African, and, most recently, Latino/a experiences into her depiction of African American experiences. Similar to the work of African American writers including Audre Lorde, Assata Shakur, and Alice Walker, Jones, too, has pushed African American literature beyond the category of U.S. literature into that of "world literature." In *Liberating Voices*, she argues against maintaining rigid boundaries between African American literature and other world literatures. The problem of the "freed voice" endemic to African American literature, she argues, is also an issue for other world literatures:

> the problems of the freed voice apply not only to African American literature and criticism, but to all the world's literatures and criticisms: European versus American, Anglo-American versus Chicano, French Standard versus French Creole, ...and so on. One sees it in the dynamics of every national literature vis-à-vis another. The voices of the less powerful group, 'the other,' always must free themselves from the frame of the more powerful group, in texts of self-discovery, authority, and wholeness. (Jones, *Liberating Voices: Oral Tradition in African American Literature*, 192).

Thus, Jones's critical text sets the stage for *Mosquito*, in which she concerns herself with the problem of expressing oneself as a person of color (be one of African American, Latino/a, Chicano/a, Native American, biracial, or multiracial descent) in the United States.

In her earlier works, Jones demonstrates her commitment to uncover and iterate the Africanist presence in South America, thereby extending traditional conceptions of the African Diaspora. Consequently, she expands the definition of "African American" and resists limiting notions of blackness and authenticity. In explaining Jones's response to the cultural nationalism espoused during the Black Power movement of the 1960s, critic Ashraf Rushdy contends that, with *Cor-

regidora and *Song for Anninho*, Jones "complicates the racial formation operative in Black Power by exposing its historical roots, by dwelling on the ways that contemporary concepts of authenticity in black communities are connected to historical master documents on plantations." Her work "challenge[s] the constricting parameters of racial formation" (Rushdy, 288). In her 1982 interview with Charles Rowell, Jones expressed her frustration with the limitations placed on U.S.-based writers who attempt to write about the "American" experience. She implicitly argues for expanding this vision to include peoples and experiences beyond U.S. borders by stating that "I'd like to be able to deal with the whole American continent in my fiction—the whole Americas—and to write imaginatively of blacks anywhere/everywhere" (Rowell). With her latest novel, Jones comes closest to reaching this goal.

As an African American writer, Jones's interest in Brazil is historically in keeping with the African American literary tradition. Similar to Cuba, Brazil has long fascinated African American writers, scholars, and activists. For decades, Brazil was hailed as a "racial paradise"—a place where one's dark skin need not be a source of prejudice and discrimination. Over the years, though, it became apparent to many writers, scholars, and activists that skin color did indeed matter in Brazil and that those with darker skin were more likely to suffer socio-economically as well as politically (Hellwig).[5] Jones reveals the reality of prejudice, discrimination, and abuse inherent in this mythical racial paradise in her works, including *Corregidora*, *Song for Anninho*, and, most recently, *Mosquito*. In *Mosquito*, she goes so far as to openly refute claims about racial harmony in Brazil by contending that "Brazil ain't no racial paradise; they just let more people play white than in America" (Jones, *Mosquito*, 27). She fleshes out this assertion by stating that you "don't know who white and who ain't in Brazil. And don't you be [going] to Brazil assuming that colored people is colored, 'cause [there] a lot of colored people is white, and a lot of white people is colored" (Jones, *Mosquito*, 215).

Jones has often been hailed as a revisionist writer—in particular, one of feminist import. I would argue that she takes this revision one step further to include a historical revisioning. Critics, as well as Jones herself, have remarked upon the importance of telling the untold tale in her work. In order to reveal the untold tale, Jones most often turns to oral and vernacular folk forms. For her, the oral is more genuine and politically significant, as it is linked to persons of color or those without access to traditional Western modes of literature. Most often it is those persons whose story is often negated or, worse, obliterated by traditional historical and literary accounts—an issue that comes up in *Corregidora* and *Song for Anninho*. In both of these texts, Jones concerns herself with rewriting master narratives in order to reflect the stories of those most often erased from history: women and persons of color. These works center on countering official histories and documents with personal tales of anguish and triumph. *Song for Anninho* opens with the official account of the defeat of the Palmares tribe in Brazil, as presented by Domingos Jorge Velho in 1695 to the Portuguese king. However, the bulk of the narrative centers on the story of Almeyda, a member of the Palmares tribe whose slain husband, Anninho, was a former tribal leader. Through Almeyda's account, Jones is able to imagine what Palmares was really like for its members and counter the myths presented in "official" documents. Similarly, in *Corregidora*, Ursa, the protagonist, struggles to bear the story of her family history that has been deliberately passed on through generations in order that the horrors and abuses suffered at the hands of a Portuguese slavemaster shall never be forgotten. This task is made all the more urgent by the fact that official records documenting the atrocities of slave life have been destroyed. The Corregidora women, thus, are left with the terrible task of literally bearing witness to the pain since, as Ursa has been told, "when they did away with slavery down there [Brazil] they burned all the slavery papers so it would be like they never had it" (Jones, *Corregidora*, 9). The abuse that they suffered must, instead, be kept alive via the stories handed down from one generation to the next. These stories present an alternative account to official ones recorded in history books.

Jones continues to reveal untold tales with *Mosquito*, in which she explores the oft-ignored subject of Afro-Latino/a cross-cultural identifications. She revisions African American culture by emphasizing its connections to and intersections with Latino/a and Latin American cultures worldwide. Jones's latest text accentuates her belief that traditional racial categories fail to explain adequately the multi-faceted ethnic categories that people embody. Instead, she advocates taking a multicultural and multiracial approach to the world and commits herself to representing a multitude of peoples as well as cultures. Her work privileges the contemporary multicultural experience of African Americans in order to better represent their complex ethnic heritages. At the same time, she explores the issue of borders—geographical, racial, and cultural. These borders are both literal and metaphorical. Appropriately in keeping with her focus on borders, her text is, on one level, a commentary on U.S. immigration policy and the mistreatment of illegal aliens. In this work, she tells the tale of illegal aliens, in particular that of Mexicans. As such, she produces a counter-narrative to that presented in mainstream U.S. media, much as she tells a counter-narrative about Brazil in *Corregidora* and *Song for Anninho*.

The myth of U.S. racial purity has long been a subject of fascination for Jones. In examining Jones's oeuvre, one can trace a clear progression in her growing exploration of this phenomenon. This exploration culminates in her latest novel, in which she foregrounds the complexity of ethnicity and privileges multiracial, multicultural American experiences. Delgadina, a Chicana woman, is the one whom Mosquito, the novel's protagonist, most respects and is closest to. Their friendship represents a bridging of two cultures—African American and Chicana. Mosquito herself is very concerned with the concept of multiculturalism and cultural intermingling and spends much of the novel educating herself about different ethnic groups, in particular Latino/a, Chicano/a, and Native American cultures. In doing so, she learns that people's ethnic heritages are so intricately intermingled that one can neither neatly compartmentalize one's ethnicity nor make grand claims about ethnic purity. For instance, in a telling moment, Mosquito listens to the tango, a conventional Latino/a/Brazilian musical form, and compares it to rap, a traditionally African American cultural form, and looks for "the tango base in the rap, or the rap base in the tango" (Jones, *Mosquito*, 109). By doing so, she identifies alliances between these two cultures as evidenced in their popular musical traditions and suggests implicit connections between them. Furthermore, as her statement suggests, one cannot clearly identify which culture influenced the other—an undeniable testament to the impossibility of racial or ethnic purity. As Delgadina resolutely proclaims, there is no such thing as "'pure' Americans" because "racial purity a myth or some shit" (Jones, *Mosquito*, 191). Significantly, Mosquito watches a play entitled *La Raza Pura*, which satirizes the American melting pot, and says, "I gots to tell y'all about that play, 'cause it's about America. 'Cept it's about the American myth, the American myth of race that say that they's racial, cultural, and social purity in America" (Jones, *Mosquito*, 337). With this novel, Jones attacks and explodes the American myth of "racial, cultural & social purity" (Jones, *Mosquito*, 337). Jones also challenges the notion of one "authentic" black identity with her insistence that all Americans are multiracial, while aligning herself broadly with "the colored peoples of the world" (Jones, *Mosquito*, 137). In so doing, she contends that race is a learned construct and, ultimately, critiques essentialist notions of blackness.

Coser has provided a particularly relevant analysis of Jones's interest in Latin America and her connection to Latin American writers, in particular, Gabriel García Márquez and Carlos Fuentes. Coser asserts that in both *Corregidora* and *Song for Anninho* Jones creates "inter-American bridges to Brazilian history and Latin American literature" (Coser, 120). Coser presents a coherent analysis of connections between Márquez, Fuentes, and Jones. In particular, Coser points to elements of magical realism in Jones's work that corresponds to those in Márquez and Fuentes:

> Like them, Jones also combines historical accounts, dreams, obsessions, and the stories of mothers and grandmothers to create her own tale. Recalling the use of ambiguity and paradox in Fuentes, Jones is interested in several different but complementary dimensions of reality and in open-ended stories that keep bringing the past into the present (Coser, 145).

Corregidora, he also contends, can be read as a response to Brazilian writer Gilberto Freyre's *The Masters and the Slaves*, in which Freyre claims that couplings between slaves and their Portuguese masters were non-violent, if not peaceful, unions (Freyre).[6] With her book, Jones counters Freyre's claims of a "peaceful" miscegenation through her depiction of the incestuous and diabolical Old Man Corregidora and the destruction his sexual exploitation wreaks on generations of black women. Coser aptly concludes that "aspects in which Latin

American novelists have affected Jones's writing include the blend of history and myth in language and the shifts in time and space allowing for broader and deeper perceptions to be translated into writing" (Coser, 145). Although Coser's contention that "Jones shares with Latin American writers the wish to write a new *American* narrative" is well taken and articulates Jones's multiracial and multicultural take on the United States in her most recent novel, his belief that she modifies this intention by "recognizing its connections with European literary history" fails to fully recognize the pervasiveness of African American folk culture in Jones's work (Coser, 145). In addition to her depiction of what I would term an Afro-Latino/a perspective, Jones always remains true to her African American roots and foregrounds a black cultural aesthetic, most often manifested through her incorporation of the blues and the vernacular in her writing.

In regards to Jones's decision to focus on Brazil while exploring the subject of slavery in *Corregidora*, Coser contends that Jones deliberately focused her story on a Brazilian slavemaster rather than an English one, as is typical in most U.S. slave narratives, due to the higher instance of miscegenation and concubinage in Brazilian society. In comparison, American slaveholders were less likely to admit to having sexual relations with their slaves due to the stigma attached to miscegenation in the United States. However, as Coser notes, Jones does not make strict distinctions between Brazilian and U.S. slavery. Instead, she connects the two experiences by centering her story on Ursa, a black woman living in the United States, thereby broadening the U.S. slave experience beyond its traditional geographical borders.

In exploring Afro-Latino/a identifications in *Corregidora*, it is also significant to note that Ursa physically resembles Latinas—indicative of Jones's interest in mixed racial heritages and lineages, something she explores in depth in *Mosquito*. Ursa is coffee-bean-colored, as are all the Corregidora women. People often mistake her as being Hispanic or Spanish because of her skin color. For instance, Sal Cooper comments on Ursa's light skin and questions her about "passing." This is not unusual, considering that many light-skinned black women can pass for white. However, Sal's questions *are* unusual in that she does not ask if Ursa has passed for white. Rather, she says, "I don't mean passing white. I mean passing for Spanish or something, you know" (Jones, *Corregidora*, 70). Instead, Sal wonders if Ursa has ever thought of passing as a Spanish woman. Here, Jones complicates racial issues with her suggestion that such things are not limited to matters of black and white but are, instead, much more complex, involving varying shades of black, white, and brown. As Coser contends, in Jones's work, "the black-white dichotomy is explored and broken apart in its many hues and nuances" (Coser, 167). Tellingly, though, Sal is correct in her observations, for Ursa is in fact of Portuguese and Spanish descent. However, given Corregidora's legacy of abuse, Ursa privileges her national identity as an American over her mixed racial background. When two men she meets while walking down the street question her racial identity, she answers, "I'm an American." They counter her assertion by questioning her nationality: "You Spanish?...You look like you Spanish." To which Ursa immediately replies "Naw" (Jones, *Corregidora*, 71). Again, she demonstrates her unwillingness to claim her Portuguese and Spanish heritage. Her coffee-bean-colored skin, however, belies her mixed racial heritage, rendering it inescapable.

Jones explodes black-white dichotomies with her depiction of an Afro-Latino/a character and reveals her interest in probing issues of racial purity and interracial complexities. Ursa's tawny complexion also symbolizes Jones's fledgling distrust of skin color as a reliable racial indicator due to its inherent deceptiveness. Not coincidentally, Old Man Corregidora's skin color is also in question. He prides himself on the purity of his Portuguese heritage—a heritage that renders him a master, even though some of his African slaves are lighter than he is. Great Gram reveals this paradox, recalling that "Corregidora himself was looking like a Indian...so that this light black man looked more like a white man than he did" (Jones, *Corregidora*, 124). Again, Jones complicates skin color as a racial marker, since Corregidora's power is not derived from his complexion but from his assertions of racial superiority. Similarly, the enslaved are chosen not based only on their dark skin but on their racial status as well. Corregidora sets himself up as the gatekeeper of miscegenation due to his strict policing of who he will allow his prostitutes to service. Although he routinely engages in sex with black women, he resolutely forbids them to sleep with black men: "He liked his women black, but he didn't wont us with no black mens." As Great Gram astutely contends, Corregidora's actions lay bare the complexity of racism, for "it wasn't color [that he based his rule on] cause he didn't wont us with no light black men" (Jones, *Corregidora*, 124). Corregidora's rule reveals that racism is not necessarily based on skin color, given its status as an indeterminate symbol of a person's race. Race is something much more complex and not necessarily perceptible to the human eye. More than likely, Corregidora's rule has as much to do with his insecurities about his own mixed racial heritage as with his desire to keep black men from becoming intimate with the black women on his plantation.

Significantly, as opposed to Jones's emphasis on African retentions in *Song for Anninho*, in *Corregidora*, she highlights Brazilian, or what I would term an Afro-Latino/a, heritage (Coser, 141). She does, though, make reference to enslaved Africans in her allusion to the legendary Palmares that she explores in depth in her later work. Great Gram recalls a young black boy who dreams of escaping and running away to join the Palmares tribe, where he can be free and "have him a woman." Although she tells him that Palmares no longer exists, he counters her by asserting that "Palmares is now" (Jones, *Corregidora*, 126). Even in this early work, Jones privileges Palmares as a place of peace and unity between black people, particularly between black men and women. Great Gram's Brazil, ruled as it is by the Portuguese Corregidora, offers no such sanctuary for African peoples. Rather than a racial paradise, Jones presents Brazil as a place fraught with racial and sexual violence, where all peoples, black, white, and brown, are scarred by the legacy of slavery and oppression. For Ursa, given the evil legacy of Corregidora's abuse, embracing her Portuguese ethnicity is not an option. Here, Jones remains focused on the negative aspects of a mixed racial heritage given its basis in forced sexual conquest. In her later works, *The Healing* and *Mosquito*, Jones expands her depiction of complex racial identities in order to embrace them as a means of decrying authenticating notions of blackness and countering the myth of racial purity.

Although *Song for Anninho* takes place in Brazil, in this work Jones focuses on connections to Africa by rewriting official Brazilian records of the defeat of Palmares in 1695. Throughout this prose poem, Almeyda compares Brazil to her African homeland and concludes that "this is a good place, because it is like the place we lived before; like our own country" (Jones, *Song for Anninho*, 1). However, it is most certainly not a good place, as it is where Africans have been enslaved, and it later becomes the site of the destruction of the Palmares tribe, to which both Alymeda and Anninho belong. Despite Jones's emphasis on Africa in this work, there are allusions to her growing interest in racial mixing and her desire to embrace persons of all colors and races. Early on, Almeyda states that "the blood of the whole continent [is] running" through her veins (Jones, *Song for Anninho*, 6). Almeyda's statement demonstrates her connection to all persons on the South American and African continents, regardless of their race or skin color. However, Almeyda, despite clearly identifying herself as an African, also considers Brazil her land: "This is my place. My part of the world" (Jones, *Song for Anninho*, 13). Again, this is indicative of a melding of African and Brazilian cultures. Throughout this work, Jones places a premium on wholeness, in particular, the union of a man and a woman. One could also read this wholeness as a search for cultural/racial wholeness that would necessitate a reconciliation and embrace of one's Afro-Brazilian heritage.

Despite allusions to cultural wholeness, Jones clearly underscores the cruelty of the Brazilians. They cut off women's breasts and mutilate dead bodies by putting decapitated heads on display. This inhumanity is contrasted with the civility of the Palmares, who would only kill "when it was necessary" (Jones, *Song for Anninho*, 32). This cruelty does not end with the destruction of the Palmares tribe. Almeyda's grandmother rightly predicts that "the Portuguese who fight us here will fight others like us, others with the same flesh and blood and dreams" (Jones, *Song for Anninho*, 55). The destruction of dark-skinned peoples will continue as demonstrated in *Corregidora*, which also takes place in Brazil, although almost two hundred years after the defeat of Palmares. In keeping with an emphasis on the melding of races and cultures in this work, Palmares presents an open attitude towards persons of other cultures. Palmares included African, biracial, indigenous, and white persons. Zumbi, the tribe's fearless leader, captures a fair-skinned woman, subsequently referred to as Reina Blanca ("fair queen"), and takes her as his lover. Jones raises the possibility that women are more capable of embracing persons of various racial backgrounds: "the women become a part of whatever people they come among. It does not matter if the woman is blanca or negra, women are different" (Jones, *Song for Anninho*, 91). Coser argues that "In her poem, only women are truly capable of mixing with other races ...Jones imagines a healthy environment and a strong support group for the common women in that society" (Coser, 157). However, I would counter his argument as being too simplistic. Jones is far from an idealist and revels in depicting the complexities and paradoxes inherent in human life. Thus, although the women are charged with being "different" and, therefore, more open to embracing persons from different racial backgrounds, they are not without jealousy over the introduction of the Reina Blanca into their midst—a much more realistic response. Reina's long hair and fair skin threatens the other Palmares women, who wonder, "What can you do when there's a fair-skinned woman with long hair among you?" (Jones, *Song for Anninho*, 103). Almeyda even becomes jealous of Anninho's interactions with Reina. Here, Jones presents the difficulty of accepting the "other"— someone who is from a different culture—into one's fold. Almeyda expresses the complexity of race relations as she recounts the irony of fair-skinned women tanning their skin, rendering "themselves dark like our women. They had burned their skin dark. No, these are not colored women. They found a day that was bleeding and hot, and made themselves dark, and pretended" (Jones, *Song for Anninho*, 115). Converse to Ursa's ability to pass as a Spanish woman in *Corregidora*, here we witness white women attempting to pass as African. Interestingly, Jones presents an oft-ignored aspect of passing, namely, the desires of white women to pass for black. Such a depiction exemplifies the complexity of ethnic and race relations.

In examining Jones, Coser places her work within what Immanuel Wallerstein calls the "extended Caribbean" that "stretches north and south along the Atlantic and spreads its influence beyond the core plantation-slave region" in order to describe the geographical bridges that her work promotes between African Americans and Latin Americans (Jones, *Song for Anninho*, 172). However, with *Mosquito*, much of which takes place in the southwestern United States along the Mexico-Texas border, I maintain that Jones moves outside the "extended Caribbean" paradigm, thereby extending her geographical bridges into relationships between African Americans and Latino/as. With its opening lines, *Mosquito* establishes borders, both literal and metaphorical, as its subject as Jones proceeds to interrogate the contemporary experience of non-white persons living in the United States. This experience, she contends, is best depicted as one situated, sometimes literally, on the border. Jones's narrative begins with her protagonist, Mosquito, a thirty-something female African American truck driver, traveling her regular route through southwestern Texas: "I was on one of them little border roads in South Texas, you know them little narrow roads that runs along the border between South Texas and northern Mexico" (Jones, *Mosquito*, 1). This setting is not coincidental as in this novel Jones foregrounds relationships on the U.S. border between Latino/as and African Americans, as well as those between members of various other racial groups. Fundamentally, Jones makes a strong case against the myth of racial purity thereby enabling herself to expand the definition of the African American experience to include the related experiences of various other racial groups and to counter claims of an authentic blackness by depicting persons of various racial backgrounds including Afro-Brazilians, Portuguese Africans, Native American/African Americans, among others. It is also significant that Jones places her protagonist in the southwestern United States—not an area that is commonly depicted by African American authors. Mosquito, however, proudly claims a close familiarity with South Texas in her proclamation that "I knows the Southwest" (Jones, *Mosquito*, 3). On the other hand, the Southwest, given its position on the literal border between two countries, is perhaps the perfect place for Jones to interrogate and revise the African American experience. As Mosquito declares, "when you gets to the Southwest it got it own distinctive landscape, and you knows you's in a different country" (Jones, *Mosquito*, 2). Jones uses this pretense of being in a "different country" to present a unique account of life in the United States—one that counters official histories of American life much as she countered official Portuguese documents in *Song for Anninho*. Nothing is sacred to Jones, and she proceeds to dispel almost every American myth, beginning with the standard depiction of all cowboys as white. Mosquito reflects upon the "real cowboys" as being "Mexicans and Navajos and Zunis and Cherokees among the whites and

'Oklahoma Africans' I calls the others, 'cause the first black cowboys I seen was in Oklahoma" (Jones, *Mosquito*, 4). Rather than upholding the traditional image of white cowboys presented in Hollywood films, Jones reverses this stereotype by claiming that the "real" cowboys were most likely other than white, while the "pretend" cowboys are those we see in the movies. Jones also redefines derogatory American racial slurs, such as the term "nigger." According to what Mosquito has learned, the term now refers to "them that can't play white in America or refuses to play white" (Jones, *Mosquito*, 9). Conversely, the term "gringo" also gets rewritten as a possible referent to any person prejudiced against people of color, regardless of the whiteness of their skin, since, as Delgadina contends, "gringoism ain't a color, it a state of mind" (Jones, *Mosquito*, 126). The above examples of redefining and rewriting American terms and icons lay the groundwork for Jones's greater project, namely, the expansion of the African American experience through her establishment of Afro-Latino/a cross-cultural connections.

Mosquito's choice of relationships reflects her allegiance to a variety of racial persons and illustrates Jones's desire to forge connections between African American and Latino/a communities. Her closest friend, with the exception of her childhood best friend Monkey Bread, is Delgadina, a Chicana, and she routinely transports a trio of men consisting of a Navajo, a black man, and a white roustabout from Texas to Albuquerque, New Mexico. Similar to these relationships is the concern that she displays for the safety and well being of various ethnic persons. For example, upon meeting Leonora Valdez, a young Native American/Chicana woman, in a McDonald's restaurant, Mosquito offers Leonora a ride to New Mexico, her final destination, and then makes sure that she has enough gas money once she arrives. More important, though, is her relationship with Maria Barriga, a pregnant illegal Mexican immigrant, whom she accidentally smuggles across the U.S. border. Upon discovering Maria hidden in the back of her truck, Mosquito exhibits remarkable tenderness and compassion towards her and eventually delivers her to safety. Her interaction with Maria leads her to join the Sanctuary Movement—an undercover organization (dubbed "the new Underground Railroad") that aids illegal immigrants in entering the U.S. and defends the rights of ethnic peoples in numerous third-world countries. Her job as a member of this organization is to transport illegal immigrants across the U.S.-Mexico border. Mosquito also demonstrates her commitment to other racial groups in her willingness to educate herself about such peoples. Throughout the novel, we see Mosquito learning from various characters, such as Delgadina or Ray, her Filipino/African American lover, about different cultural traditions. Among the things she learns are different native customs, beliefs, and languages. Not coincidentally, Jones peppers her narrative with a variety of languages, including Spanish, Chicano English, and various Native American dialects, which also demonstrates Jones's desire to test her readers' expectations of an African American novel. Through her inclusion of these languages in her novel, along with her subject matter, namely relations and connections between various ethnic groups in the United States, Jones implicitly expands our understanding of the typical African American novel.

As she has done in her previous works, with *Mosquito*, Jones again engages in the project of revising official history to include the neglected histories of persons of color. Mosquito also defies traditional U.S. history in her claim that America's land was stripped from its original and rightful owners: "I thinks about this whole land when it were just the lands of the Kiowa, Cheyenne, Arapaho, Comanche, Apache and what Delgadina calls the Clovis Culture before them" (Jones, *Mosquito*, 14). She, herself, fantasizes about being part of this legacy stating that "I daydreams of myself sometimes, riding the prairies on a wild Spanish mustang" (Jones, *Mosquito*, 14). Although a seemingly simple act, it is significant in that in doing so Mosquito ignores traditional racial barriers as she inserts herself, an African American woman, into a Native American version of history. She privileges this non-white version of U.S. history, stating that "I ain't like to hear the white man's version, 'cause everybody know that. I likes to hear the other people's eclectic stories of the Southwest" (Jones, *Mosquito*, 14). Mosquito continues by refuting the traditional story of the so-called discovery of America with her statement that "Maybe Columbus discover the white man's America, but he ain't discover they [Native Americans'] America. And they America ain't even America" (Jones, *Mosquito*, 63). Here, Mosquito also makes an important distinction between the terms "America" and "the United States," driving home the point that "America" encompasses all of North and South America and, therefore, all inhabitants of either continent are entitled to refer to themselves as "Americans." By collapsing the terms "America" and "the United States," Jones contends, we deny people outside of the United States their rightful status as "Americans." Thus, throughout this novel, Jones not only carefully recuperates the history of African Americans and Latino/as in the United States, but, moreover, she privileges the indigenous history of both the United States and Mexico.

In an attempt to defend the importance of building bridges between African American and Latino/a cultures, Jones highlights the lack of interaction between these groups—something that is all too familiar. In doing so, Jones addresses another border issue, namely those seemingly immovable borders between different racial communities. Delgadina is particularly aware of border wars between various racial groups and compares it to "how people behave during wartime." This is not unusual, she contends, by stating "that how it seem like certain minorities behave with each other all the time" (Jones, *Mosquito*, 126). She also goes on to affirm that such disparities exist between African Americans and Latino/as. Mosquito relates that Delgadina "[is] talking like the African Americans they the gringo too, and in the Southwest they's African Americans that looks at them Mexicans and Mexican Americans like they's second- or even third-class citizens, 'cause that gringoism a state of mind" (Jones, *Mosquito*, 130). Moreover, although some may eat at Mexican restaurants, few, if any, African Americans frequent the cantina where Delgadina works as a bartender. It is this fact that causes Delgadina to suspect initially that Mosquito is an immigration officer. She explains her mistaken assumption to Mosquito by stating that "I thought you were immigration, because aren't many African Americans come in here. Some of the tourists come in here, but not many African Americans from the area," further underscoring the palpable separation between these groups (Jones, *Mosquito*, 143). In regard to her status as a feminist, Delgadina is at a loss to find a word that refers specifically to her struggle as a Chicana feminist. As she talks about the double oppression experienced by women of color, as women and as persons of color, Mosquito relates Delgadina's thought process: "So us can't be the same kind of feminists as gringo feminist, if us consider usselves feminists at all. She be talking about that Alice Walker word *womanist*, but then she be saying that womanist ain't her culture neither, so she can't be calling herself no womanist neither" (Jones, *Mosquito*, 54-55). Delgadina critiques Alice Walker's use of the word "womanist" to refer to African American feminists due to its exclusive reference to black feminists rather than to all women of color. In her rejection of the term "womanist," Delgadina makes implicitly clear the barriers that exist between different racial groups. Similarly, in her reference to some African Americans as "gringos," Delgadina implies that some African Americans treat Chicano/as in a manner similar to the way whites mistreat persons of color. She solidifies this claim with her contention that "they's even African Americans in South Texas that's got they own brand of gringoism" (Jones, *Mosquito*, 153). Although Mosquito does learn some Spanish words and familiarizes herself with Latino/a culture, it is Delgadina, a Chicana, who educates herself about African American literature and racial politics. Notably, Jones seems to lay the blame for the border wars between African Americans and Latino/as on African Americans, since Delgadina is most aware of the animosity present between these groups and educates Mosquito about its existence—a possible wake-up call to the black community.

Jones also contests the rigid separation between African American and Latino/a cultures in regard to the academy (perhaps asserting her position as an African American writer who incorporates Latino/a life and culture into her work). For example, Delgadina tells Mosquito about an African American scholar who specializes in Chicano/a literature and recounts the constant criticism she endures because "everybody be wondering why she ain't specialize in African-American literature. Even Chicanos be wondering why she don't specialize in African-American literature" (Jones, *Mosquito*, 75). With this admission, Jones may be making a case for herself as an Afro-Latino/a writer. Perhaps to counter similar questions about her authenticity as an African American writing about Latino/a experiences, Jones underscores the overlap in the experiences of persons from both these communities due to their similar positions as persons of color in the

United States. She also refutes claims that one must possess the same racial background as that which he/she studies in order to fully understand or appreciate such work. Not coincidentally, it is Delgadina, a Chicana, who educates Mosquito, a black woman, about African American literature and racial politics. Delgadina takes many classes in race relations, studies African American literature, gives Mosquito books to read by African American authors, educates her about Miles Davis, Louis Armstrong, and minstrelsy, and even knows some of the Swahili language, which she teaches to Mosquito. Delgadina also regularly expresses her familiarity with canonical black writers, including LeRoi Jones and Langston Hughes. In fact, it is her familiarity with such texts that leads students in her class to mistakenly presume that she is black. Delgadina's professor recalls this, stating that "They [the other students] thought you were black." However, Delgadina refused to allow him to correct their mistake: "Why should you [correct them]? And, anyway, I felt like LeRoi Jones was my poet too. I would have brought up a Chicano poet if I'd known any Chicano poets in those days.... I brought up LeRoi Jones, 'cause they were talking like poetry was just themselves" (Jones, *Mosquito*, 169). This incident is important, for it emphasizes the overlap between the experiences of African Americans and Latino/as. Although LeRoi Jones is an African American writer, Delgadina, a Chicana, thinks of him as articulating her experiences as an oppressed, non-white U.S. citizen as well.

Delgadina's refusal to divulge that she is not African American to her classmates reveals the significance of passing in this novel. As she did, albeit briefly, in *Corregidora*, here Jones also interrogates incidents of passing other than the *de riguer* passing of black for white. In keeping with her desire to explode the myth of racial purity, in *Mosquito* Jones constantly emphasizes the blending of various races to the extent that one is unable to physically distinguish one culture from another. When she first describes Maria Barriga, Mosquito says that "she look as much Indian as Mexican though and maybe even a little bit Chinese" (Jones, *Mosquito*, 27). Here, she highlights Maria's indigenous heritage—again, refiguring mainstream depictions of Mexican peoples. For example, people often think that Mosquito is African, and she is mistaken for being a Portuguese-African while on vacation in Canada. People often confuse Delgadina's racial identity, as well.

Upon first meeting Delgadina, Mosquito erroneously presumes that she is an African American. She states that "when I first seen my friend Delgadina I be thinking she African American too, then she be telling me she Mexican American, I mean, Chicana" (Jones, *Mosquito*, 75). Alternatively, even Anglo-Americans can be mistaken as being of various other racial backgrounds since, as Delgadina contends, "lotta them gringa Americans look like Chicanas" (Jones, *Mosquito*, 142). Similarly, while explaining Delgadina's animosity towards Latino/a men who marry white women, Mosquito notes that "she say a lot of the good ones that don't marry gringas be getting them Mexican women or Chicanas that looks like gringas" (Jones, *Mosquito*, 150). Mosquito not only makes reference to the fact that some Chicanas look white, but, more importantly, she implicitly reveals the failure of conventional racial categories, for one can rarely accurately determine a person's racial identity based on their outward appearance or skin color.

Mosquito also acknowledges Delgadina's ability to pass, or at least defy typical Chicana stereotypes, in her discussion of Delgadina's linguistic abilities. She remarks that, granted Delagadina, as a Chicana, is bilingual, when she:

> be talking English she be talking different kinds of English. When she be talking intellectual stuff she be sounding almost like a gringa, then when she be talking everyday stuff she be sounding kinda like Rosie Perez or like María Conchita Alonso—they's movie actresses—or she be sounding like herself which is a Chicana flavor that's her individual ownself, and sometimes when she be joking sometimes or kidding with me about something or specifying or signifiying sometimes she be sounding like me (Jones, *Mosquito*, 126).

Here, Jones reveals Delgadina's linguistic chameleonism. She is capable of impressive code-switching according to her subject as well as her audience. At times, she can sound intellectual, that is, "white," or she can sound like a stereotypical Latina, a la Hollywood, or she can sound like her unique self, or, amazingly enough, she can even sound African American when engaging in specifically black linguistic practices, such as specifying and signifying. Her linguistic ability constitutes racial passing on one level. Most certainly, it demonstrates her familiarity with various ethnic speech practices and supports Jones's argument against racial purity. Although Mosquito claims that

Delgadina can accurately emulate speech patterns from a variety of racial groups, besides her own speech community, Delgadina is most familiar with African American vernacular English. Delgadina's linguistic agility, to which Mosquito's words attest, goes beyond merely repeating words common to African American speakers. Rather, she is able to successfully engage in complex linguistic practices, such as signifying, that require a close knowledge and understanding of the black community. Her ability to linguistically pass for black further suggests a close affinity between African American and Latino/a communities.

Despite Delgadina's closeness to Mosquito and the African American community, Jones refuses to simplify the act of passing. Passing, she demonstrates, is an extremely complicated practice and holds serious consequences. Acutely aware of such consequences, Delgadina sometimes "acts black" when she knows it will benefit her. This is most true in her experiences in her poetry class. There, an African American racial identity gives her cultural currency and allows her to embrace her status as "other" instead of acquiescing to Anglo-American ideals, since "I saw how the other Latinas there played it, and I didn't want to play it like that. I preferred them to think I was black than play it like that" (Jones, *Mosquito*, 170). In this instance, being culturally marked as Latina in the northeastern United States[7] affords a Chicana, such as Delgadina, the opportunity to deny her cultural heritage and pass for white, or, at the very least, embrace whiteness. Delgadina refuses to do that and, instead, identifies herself with the black community in order to distance herself from Anglo-American society and become culturally marked as "other." In distinguishing between the Northeast and the Southwest, Delgadina makes the telling remark that, had she been in a similar class at a school located in the Southwest, there would be no need for her to identify as an African American in order to be considered "other," since "we're [Latinas] niggers in South Texas ourselves" (Jones, *Mosquito*, 170). Delgadina's statement connects the experiences of both African Americans and Latinas as "niggers" in the eyes of white America, and attests to the logic of alliances being formed between these two groups on the basis of their similar status as oppressed peoples in the United States.

The complexity of Delgadina's passing is also demonstrated by the fact that, although she often embraces her mistaken identity as an African American, at times Delgadina does *not* want to be mistaken for being African American—a fact that Mosquito reveals when she hesitates to tell Maria that her baby looks slightly African.[8] Mosquito states that she refrains from revealing this piece of information "'cause after reading that Delgadina notebook, about not wanting people to mistake her for no African American, I be thinking that Maria not want me to say her little boy remind me of a lot of little African-American babies with his reddish-brown complexion and curly hair" (Jones, *Mosquito*, 207–208). So, although sometimes Delgadina does not object to being considered African American, in other instances she refutes this mistaken identity. Her objection to being mistaken as African American attests to the significance of one's racial identity for it influences how one is perceived by others. Delgadina astutely notes, "If somebody tell you they Chicana, then you be looking at them like they Chicana. And you be having different ideas of who they are and they possibilities" (Jones *Mosquito* 142). As she contends, how one is perceived racially does affect our expectations and assumptions about them. Unfortunately, such assumptions are all too often negative and can severely hinder one's aspirations and achievements. Delgadina's refusal to be mistaken as an African American also demonstrates the unease with which these two racial groups often approach the project of forming cross-cultural alliances, as well as the underlying prejudices each group possesses about the other.

Similar to Delgadina's command of African American vernacular English, Mosquito, too, expresses a remarkable willingness to embrace other cultures and incorporate them into her own unique persona. Just as Delgadina is familiar with African American literature and culture, Mosquito has also picked up some traits from the Chicana community, among others. Besides peppering her conversations with various Spanish words, she refers to herself as a *"trabajadora"*— the Spanish word for "working-class woman" (Jones, *Mosquito*, 240). Mosquito explains her cross-cultural connections stating that:

> I do know something about Latin and general science, a little about history, but from my own interpretation. I knows a little Spanish which I been

> learning.... I knows the English that I don't resist to know, I knows how to dance the Argentinean tango, and I knows the difference between Taco Bell tacos and real tacos.... I knows a little Italian 'cause I knows some Italians who is as much colored as they's Italian (Jones, *Mosquito*, 240).

With this statement, while tacitly contesting the use of the term "colored" to describe only African American peoples, Mosquito presents herself to be quite a culturally well rounded woman who, in particular, favors Latin American and Chicano/a culture second to her own. Moreover, Mosquito claims to have had a life-long appreciation for Mexican culture. She states that "I ain't never had that typical American attitude towards Mexico myself, even before I met Delgadina. I ain't know why I always liked that Mexico. I ain't never been to Mexico" (Jones, *Mosquito*, 316). Furthermore, she lays claim to her own Mexican heritage by contending that "Us family history say that some of us Johnsons originated in Mexico, that we was originally Mexican Africans.... I know I don't look like no Mexican, but family history say that there's a little Mexican in me" (Jones, *Mosquito*, 317). With Mosquito's admission of her own Mexican heritage, Jones reveals an often overlooked or denied connection between African American and Latino/a peoples, namely, the existence of persons of Afro-Mexican or Afro-Latino/a descent. Mosquito's admission allows her to reclaim her Mexican heritage and further strengthens Jones's argument against the representation of a monolithic blackness. Although Mosquito may appear to be African American, in truth, she also possesses some Mexican heritage and, thus, could be conceived of as "Afro-Mexican" or "Afro-Latino/a." Perhaps it is this realization that prompts Mosquito finally to refer to herself as a "New World African," rather than simply as an "African American."

In addition to claiming a Mexican heritage, while in Canada, Mosquito meets a man of Portuguese/African descent who also makes a strong case for the existence of Afro-Latino/a connections. He refuses to be called "Portuguese African" and refers to himself simply as "African." He makes an implicit reference to the Palmares tribe and then contends that "he could claim to be Brazilian as much as he could claim to be African." He then educates Mosquito about the "Africanization of Brazil." With this statement, he implies that borders, geographical or cultural, are incapable of keeping various racial groups rigidly separated. Furthermore, he contends that there are stronger connections between Africans and Latin Americans than people most often acknowledge. He declares that when he is in Brazil he feels as if he is in Africa and that "they got towns all over Latin America like that, even Mexico, and...he been in them towns and think he still in Africa" (Jones, Mosquito, 289). His comments demonstrate the fluidity of cultures and the similarities between African and Latino/a peoples. Like Mosquito's claims to a Mexican heritage, he, too, demonstrates cultural links between these two groups.

In keeping with Jones's belief that traditional racial classifications fail to adequately articulate the complexity of people's identities, Mosquito finds such categorization problematic as well. In her final letter to Ray, she counters fixed racial categories by compiling a list of the various racial identities that people of color choose for themselves. She states that some

> are Negroes, others is colored peoples, others is blacks (with a small *b*), others is Blacks (with a big *b*), others is Afro-Americans, others is African-Americans (hyphenated), others is African Americans (unhyphenated), others is Just Plain Americans, others is New World Africans, others is Descendants of the Victims of the African Diaspora Holocaust, others is Multiracialists, others is Multiethnics, others is Sweeter the Juice Multiracial Multiethnics (these are people like myself who have other races and ethnic groups, like Mexicans, Irish, Greeks, and Italians in they ancestry but who resemble pure African gods and goddesses) (Jones, *Mosquito*, 613).

Here, she presents, in typical Jones's tongue-in-cheek fashion, the complex variety of designations that people bestow upon themselves. With this, Jones underscores her desire to refute claims of a monolithic African American identity. Instead, she privileges a multitude of black identities and refrains from imposing a singular, specific designation upon them. Jones also disputes claims of a monolithic whiteness, since when many whites trace their roots they "discovered that they own roots led them to Africa. That not all they roots led them to Europe. Some of they roots even led them to Asia.... A lot of the peoples that they thought was white they is discovering resembles more the colored people of America than the so-called whites." Even the designation of "white" is no longer a reliable racial marker, since most whites are as racially mixed as non-whites are. Mosquito professes that "I think everybody's got a little nigger somewhere in their woodpile" (Jones, *Mosquito*, 536–537). Consequently, in the end, Mosquito contends that there needs to be a new definition of the term "American" that encompasses persons of a variety of racial backgrounds.

In the end, the publication of *Mosquito*, Jones's most recent novel, demonstrates her commitment to revising the African American novel to include the "experiences of blacks everywhere" within and without traditional U. S. borders. Moving from her earlier interest in interrogating the diasporic roots of African Americans by depicting Afro-Brazilian experiences, Jones has returned to U.S. soil. Yet she continues to expand the literary representation of the African American experience by forging connections between African American and Latino/a peoples, all the while remaining true to her original desire to refute monolithic claims of an authentic blackness. With *Mosquito*, Jones does important cultural work in presenting a strong case for the importance of establishing connections between various oppressed peoples, specifically African Americans and Latino/as, within the United States. Overall, the intense friendship between Mosquito, an African American woman, and Delgadina, a Chicana, while underscoring the failure of conventional racial categories to adequately identify one's racial background, demonstrates the importance of forging cross-cultural alliances between African American and Latino/a communities. This book, taken in the context of her earlier work—both critical and fictional, firmly establishes Gayl Jones as an essential and integral figure in expanding the representation of the African American experience to include Afro-Latino/a experiences.

Notes

[1] See Gloria Anzaldúa and Cherríe Moraga, eds., *This Bridge Called My Back: Writings by Radical Women of Color*, second ed. (New York: Kitchen Table: Women of Color Press, 1983).

[2] See also Jones's poetry volumes *Xarque and Other Poems* (1981), *The Hermit Woman* (1983), as well as her short story "Ensinaca" in *Confirmation: An Anthology of African American Women* (eds. Amiri and Amina Baraka, 1993).

[3] Palmares was a tribe of Africans, comprised of both runaway slaves and freed persons, located in the mountains of Brazil in the late 1600s. They were defeated by the Portuguese in 1695

[4] In this essay, I use the term "Afro-Latino/a" to describe authors, either African American and/or Latino/a, who make connections between African American and Latino/a cultures and experiences in their writing. Others also use this term to refer to persons of African American and Latino/a descent.

[5] For a historical overview of Brazil's paradisical status for African Americans see *African-American Reflections on Brazil's Racial Paradise*, ed. David J. Hellwig (Philadelphia: Temple University Press, 1992).

[6] Freyre contends that Portuguese planters actually preferred mulatto women to their Portuguese wives and that, although planters engaged in sexual relations with their African slaves as a means of increasing their holdings, miscegenation was peaceful and encouraged by the Catholic Church.

[7] Delgadina's poetry class was located at a university in Connecticut.

[8] This, in and of itself, is significant for Maria's baby's complexion implicitly reveals the Africanist presence in Mexico and suggests further evidence of the existence of Afro-Latino/a peoples.

Works Cited

Anzaldúa, Gloria, and Cherríe Moraga, eds. *This Bridge Called My Back: Writings by Radical Women of Color*. second ed. New York: Kitchen Table: Women of Color Press, 1983.

Coser, Stelamaris. *Bridging the Americas: The Literature of Paule Marshall, Toni Morrison, and Gayl Jones*. Philadelphia: Temple University Press, 1995.

Freyre, Gilberto. *The Masters and the Slaves: A Study in the Development of Brazilian Civilization*. Berkeley: University of California Press, 1986.

Hall, Stuart. "Subjects in History: Making Diasporic Identities." *The House That Race Built*. Ed. Wahneema Lubiano. New York: Pantheon Books, 1997. 289-299.

Hellwig, David J., ed. *African-American Reflections on Brazil's Racial Paradise*. Philadelphia: Temple University Press, 1992.

Jackson, Richard L. "Remembering the 'Disremembered': Modern Black Writers and Slavery in Latin America." *Callaloo*.

Jones, Gayl. *Corregidora*. Black Women Writers Series. Boston: Beacon Press, 1976.

———. *Liberating Voices: Oral Tradition in African American Literature*. Cambridge, MA.: Harvard University Press, 1991.

———. *Mosquito*. Boston: Beacon Press, 1999.

———. "The Quest for Wholeness Re-Imagining the African-American Novel: An Essay on Third World Aesthetics." *Callaloo* 17.2 (1994): 507-518.

———. *Song for Anninho*. Boston: Beacon Press, 1981.

Rowell, Charles. "An Interview with Gayl Jones." *Callaloo* 5 (1982): 32-53.

Rushdy, Ashraf H. A. "'Relate Sexual to Historical': Race, Resistance, and Desire in Gayl Jones's *Corregidora*." *African American Review* 34.2 (2000): 273-297.

CHAPTER FIVE

"reads kinda like jazz in they rhythm": Gayl Jones's Recent Jazz Conversations

Jill Terry

Gayl Jones's most recent novel, *Mosquito*, published in 1999, has been described as a "literary tour de force."[1] Over 600 pages long, it seems likely that it is the product of the many years in which Jones has been hidden from the public eye, for it has an astonishing breadth of subject matter and includes myriad cultural references. *Mosquito* is, first and foremost, a narrative of storytelling. It is narrated in the first person in a southern vernacular conversational style by protagonist Sojourner Jane Nadine Johnson, who originates from Covington, Kentucky. Sojourner is an appropriate name for a character of such wit, intelligence, and commitment to human rights. In particular, her political viewpoint accords with her name "Sojourner"—Sojourner Truth is a foremother who is a familiar reference in Jones's work. While Sojourner is called by each of her names according to the ways in which different people "read" her, the name most often adopted by her and her friends is the nickname Mosquito, a name seemingly quite inappropriate, for she is neither small nor blood-sucking. Mosquito is a thiry-ish African American woman who, like the original Sojourner Truth, is unusually tall. She is also highly curious. Rather than absorbing blood, she is constantly absorbing knowledge from those around her. By what her friends tell her, rather than from the books she reads, she seeks self development as she mistakenly believes that she is "ignorant" due to the lack of educational opportunity for one of her race and social class. *Mosquito* presents an optimistic and assertive view of black femalehood in contemporary America and, therefore, a different perspective to that presented by the traumatized, needy, protagonists Ursa Corregidora and Eva Medina of the 1970s novels. With Mosquito, as with her character Harlan in *The Healing*, Jones demonstrates that she has established a new confidence in the ability of a black woman to move on from a position of reaction to one of self-determined action.

For each of Jones' childless protagonists it is important to find alternatives to the traditional means of passing on oral culture. For them, the community in which the oral culture circulates must be one that is outside the immediate family and one that can be approached through the telling of stories. For the author, the writing of books serves a similar function; as Gunilla Kester argues, books are now the main body and repository of women's culture.[2] The first-person vernacular voice characterizes the novel as oral; it is a "speakerly text" that privileges the linguistic features of oral speech. Mosquito's narrative is, in parts, like that of a travel writer who knows her landscape intimately; she discourses on the flora and fauna of the Southwest, its archaeology, history, and people. Mosquito travels through the landscape as the driver of a truck that she is very proud to own. It is her truck that gives her the independence that is her most striking characteristic, as it is also truck driving that brings Mosquito into contact with the people of the regions through which she travels. She emphasizes their complex ethnic/racial makeup to include Black Mexicans, Chicano/as, Latino/as, Hispanics and Latin Americans, and Native Americans.

With Mosquito's sympathy towards indigenous peoples and her relationship to the land, it is not surprising that she helps in the movement of people who may be illegal aliens in the country. She manages this under the protection of her legitimate cargo of industrial detergents. It is also unsurprising that she becomes recruited to the "new Underground Railroad"—Sanctuary, an organization which serves a similar function to that of the Underground Railroad in the time of slavery.

The novel revisits, and re-emphasizes, a number of themes and literary techniques that are significant in Jones's earlier work. First, with the self agency of a developing female narrator telling her own unmediated story, Jones reconfirms the narrative point of view established in *Corregidora* (1975), *Eva's Man* (1976), and *The Healing* (1998). This is a narrative technique that is advocated by Jones in her work of literary criticism, *Liberating Voices* (1991). Second, this novel re-emphasises a commitment to representing the multicultural, multiracial nature of American society as acknowledged in the postscript to *Liberating Voices*, in which Jones advocates applying the problems of the "freed voice" to "all the world's literatures and criticisms."[3] Third, the novel develops and emphasizes a theme which Jones introduced in *The Healing* namely, that the categorization of people according to race is untenable. In both the recent novels Jones foregrounds the practice of stereotyping as the main example of the static, overdetermined categories of identity that she interrogates, implying that these categories impose a constricting idea of blackness. Last, the novel is inscribed with representations of the musical forms that have particular significance for black culture, for example, spirituals, the blues, jazz, and rap. What is perhaps the most striking feature of the novel is the way in which *Mosquito* accommodates both a connection to the particular history of black people in the South, and their continuous history of oppression (a history evoked by the novel's relationship to, and representation of, black music), yet, concomitantly, concentrates on the contemporary multicultural experience. To this end, references to African American musical culture are juxtaposed with representations of a panoply of high and popular cultural forms, from American television and film to salsa recipes and canonical literature. The astonishing range of subjects and the plurality of referents, juxtapositions, and pastiche, make this a postmodern polyphonic novel.

The reader might easily become lost in the novel's profusion were it not for the one stable point of connection: that provided by the controlling voice of Mosquito. Although it is not at first apparent that the narrative is retrospective, this becomes evident in moments when some distance between the delivery of the narrative and the events it portrays are indicated. For example, we learn in a brief comment that

Mosquito is now the joint owner of a motel and has her own truck company, this is reinforced by a small reference to "years later" (381). The majority of the narrative reads as if it is a moment-by-moment account which is being narrated as told in the immediate narrative instant. The free and direct discourse of Mosquito "speaks" to the reader/listener, immediately drawing the reader into a position aligned with an implied reader who is part of an interpretative community that is constructed as an audience. The reader is apparently sharing knowledge with a narrator who is already known, for Mosquito is not ever introduced to the reader (except by what we learn when she introduces herself to a character, a truck stowaway, some thirty-six pages into the narrative.)

This narrative style is maintained throughout the novel with intermittent direct addresses to the reader/listener, which include, for instance, shared knowledge of films: "Y'all remember that scene..."; "You remember that movie" (33, 118). She shows her awareness of a possibly skeptical audience: "I know there is some amongst y'all that ain't going to believe me" (90); and assumptions are made about the implied audience's political perspective: "I know some of y'all wants me to identify that star as a true racist" (403). Further, Mosquito is aware that the audience is likely to become tired of the overlong digressions in which she and they lose the thread of the narrative: "I spent so much time telling y'all about Delgadina, y'all probably forgot about that priest. But that's the way true stories is" (121). This self-referential knowledge about the implied reader/listener is restated at several points, as the narrator is explicit in addressing an audience of "listeners" who may not all be trustworthy and to whom she cannot reveal full details about the New Underground Railroad, but who are called to respond as coproducers of the text.

In that vein the novel opens with the voice of Mosquito addressing her reader in a conversational tone in the midst of what appears to be a flowing dialogue:

> I was on one of them little border roads in South Texas, you know them little narrow roads that runs along the border between South Texas and northern Mexico. Maybe that Dairy Mart Road, probably that Dairy Mart Road, though all them border roads in them border towns looks alike. (1)

These first lines immediately effect an illusion of intimacy with the reader and the place described; they also imply that you can never really be sure where you are, or if what you think you see *is* what you see. The reference to border towns is the first clue that the novel will take the reader on a journey in which the idea of a border has particular resonance in signifying the issue of U.S. immigration policy. The processes of migration and border crossings contribute to the novel's thematic concerns with multiplicity as it confronts flaws in the American dream. As Mosquito's friend Delgadina puts it: "Like I can't even go out and collect my wildflowers without some border patrol wanting to see my identification. Those people who think it's not a war, and that America's not a war zone, just don't know who they're dealing with" (136).

The status of all knowledge is thrown into question in the novel as people, events, and narratives are in disguise, have aliases, or are represented by code. While foregrounding its fabrication, the novel also establishes status as an artifact, record, or testimony to the subjects, events, people, and conversations that it portrays. It soon becomes apparent that through the narrator the reader will be plunged into a world of indeterminacy, where it is often difficult to know whether Mosquito is recounting a dream, an event, or a recollection. Among the narratives included in the pastiche are a play script (written in rap rhythm); a newsletter (which may or may not be signifying and "confabulatory"); a series of letters between her friend Monkey Bread and the narrator on subjects which range from the diversity of African ethnicities to jazz, film, and *Oprah*; letters to her lover, Ray, in which events from her childhood are described by Mosquito, including songs, spirituals, and the "root" woman; and extracts from a notebook of her friend Delgadina, containing her source materials for her writing. All narratives are equal and all are destabilized, while all finally achieve the fictional status of an authentic record despite the unresolved threads, incomplete characterizations, and lack of closure. These defamiliarizing devices are explained by the narrator as being justified due to the danger of exposure faced by the narrator and others who work in the new Underground Railroad:

> I's told y'all the true truth about most of the peoples in this story, although I ain't told y'all the whole truth about none of the peoples in this story. Or

perhaps I've told y'all the whole truth without telling y'all the real truth. Like I said, my mama didn't raise the sorta fool that would tell y'all the whole story, 'cause that would be like if I was a fugitive during the time of the old Underground Railroad I got myself free, then I comes telling everybody my secrets. I gots to defend the rights and freedoms of them that ain't got they freedom yet. I'm only telling y'all as much as I am telling y'all because this is supposed to be kept in the archives of the Daughters of Nzingha. The archives keeper is supposed to be trustworthy, but being a hidden agenda conspiracy specialist I have still employed everything that I've learned. My first love is the love of language, though, and whilst I defends the rights and privileges of the new Underground Railroad and maintains as much of they secrets that they ain't revealed they ownselves, I wants to maintain they privacy, conquer my own ignorance, and to tell y'all a story about South Texas. (601-602)

The prefatory comment to *Mosquito* notes that "This book is from the Daughters of Nzingha Archives." This is explained only when the reader arrives at the Epilogue and discovers that the narrative they have been reading is the one that is supposedly lodged in these archives. However, it seems that the text we are reading represents an audio book which has been recorded on tape for the archive. This corresponds to the oral mode that is privileged throughout. Therefore, the challenge of interpretation that confronts the reader of this novel is partly explained *by* the novel as being due to the peculiar circumstances of the narrative's recording and preservation.

The most prominent and insistent theme of the book concerns race. As nothing is ever what it seems, as you can never really know what or who anything is, so race, color, and ethnicity are all unstable signifiers in this text. It develops the view that all Americans are multiracial, even while different groups will, for their own purposes, project particular identities. Mosquito maintains that "America ain't just black and white. But there's still them that wants to portray America as just black and white. First they wanted to portray it as just white, then they wants to portray it as just black and white" (27). *Mosquito* is peopled with characters who represent a variety of ethnicities; the fact of their ethnicity is forcefully reiterated because Mosquito tries to learn the different languages of the different characters. The result is a polyphony of language and voice filtered through Mosquito's story into the narrative. The affirmation of multiple black identities that Jones establishes offers a resistance to a colonizing notion of "authentic" blackness. It is characteristic of her postmodernist approach that she has produced a novel peopled by black characters, suffused with black culture, and which, at the same time, emphasises the heterogeneity of black. *Mosquito* might thus be the novel that speaks for itself in the idiosyncratic article that Jones wrote in 1994:

> I do not wish to see myself in terms of duality. There are not just Africans and Europeans in the New World, but Asians and Mexican-Americans and the Original People. And of these there are many kinds of people within peoples…. I am a multicultural, multilinguistic, multi-vernacular novel and at the same time, I am a self-defined African American novel…an African novel born in the New World.[4]

Concerned with borders—geographical, racial, psychological—Mosquito describes the "real border," the "metaphorical and cultural borders," and her "own borders." She says she "knows America like I knows myself. I knows if the colored peoples of the world writes they view of history it is a different history" (137). By using the expansive description: "colored peoples of the world," Mosquito allows for a cultural heterogeneity of color and clearly signifies that for this African American writer, color moves beyond the racial, geographical, or psychological borders of absolutist African Americanism blackness. Furthermore, the extreme sensitivity that Mosquito shows towards the racial roles that people occupy is directed against the operation of stereotypes, both in popular cultural representations and in the daily lives of people who either adopt, or deliberately avoid, stereotypical classifications of ethnicity. In the cantina, where Mosquito's Chicana friend Delgadina works, and where Mosquito is frequently to be found, this extends to food:

> Mexicans likes jalapenos but don't eat them because they thinks they be stereotyping themselves, like African Americans that don't eat watermelon and they don't eat them tacos neither. They likes tacos but don't eat them. But she be saying they's two kinds of stereotypes, though, them based on falsehoods and them based on some kinda reality, when they vulgarizes another people's culture, so when people be running from them stereotypes based on some kinda reality a lot of times they be running from they own culture, they be running from theyselves. Like in Africa, North and South, you see them women wearing them headscarves, 'cause that's part of either they culture or they religion. But then in America they be stereotyping that, even the Africans themselves, and just be thinking Aunt Jemima or they be calling people handkerchief head, and that's they own culture or they own religion. (44)

Stereotypes are inescapable, as Mosquito knows, "'cause that's the only way them others has of perceiving the people is via the stereotype....that's how the dominant culture enforce that stereotype by having the people see themselves as the stereotype" (134). This piece of Delgadina's wisdom extends to her view of Mosquito: "All the people hear is the stereotype. You know, the southern Negro. To tell you the truth, sometimes when I'm listening to you, it's sorta like when I was taking this course in African-American literature and we had to read slave narratives by women who were slaves in the Old South, and sometimes when I'm listening to you it's kinda like those old slave women might sound, if you hear them talking. You even resemble some of those old photographs" (182). Mosquito recognizes that Delgadina matches the stereotype held of the Chicana as a bartending Mexican woman but, as with the sensitive, independent, intelligent, truck-driving, linguist, griot, Mosquito herself, every facet of the novel's complicating treatment of its characters deconstructs those stereotypical images of ethnicities. For example, rather than Mosquito simply occupying the role of griot as part of a continuum linking back unproblematically through her foremothers to Sojourner Truth, the novel highlights the complexity of her black identity, exemplified by the different resonances of the parts of her full name Sojourner Jane Nadine Johnson. Mosquito challenges us to understand and accept the importance of self-identity and difference in a world that places limits on individuality. She acknowledges that "the natural self has got to be like jazz, 'cause there is complexities in America" (140).

The plot concerning the illegal immigrants who are being helped by Sanctuary highlights a perennial problem about the perception of peoples of color by the dominant white population who see Latin American immigrants as a threat to "so called American values" (76). This is an accusation familiar to African Americans. We are shown that racist stereotypes are constructed from fundamental distortions and errors about racial purity and racial difference, but that they can be reclaimed. An example is the African American professor who has taught Mosquito that the Aunt Jemima stereotype had a basis in reality, and one that ought to be reclaimed, for "in Africa they's true women" (253). The passing on of this account enables Jones to make a statement through her book that, due to the storytelling narrative technique, appears as wisdom instead of a preached polemic. This wisdom is continually surfacing through examples such as in the case of the pregnant Latino refugee whom Mosquito helps and who tells Mosquito her own story. Relayed to the reader by Mosquito, the refugee's story shows how she is discouraged from describing the harsh conditions of her country "for they say it feeds the stereotypes of Latin America, that it feeds the prejudices, but not for those of us who know who we are, who have learned who we are" (376), "They had taken something that had a basis in our reality and perverted it into a stereotype" (252). The effect which Jones achieves is the reclaiming stereotypes—her "talking back" is the same as the resistance described in the narrative.

The novel similarly demonstrates its preoccupation with racial categories through the lengthy conversations on the subject between Mosquito and Delgadina as they discourse on the multiple origins of Americans. The novel reiterates the view that "racial purity's a myth" (191). A play directed by Delgadina is about "America. 'Cept it's about the American myth, the American myth of race that say that they's racial, cultural and social purity in America. Naw, that ain't what it's saying. It's saying that the myth of racial, cultural and social purity is supposed to be the basis for prejudice in American society" (337). The play produces a performance of races and thereby conceptualizes racial identity as a pattern of behavior. Edward Said is invoked as an authority who "has spoken of the 'monocultural myth' of American society" that the "play debunks" (339). Pressed for clarification, Delgadina states that the play is saying "That we're not made differently from anybody else" (343).

In a letter, contained in the epilogue of the novel, Mosquito talks about her role as an official griot with the Perfectibility Baptist Church. As a griot and inheritor of the storytelling tradition, Mosquito says that "we has got to know that the listener is as important to the story as the storyteller" (614). This echoes the relationship which Jones has advocated between the "teller and the listener," an analogy for the ideal relationship between writer and reader familiar from Toni Morrison (Gayl Jones's original editor) who promotes this relationship:

> In the same way that a musician's music is enhanced when there is a response from the audience,....to have the reader work *with* the author in the construction of the book—is what's important.... To construct the dialogue so that it is heard.[5]

Mosquito's digressions throughout the novel effect a mimicry of the kind of digressions that people are diverted by as they speak, or gossip, with a friend. In this way the novel exemplifies the critical view that narrative technique can mimic oral storytelling. This view also forms the subject of *Liberating Voices* in which Jones continually returns to the technical problem of writing "orally," that is, to "break out of the frame" of the European literary tradition, when inscribing the oral tradition.[6] However, in this experimental novel Jones extends the limits of the writerly text in creating a continuous demand upon her reader to coproduce the narrative in her attempts to actualize her idealized relationship. Of course, in the face of the excesses and plethora of images, the reader may become distracted and interpretation frustrated. Jones apparently anticipates this response from her reader as, in the guise of Mosquito, she offers an explanation for, and defense of, the narrative method she has chosen by distinguishing between literary realism and her own more true to real storytelling mimetic approach. In the process she recalls decades of literary critical debates about the relative virtues of realism:

> Some of y'all listeners confuses me when I'm talking to you. You wants me to clarify this and wants me to clarify that and wants me to clarify where I am and wants me to clarify who I am....Contradictions in reality don't mean it ain't real. Maybe it's some of y'all who don't know who y'all is and needs to clarify yourself. I'm just kidding with y'all. I don't mind clarifying what peoples needs to know. Maybe modern stories just looks at theyselves, but I always prefers the storytellers that looks at them they's talking to, and acknowledges what other peoples needs to know. (420)

It is to Delgadina that Mosquito defers for her words of wisdom and, as much of the narrative is made up of conversations between the two women, the voices of Delgadina and Mosquito blend and become almost indistinguishable as speech marks are omitted. We learn that Delgadina's ideal type of novel is:

> a novel where you could read any chapter when you wanted to and where you wanted to read it. After you read the first chapter and got introduced to the principal characters, you didn't have to read the novel chapter by

chapter. Ideally, you didn't even have to start reading the beginning first. For her that the ideal novel, the ideal way of telling a tale (181).

The reader of *Mosquito* can adopt the idealized role in their response to the novel's call but they are not freed to play an entirely different tune for, as this novel illustrates, the ideal of giving freedom to the reader can only ever be a Barthesian illusion of the reader's birth. Control is effectively manipulated by the narrator's lead and this is dramatized when Mosquito begins to describe something and then withholds the information: "I prefers not to describe my truck" (7), or, "but that's a tale for her to tell" (53). Yet, in these and other examples, having refused the information, Mosquito generally goes on to spill the beans. Of course, this might be said to be a good imitation of a gossip's method of retaining the attention of the audience and generating suspense. But, as other practitioners of the postmodern novel have demonstrated, the development of techniques to allow freedom for the reader must, to an extent, be illusory. *Mosquito* illustrates that the oral can only be represented by literature and not enacted by it; a written narrative cannot achieve the ideal toward which Jones's novels have increasingly striven:

> When you's talking to people, though, you can tell them anywhere in the tale you wants to tell them, and you don't even have to tell them all of the tale. And then they can ask you questions and have you clarify. (181)

The problem on which Mosquito muses is the problem the writer faces: "you ain't supposed to tell written stories like people tell real stories" (298). This self-reflexivity in *Mosquito* suggests that Jones is working with the same generic formulation as Toni Morrison who stated that her book *Jazz* is "really a book about the processes of its own construction."[7] Jones noted in *Liberating Voices* that "the oral tradition is a laboratory for making experiments with Western literary tradition" (86). This seems to support the experimental nature of the novel's exploratory blurring of binary distinctions between orality and literacy that produce an uncertainty surrounding the issue of whether the character Mosquito has produced an oral or a written text. In the process, the novel does offer encouragement to suspend the belief that it is a novel we are reading:

> I know that some of y'all don't think that just them letters and even that story from Monkey Bread is enough and y'all want to see her for yourself. Well, stories ain't like them novels where there's plot unity and coherent scenes, when you's telling a true story, you don't always get to meet the folks you want to meet (397).

However, as this "true" story continues to declare its realism, its insistence paradoxically draws attention to the constructed nature of the fiction and away from the kind of oral story, which the novel both advocates and exemplifies, as in the example of Ernest Gaines:

> I likes the stories myself, the Ernest Gaines stories, I mean the stories he tells. I likes to listen to that tape and them storytellers on that, 'cause they sounds like true storytellers, and they don't tell nobody nothing that don't need to be told (423).

Jones frequently exploits such examples of the direct address to the reader/listener to embark on a discourse about the nature of storytelling that is strongly suggestive of an authorial point of view and gives some insight into her aims and methods. Ironically, it seems that this *is* a novel that looks at itself. It is a particular object of the novel's self-reflexivity that a dichotomy and hierarchy is established between the oral and the literary, whereby the oral is favored as more genuine. This has extraordinary resonance for a culture in which historical accounts have been falsified and where writing has carried authority to the detriment of the illiterate and enabled human rights abuses. An example is when Mosquito overhears a Sanctuary worker describe his experience to Ray, Mosquito's lover. Ray is a leader in the organization and conductor on the new Underground Railroad, who disguises himself as a priest. The reference to documents here recalls the issue of the destruction of records of abuses in slavery; an issue also treated by the novel *Corregidora*:

> That's how they use their literary tradition—they go by what's written down, not by what people say, even if the people falsified them documents....But every African-American family in the South has got the same tale, part of their family history and folklore. Call it folklore 'cause it ain't written down....You be with somebody in Georgia or somewhere and they say, Look at that land over there, that usedta be us family land, and then they be telling you they history.... 'Cept they ain't got the documents or the documents they do got is falsified (254).

The significance of passing on histories through oral narrative is developed in the novel by its form, themes, and specific incidents, as the structure of *Mosquito* allows for the inclusion of a chorus of voices and stories. Mosquito's other important friend and confident, Monkey Bread (now working for a "star" in California and member of the Daughters of Nzingha), has her own story inserted within the narrative (393). A Native American Indian man, Saturna, who frequents Delgadina's bar, makes a strong impression on Mosquito by the tales he tells and the particular story of "his people...banded together to fight the white man before the Civil War" (82). The Indian seems to Mosquito to be a Spirit Talker or Shaman, and the stories he tells are about the gross deception practiced by the white man on the tribes. Even though Mosquito does not share the same tribal inheritance, she feels that she has been "resanctified" through hearing the stories. The importance of her hearing and remembering, and passing on these stories as she does through the book, is emphasised by Saturna's repeated insistence for her to remember the people of the stories until she responds in a dialogue whose repetitions effect the rhythms of an incantation: "Remember the Story of Chief Nigger Horse, he say. Okay, I says, and sips some of the Mogen David-tasting Budweiser" (89-90).

The priority of the oral is further reinforced because of Mosquito's extraordinary auditory gift, which allows her to remember, and then retell, everything she has heard (a skill she is using in the above example): "I know I read it somewhere, about that jazz music, 'cause if I heard it I be remembering all of it, so I musta read it somewhere" (93). No matter who she is with, Mosquito drifts off from reporting the event and conversation taking place into her daydreams of memories, events, conversations, ideas, dream sleep, which have been prompted as if by thought association. This method serves to fully realize the identity of Mosquito in all her levels of consciousness, her thoughts and ideas. Rather than a descriptive characterization, this is a fictional autobiography that records moment by moment what Virginia Woolf described as "moments of being." Indeed, the technique of not separating dialogue from direct address or from thought emulates Woolf's modernist technique and can be compared to "free jazz" in its escape from literary convention and formal structure. Her numerous digressions are like improvisations "in the break" in a jazz piece, as Jones realizes in this fiction her view that music is the African American writer's "most significant extraliterary model." Moreover, she argues that the "standard set by African American music seems the highest artistic standard developed within the African American culture, so it is important to continue to discover ways in which it can be translated into words and literature."[8] In an early interview with Michael Harper, Jones described her own writing as "improvisational."[9]

As the novel makes frequent use of analogies with jazz, and in its sustained striving for a dialogue with the reader, it operates as a metaphorical "conversation," which is of course the major metaphor used to describe jazz. Mosquito describes the switching between time frames as writing in "virtual time," which "reads kinda like jazz in they rhythm" (421), and the novel further mirrors its many descriptions of jazz as "[p]laying that jazz you supposed to be able to move freely in every which direction" (305). Through her ruminations on whether it is possible to "tell a true jazz story," Mosquito effectively describes an idealized scenario for the method of the novel we are reading:

> The story would provide the jazz foundation, the subject, but they be improvising around that subject or them subjects and be composing they own jazz story. If it be a book, they be reading it and start telling it theyselves whiles they's reading. For example, if they gets to a part of the book where I talks about my daddy, say if I was the storyteller, then they ain't just have to read about my daddy, they can start talking about they own daddy or other people daddy or even they Spiritual Daddy..., so they be reading and composing for theyselves, and writing in the margins and ain't just have to write in the margins, 'cause ain't wanting my listeners to just be reserved to the margins, but they writing between the lines, and even between the words....I ain't know if I wants them peoples to be changing names, though they can compose around the themes, but they could still bring they own multiple perspectives everywhere in that novel, and they own freedom. (94)

What Mosquito seems to describe here is a relationship between the storyteller and the reader/listener, which goes beyond an effect analogous to call-and-response, but is one in which the reader is as if part of a jazz jam session and has the actual freedom to improvise around the themes that have been introduced. Thus it is a "polyphonic story" (522). The polyphony of music is achieved by collective improvisation—that is, by each player or performer embellishing the melody by adding extra notes and alternating note values, but in such a manner as to retain the essential shape of the original melody.[10] Mosquito describes jazz as "original and originating music...it makes every musical influence its own" (134). She might be talking about her own narrative voice.

Jones represents jazz to suggest a particular mood and cultural milieu, or to stand for elements of characterisation and to suggest levels of experience. In the case of John Henry Hollywood, a former lover and the subject of many of Mosquito's digressions into past experiences, the fact that he puts on "that real avant-garde-type jazz" when alone with Mosquito is allowed to stand for a wealth of missing detail, including their lovemaking. Mosquito tells the reader "y'all might be a little too young to hear me talk about some of the things we was doing or to be doing some of the things we was doing" (178). While Mosquito is making love with Ray in her truck she feels that she is "still that jazz musician and them womens is still saying they same song" because like a musician, Mosquito is playing the leading melody, but always her thoughts contain the voices of others. Ray's voice interjects at another level as he tries to pull Mosquito back to the main theme, while a further sound is added by the truckers who pass and "honk" to Mosquito, a "honk" that rhythmically interrupts the narrative every few lines (315, 318). This image also represents the narrative structure of the novel as a whole as voices filter into Mosquito's narrative that are fluidly responsive to moves between ideas and rhythms. So, while making love with Ray, Mosquito says that she "can still hear them peoples talking.... We's making love and I'm hearing conversations. Which don't mean we ain't making good love, but them womens is still having they conversations....I'm trying to think about me and Ray, and us loving, but I'm still that jazz musician and them womens is still saying they same song" (315). Similarly, the effect of Mosquito's digressions which follow her thought associations can represent what Townsend defines as "lateral improvisation"— when a soloist is "driven by something in the dynamics, in the drama, of the moment."[11]

That the voices which Mosquito tunes into in the truck are "womens" might suggest a collective, womanist experience except that Alice Walker's term "womanist" is put under interrogation when Mosquito's friend, the Chicana woman Delgadina, tells her that "they can't be the same kind of feminists as gringo feminists," and they can't be what Alice Walker calls *"womanist...because womanist aint' her culture neither"* (50). Jones thus draws the reader's attention to debates which circulate within feminist discourses in suggesting that the term "womanist" is too limiting because it refers to African American women's feminism alone, and we are again reminded of the limitations of racial categories.

The novel is grounded in the contemporary milieu by references to rap, along with references to a range of performative media: the radio, audiotapes, CD, and live performance. Popular culture signifiers of blackness abound in the novel yet operate in contrast to the representations of black cultural scenarios that have traditionally been adopted in the African American literary tradition to conjure positive representations of authentic black identity, such as, for example, 1920s Harlem or southern rural folk. For Jones, the obligation to discover origins is "disconnected from their legitimation and from their enjoyment," to borrow Paul Gilroy's phrase.[12] Here the parodic impulse of rap suggests its postmodern genesis and it is, as Eric Lott argues, "one of the only postmodernisms with a conscience."[13] Rappers continue the "traditions of the African griot storyteller"; Mosquito remembers hearing some Caribbean rap and how she started singing the song herself. The song is reproduced in the text and so becomes part of the narrative technique.[14] Mosquito recounts this memory and in the telling, she digresses as she associates the memory with others that the first suggests; she thus achieves her improvisatory affect. As the rap evokes thoughts of the oratory of the preacher of the Perfectibility Baptist Church of Memphis, the black sermon becomes the narrative. This recalls once more the Caribbean rap song, which then suggests a rumination on jazz and its assumed value from the perspective of Western classical music (93). On another occasion Mosquito is listening to tango, and then rap, and "trying to hear the tango base in the rap, or the rap base in the tango" (109). These associations serve to suggest a relationship between African American and other black cultural forms which are authorized by this novel, and which refuse either distinctions between the variety of black cultural orality or, indeed, the privileging of particular forms.

Mosquito is steeped in black culture for, while this is complicated by discussions of variety, hybrid origins, and the social constructions of race, the novel is nevertheless grounded in the blackness associated with specific oralities and contextual elements from the oral tradition: the call-and-response performed by the southern black congregation, myths, rituals and folk wisdom, as well as intertextual references. All of these are passed on in, and by, the novel.

In each of the novels written by Gayl Jones the protagonists undermine narratives of sexual and racial difference that have confined, constrained, and framed the black woman as negativity. This is achieved through the inscription of non-essentialist, specific, identities using strategies of orality. As Jones notes in various interviews, she uses the first-person narration almost exclusively to achieve the effect for the reader of being able to hear, not simply read, stories which are rendered without any authorial intrusion. These are identities that are resistant to recuperation into a universalizing project as examples of ethnic "essence." If one sees the construction of identity as conscious and external, as Jones certainly does, subjects cannot be returned to racialist or essentialist notions of inferiority. While this novel exposes identity as a matter of construction, and race as a learned quality, it holds up a distinction between the original and the copy in its refusal to give up the possibility or significance of black cultural orality. Indeed, it is still vital that the black woman finds her own unmediated voice in the text and speaks in her own dialect to reclaim it. That this is still a priority for Jones is suggested by Mosquito's discussion of the minstrel nature of white literary representations of black people:

> I didn't identify with none of them colored people. Seem like whenever they is colored people in stories like that they is people of diminished humanity. Even that Faulkner that they talks about, and has got all them extraordinary stylifications in his storytelling and knows about all the stylifications and trickifications of the South and can hear the different peoples languages. Seem like the colored people in them stories has more diminished humanity than the whites in them stories, even though the stories themselves is written good. (397)

Gayl Jones raises what Paul Gilroy describes as "large questions about the direction and character of black culture and art if we take the powerful effects of even temporary experiences of exile, relocation, and displacement into account."[15] Jones's writing displays the polyphonic qualities of black cultural expression, and it identifies itself as black by its musical referents because, as Gilroy confirms, black music is the principal symbol of racial authenticity.[16] However, Jones's recent work, in its opposition to re-inscribing notions of "authentic" black identity, articulates a critique of essentialism and suggests strategies for the subversion of constricting ideas of blackness that have been imposed both from within the black academy as formulated by the black aesthetic, and from without as "natural" stereotypes in the cause of white racism; its form is in sympathy with its polemic. The multicultural, multiracial nature of American society is represented through the jazz improvisations of voices who join in the novel, called forth by Mosquito's lead voice to represent the variety of ethnicity in this complex and evolving culture. The novel presents the polyphony of black America, recognizes the importance of the fluidity of black cultural exchanges, practices and conversations, and demonstrates that a postmodern perspective on blackness includes variety of experience and voices. In his most recent work, Paul Gilroy has described "the density of today's mixed and always impure forms [that] demands new organic and technological analogies." He notes that "[i]ts poetics is already alive and at large." In *Mosquito* we can see that Gayl Jones is a practioner of such poetics, for she has left behind "modernist obsession with origins" and yet, in her employment of a multicultural aesthetic, she retains cultural integrity and cultural value, showing that race still matters.[17]

Notes

[1] Gayl Jones, *Mosquito* (Boston: Beacon Press, 1999). All following citations are to this edition and page numbers are given parenthetically within the text.

[2] Gunilla T. Kester, *Writing the Subject* (New York: Peter Lang, 1995), 81.

[3] Gayl Jones, *Liberating Voices: Oral Tradition in African American Literature* (Cambridge, MA: Harvard University Press, 1991), 194.

[4] Gayl Jones, "The Quest for Wholeness Re-Imagining the African-Novel: An Essay on Third World Aesthetics." *Callaloo* 17.2 (1994): 507-518.
[5] Toni Morrison, "Rootedness: The Ancestor as Foundation" in Mari Evans (ed.), *Black Women Writers: Arguments and Interviews* (London: Pluto Press, 1985), 341.
[6] Jones, *Liberating Voices*, 178. Jones refers to John Wideman's influence here.
[7] Christopher Bigsby, "Jazz Queen", *The Independent on Sunday*, 26 April 1992, 29.
[8] Jones, *Liberating Voices*, 92, 187.
[9] Michael Harper, "Gayl Jones: An Interview", *Massachusetts Review*, 1997, 18.4, 692-715, 695.
[10] See Eileen Southern, *The Music of Black Americans* (W.W. Norton, 1971; 1983 second edition).
[11] Peter Townsend, *Jazz in American Culture* (Edinburgh: Edinburgh University Press, 2000), 20.
[12] Paul Gilroy, *Between Camps*, (London: Penguin Books, 2001), 251. Also published as *Against Race*, (Cambridge, MA: Harvard University Press, 2000).
[13] Eric Lott, "'Response to Trey Ellis' 'The New Black Aesthetic'", *Callaloo*, 1989, 12.1, 233-247.
[14] Paul Gilroy, *The Black Atlantic: Modernity and Double Consciousness* (London: Verso, 1983), 108.
[15] Gilroy, *The Black Atlantic*, 15.
[16] Gilroy, *The Black Atlantic*, 32.
[17] Paul Gilroy, *Between Camps*, 251. Gilroy critiques absolutist camps who have been divided between the multiculturalist and the homogeneitist. See, especially, Chapter 7.

Works Cited

Bigsby, C. "Jazz Queen." *The Independent on Sunday*, 26 April 1992.

Gilroy, Paul. *The Black Atlantic: Modernity and Double Consciousness*. London: Verso, 1983.

———. *Between Camps*. London: Penguin Books, 2001.

Harper, Michael. "Gayl Jones: An Interview." *Massachusetts Review*, 1997, 18.4, 692-715.

Jones, Gayl. *Liberating Voices: Oral Tradition in African American Literature* (Cambridge, MA: Harvard University Press, 1991.

———. "The Quest for Wholeness: Re-Imagining the African-Novel, An Essay on Third World Aesthetics", *Callaloo*, 1994, 17.2.

———. *Mosquito*. Boston: Beacon Press, 1999.

Kester, G.T. *Writing the Subject*. New York: Peter Lang, 1995.

Lott, Eric. "'Response to Trey Ellis' 'The New Black Aesthetic.'" *Callaloo*, 1989, 12.1, 233-247.

Morrison, Toni. "Rootedness: The Ancestor as Foundation" in Mari Evans (ed.), *Black Women Writers: Arguments and Interviews*. London: Pluto Press, 1985.

Southern, E. *The Music of Black Americans*. W.W. Norton, 1971; 1983 second edition.

Townsend, P. *Jazz in American Culture*. Edinburgh: Edinburgh University Press, 2000.

CHAPTER SIX

Interruptions: Tradition, Borders, and Narrative in Gayl Jones's *Mosquito*

Sarika Chandra

Interruptions

Gayl Jones's novel *Mosquito* (1999) in some ways can be read as a neo-slave narrative. However, it attempts to imagine the neo-slave narrative as a cross-ethnic project. The narrator, an African American female truck driver called Sojourner Jane Nadine Johnson, nicknamed Mosquito, becomes intimately connected with the Sanctuary movement that helps Latin American refugees with legal affairs and with obtaining documentation, work, and housing— that is, with a social experience seemingly "outside" her own culture and ethnicity. Mosquito compares the situation of the Latin American refugees to that of the African American slaves attempting to flee slavery in the late 1800s. This effort to construct a cross-ethnic neo-slave narrative is reflected in the novel's formal as well as political and social properties. Formally, the novel must interrupt its own plotlines to explain and theorize how a neo-slave narrative can be imagined as a project that moves across racial and ethnic lines. Politically and socially, Jones challenges or interrupts some of the dominant narratives of race and ethnicity. I will focus on two of these dominant narratives: one that might ask us to understand the narrator of the novel primarily in African American historical and cultural contexts; and another that suggests that cultural groups who live on the margins of dominant cultures should come to celebrate that marginal existence in the form of the hybrid, mestiza, or diasporic identity of the cultural borderland. In other words, Jones's neo-slave narrative is a departure from traditional neo-slave narratives in order to challenge dominant conceptions of race and ethnicity.

At the onset of the twenty-first century, Jones makes the argument that even though African American slavery has been outlawed for a long time, neo-slavery still continues in many forms. One of those forms is the condition in which Latin American refugees cross borders into and across the United States. In other words, this comparison of Latin American refugees with African American slaves as part of Jones's critical project to challenge dominant narratives of race and ethnicity requires the narrator to interrupt her plot lines and explain how this comparison is viable. Mosquito constantly interrupts and digresses from her storytelling. She begins her story by telling the reader that she makes a living transporting detergents. On one of these delivery routes she discovers that a Latin American refugee, Maria, has taken shelter in her truck. Eventually, it is through driving Maria to a place of refuge that Mosquito becomes part of the Sanctuary movement. However, instead of satisfying the reader's expectations that the novel might follow Maria's story—does she manage to get to a place of refuge and is she able to build her life in the United States?— she uses this point as an opportunity to stop and refute some of the dominant stereotypes about Mexicans. While she and Maria eat omelet sandwiches with jalapeños, Mosquito says: "Them jalapeños little too hot for me, though, but I figures she like them jalapeños being Mexican" (44). But she catches herself and says: "I ain't mean to stereotype her, though." From here she moves on to relate conversations she has had with her friend Delgadina about stereotyping: "[S]he be telling me they's some agringado Mexicans like jalapeños but don't eat them because they thinks they be stereotyping themselves, like African-Americans that don't eat watermelon, and they don't eat them tacos neither.... But she be saying they's two kinds of stereotypes, though, them based on falsehoods and them based on some kinda reality... (44). The engagement with immediate concerns, such as the presence of Maria in her truck, is deferred until later, while we get Mosquito's thoughts on the nature of stereotyping. In fact these interruptions frustrate many of Jones's readers.[1]

The fact that *Mosquito* does not consistently follow particular characters or unfold their story in a linear fashion, that it digresses from a standard plot development to deliberate on various contemporary issues may be required in order to carry out the project of the departure from the traditional neo-slave narrative in more consciously critical ways. Through juxtaposition of personal experience, academic discourse, and allusions to popular media, such as film and television, the narration demonstrates how one participates simultaneously in many different cultural contexts. Mosquito is concerned not only with how dominant representations of racial minorities are stereotypical but also how she might be perpetuating them herself. *Mosquito* disrupts these narratives by suturing together a neo-slave narrative that not only involves a dialogue about African American historical and cultural contexts but also about those of other groups as well, specifically with the Mexican and Chicano/a communities in Texas.

Recovering Tradition

Since the historical and cultural traditions of minorities have been relegated to the margins, there is a strong desire on the part of minorities to recover, imagine, and bring their cultural traditions to the forefront. This is one of the significant projects in a neo-slave narrative that might expect African Americans to connect only to their own cultural practices and histories. The more traditional neo-slave narrative charged with the task of narrating silences in the antebellum slave narrative as well as with the construction and maintenance of an African American literary tradition effectively engages in contemporary political issues relevant only to African Americans. Thus the political and formal properties of the neo-slave narrative consciously connect only with black—or with black vs. white—literary and cultural traditions due in part to the reading and writing practices that have emerged regarding minority texts. In his book *Neo-slave Narratives* (1999), Ashraf Rushdy has noted that, at times, African American texts, such as those by Toni Morrison, are primarily read in comparison with white canonical writers, such as William Faulkner. Rushdy suggests that Morrison herself considers this move to effectively ignore black cultural practices as detrimental, and that Morrison herself insists that she writes "irrevocably, indisputably Black" texts (10-11). Consequently, non-African Americans can and do imagine these texts as written only for blacks and whites. Moreover, many of the neo-slave narratives that are part of a university curriculum are more likely to be part of those courses that primarily theorize African American histories, experiences, and cultural practices. As a result, the writing as well as reading practices of African American recovery texts may simultaneously enforce what we might term a condition of racial enclosure.

Examining properties of traditional neo-slave narratives in general will allow us to see how *Mosquito* is in some ways a part of the African American recovery tradition and yet, as a cross-ethnic neo-slave narrative, a departure from those dominant discourses on race and ethnicity that lead to racial enclosure. Rushdy argues that the neo-slave narrative, though it connects to an earlier time, emerges out of and makes an intervention into current political debates on race and ethnicity. In *Beloved*, for example, we see how the ghost of slavery comes back to haunt Sethe, a former slave, in the form of her daughter's ghost—a daughter whom she had killed to save her from slavery. The ghost of slavery then allows Sethe to come to terms with her present.

Neo-slave narratives have also made an intervention in contemporary debates on literacy. In "Memory, Creation, and Writing," Toni Morrison has suggested that the ideal reader for her novel is "illiterate" (387). This ideal readership is an obvious critique of the state of schooling for African Americans. However, her novels, especially *Beloved*, follow in the literary tradition of antebellum slave narratives—narratives that were aimed at literate audiences and that helped to plead the case with them against slavery. For example, in "'Mr. Editor, If You Please': Frederick Douglass, *My Bondage and My Freedom*, and the End of the Abolitionist Imprint" John Sekora recounts that Frederick Douglass's *Narrative* was published by the American Anti-Slavery Society and that such publication required Douglass's narrative to be heavily controlled by the editors. Therefore, Douglass's ongoing efforts to establish an independent literary career by establishing the newspaper *North Star* in 1847 meant for him "not only the ability to select his own words, but also to determine their final form and disposition" (614). In this manner, the neo-slave narrative stays within a heritage of literacy and the literary, and yet tries to refigure conventions of antebellum slave narratives and to intervene in the politics of its time. Its particular project then helps African American writers to recover and foreground previously marginalized narratives and to maintain a particular kind of African American literary tradition, even if that tradition has to be reshaped in contemporary terms.

Jones also intervenes into the present political issues. As stated earlier, Mosquito makes an obvious connection between the situation of the Latin American refugees and that of the African American slaves in the 1800s. Referring to Maria, she says: "I be thinking about harboring that fugitive Maria, but then I be thinking she ain't no modern fugitive Maria but one of them fugitive Africans..." (597). This comparison suggests that not only is Mosquito pointing to similarities between the two situations but also pointing to a way of imagining and recovering the escape narrative of the African American slaves. Moreover, she says: "[T]his new Underground Railroad have got to be maintained like the old Underground Railroad. When y'all is reading them slave narratives, y'all that reads them slave narratives, them fugitive and escaped former slaves don't tell y'all everything" (551). *Mosquito* can be understood as what Rushdy calls a palimpsest narrative. In his later book *Remembering Generations* (2001), he defines a palimpsest as "either a parchment on which the original writing can be erased to provide space for a second writing or a manuscript on which the original writing is written over an earlier effaced writing" (7). In this manner Rushdy goes on to suggest that a palimpsest can serve as an effective metaphor for the "first-person novel representing late-twentieth-century African American subjects who confront familial secrets attesting to the ongoing effects of slavery" (8). A palimpsest metaphor also applies to *Mosquito* in the sense that the narrator attempts to imagine African American slavery through contemporary issues. However, the cross-ethnicity of the novel intervenes into forms of neo-slavery that are not merely African American. Clearly one of the contemporary forms of slavery is wage labor. Although there is much statistical evidence that neo-slavery continues for African Americans by keeping a high percentage of them in low-paying jobs, this condition is exacerbated for those who are undocumented in the United States.

I will return to this form of neo-slavery, but first I want to discuss how the more traditional neo-slave narratives often seemingly take up contemporary political issues that affect only black or only black and white people. According to Rushdy, some of the neo-slave narratives, such as Charles Johnson's *Middle Passage* and *Oxherding Tale*, intervened in the debates regarding racial politics and affirmative action in the 1980s. The race debate in the 1980s between progressives and neoconservatives divided people into one of two camps: those who argued that race was no longer a "viable social category for political legislation" and those who argued "against ahistorical and unreflective thinking about race," suggesting that a "color blind policy" would not eradicate racism. Rushdy maintains that while Johnson supported affirmative action thinking that blacks and whites have "different historical background[s], [he] was nonetheless troubled in trying to reconcile these beliefs with his wish for equitable, universally applicable values and principles of justice and his conviction that race was after all 'an illusion'" (202). This particular problem is reflected in the *Oxherding Tale*, where the protagonist Andrew moves from being a slave to being a property owner who passes for white. This novel, emerging in part out of debates on affirmative action, ends up for the most part intervening in debates that see affirmative action almost exclusively as a black-and-white issue. *Oxherding Tale*, like many other neo-slave narratives, by attempting to imagine the antebellum middle passages and to intervene in the racial politics of the present, at once connect to the literary form of the slave narratives and refigure them. Johnson's intervention into the 1980s debates on affirmative action is considered mostly in black-and-white terms.

Jones's effort to move out of this racial enclosure provides *Mosquito* with an opportunity to form an alliance with the Chicano/a community in ways that contemporary political debates do not allow. Debates on affirmative action, wage conditions, and job security forge a disconnection between African Americans and recent immigrants. The nature of these conversations suggests to a significant group of African Americans already in low-paying jobs that their job security is threatened by immigrants (especially those who do not have the proper documents) willing to do the same job for even lower wages. This exacerbates the conditions of neo-slavery for all marginalized groups. According to George Borjas in "The Impact of Immigrants on Employment Opportunities of Natives," "empirical evidence indicates that immigrants do not have a major impact either on the earnings or on the employment levels of natives in the U.S. labour market" (228). Arguments suggesting that immigrants are stealing jobs from citizens assume that there are set numbers of jobs or that the economy does not expand with incoming immigrants; the discourse of wage labor creates a wedge between the newer immigrants and citizens, especially those in lower-paying jobs. As Borjas points out, this concern is primarily raised in connection with Hispanic populations. He also suggests that "blacks are the groups whose economic income progress is more likely to be hurt by the entry of immigrants in the United States" (224). He goes on to show that despite the lack of data or even data that shows no effects, the debate on immigration policy has "continually used the presumption that immigrants have an adverse impact on the labour market to justify many of the restrictions in immigration law" (227).[2] Such debates have kept the conditions of neo-slavery alive for most minority groups.

Mosquito's alignment with undocumented refugees takes the form of the neo-slave narrative because Jones is intervening in the debates regarding this particular form of neo-slavery. Her cross-ethnic narrative makes it possible for her to question some of the presumptions about race relations suggested by Borjas. Mosquito says that the people in the Chicano/a community often regard her suspiciously as if they think she is "one of them spies for the immigration department or them border patrols" (75). Therefore, the fact that Mosquito shares racial marginality with the Chicano/a community as well as with other Latin American refugees does not automatically foster an alliance between them, and Mosquito's attempt to do so produces a different sort of novel.

Keeping the intervention into contemporary politics in common with more traditional narratives, *Mosquito* shifts from ethnic and racial enclosure in ways that the more traditional narratives have not been able to. Mosquito says: "America ain't just black and white. But there's still them that wants to portray American as just black and white. First they wanted to portray it as just white, then they wants to portray it as just black and white" (27). Jones's project differs formally and politically in the sense that it does not seek to recover a primarily African American literary tradition but imagines the antebellum slave narrative in intersection with her protagonist's work with Latin American refugees. Mosquito relates via her friend Delgadina a story about an African American woman at a literature conference who "specializes in Chicano literature and everybody be wondering why she ain't specialize in African-American literature. Even Chicanos be wondering why she ain't specialize in African-American literature" (75). Here Jones's text challenges the implicit requirement that individual ethnic minorities relate only to their own marginality and also challenges the reading and writing practices of the more traditional neo-slave narrative that lead Toni Morrison to claim that she writes irrevocably black texts. Mosquito carries on a dialogue that places her not only in African American history but in other people's histories as well, thus challenging and "interrupting" a certain exclusive idea of cultural boundaries. She says, at one point, after seeing a play by Luis Valdez: "I like that play, though it ain't my culture. But then I'm wondering why people have to like they own culture. Them with dominant cultures, though, it seem like they's freer to like or not like they own culture, 'cause people ain't say of them they just imitating someone else culture" (117). In this manner, *Mosquito* is able to challenge ethnic and racial enclosures that the very work of that also connects with African American literary tradition of the slave narrative — at one level the work of a "novel" itself — may spontaneously require. Jones shows how these enclosures can become burdensome and also challenges other kinds of traditional expectations such as those of gender. Mosquito says, "I don't think no truck-driving African-American woman supposed to be a stereotype except that stereotype that supposed to make a African-American woman not have no femininity, and I know I got femininity and womaninity too" (182). She further relates that she broke up with her boyfriend John Henry Hollywood because "he be start telling me how I shouldn't be driving no truck....He be telling me I'm a remarkable woman.... And how I should be more ambitious..." (106). She recounts that John Henry asks her to clean up her dialect because it is not a sign of an intelligent woman. In fact, being a female truck driver who speaks with a dialect becomes an impediment in her relationship with John Henry and interrupts a domestic narrative that might ensue from this relationship. In this way, Mosquito herself, as protagonist, sees the need for recovery of traditional narratives and yet challenges them.

Jones's argument that slavery still exists in many forms and affects not only African-Americans is well taken. However, moving out of ethnic and racial enclosures while maintaining a relationship with the neo-slave narrative remains a difficult task because the neo-slave narrative does not cease to belong in highly concrete ways to African American literary and cultural contexts. Given that *Mosquito* is a departure from the usual form of the neo-slave narrative, it understandably requires interruptions, digressions, and explanations. It is for this reason, at least in part, that the narrative we read then often tends to the metafictional and plays very casually with plotlines. Monkey Bread, a friend of Mosquito's, describes her storytelling practices as follows: "I know a lot of times even when Nadine tells stories she don't start with the story. Sometimes she starts with everything but the story" (435). Monkey Bread goes on to say that Mosquito "tell peoples stories. 'Cept sometimes she tells people's everything but the story" (435). These particular storytelling practices are determined by the arduousness of Mosquito's, and, by extension, of Jones's project. Still, this has to be attempted if one is to question the dominant *forms* of narrative as well as dominant narratives of race and ethnicity that pressure minority groups to remain within their own historical and cultural traditions—even if that means writing a "failed" novel. Therefore, in a sense, Jones and her novel must remain on the *borders* of those traditions.

Borders

If Jones is critiquing the notion of tradition and traditional neo-slave narratives, then is she moving towards a theory that celebrates borders and cultural borderlands? *Mosquito*, as a cross-ethnic neo-slave narrative, is in some ways on the borders of tradition. However, it also calls into question current notions of "border" existence that has become one of the dominant narratives of race and ethnicity.

Mosquito asks the reader to think about the line between slavery and freedom by suggesting that perhaps existing in cultural borderlands in the form of the hybrid or a mestiza is not necessarily a cause for celebration, as it becomes in Gloria Anzaldúa's work. In fact, it could be argued that minorities relegated to cultural borders live in conditions of neo-slavery. We can understand the question of borders in the novel through Gloria Anzaldúa's work. In *Borderlands, La Frontera* (1987), Anzaldúa describes the U.S. and Mexico border as a painful place where

> the lifeblood of two worlds [merge] to form a third country—a border culture. Borders are set up to define the places that are safe and unsafe, to distinguish us from them. A border is a dividing line, a narrow strip along a steep edge. A borderland is a vague and undetermined place created by the emotional residue of an unnatural boundary. It is in a constant state of transition. The prohibited and forbidden are its inhabitants. *Los atravesados* live here: the squint-eyed, the perverse, the queer, the troublesome, the mongrel, the mulatto, the half-breed, the half dead; in short, those who cross over, pass over, or go through the confines of the "normal." (3-4)

Jones's novel participates in Anzaldúa's world of borders but moves away from it in significant ways. Mosquito is partly on the border of certain cultural traditions and expectations. However, her borders are different from those of Anzaldúa. Mosquito's borders are not a "vague and undetermined place" but specific spaces that she must cross while helping refugees in crossing them as well. It is in this more complex way that the question of borders is formally and politically incorporated within the novel.

Indeed, one of the main reasons that certain plot lines have to be interrupted is that Mosquito does not and cannot know certain stories out of concern for the security of the Sanctuary movement, just as the slave narratives from 1800s could not divulge specific details about escape routes. This unusual narrative strategy—a telling that cannot in fact "tell"—also keeps Mosquito on the borders of the very movement to which she is significantly connected. In fact she starts to wonder whether her friend Delgadina is part of the Sanctuary movement and whether she is the one who recommended Mosquito to transport the refugees.

> I believe it were Delgadina that recruited me for the new Underground Railroad and I ain't even know it. 'Cause if she come asking me to be in the new Underground Railroad, she know I ain't going to, but if she put that

Maria in the back of my truck or tell that Maria how to get back into the back of my truck and I finds her in there, then I am going to be in that new Underground Railroad. (500)

Mosquito isn't even sure if Delgadina, whom she has thought of as her good friend, may have secretly recruited her for the Sanctuary movement. Moreover, she cannot even know for certain whether Maria herself is really a refugee. So the narrative that we get from Mosquito must deal on the practical level with the necessity of many omissions. Furthermore, Mosquito's lack of information not only parallels the situation of the antebellum slave escapees but also places Mosquito on the borders of her own work and social life in many respects. She is on the borders of the Sanctuary movement because she is not allowed into meetings where the members discuss new strategies for helping refugees. Ray, one of the key individuals in the Sanctuary movement, and who later becomes Mosquito's lover, encourages her to take on the responsibility of driving refugees but advises her that it is in Mosquito's best interest not to know very much about the system: "I'd prefer that you don't come to our strategy meetings....You are far more useful to us in the work that you do, Mosquito" (550). Ray is suggesting that her transporting refugees from one dangerous border to another is far more valuable if she herself remains on the borders of the Sanctuary movement itself and does not participate in its strategy making. Ray himself remains elusive for her. He adopts many disguises in order to work in the Sanctuary movement. Even though Mosquito and Ray are lovers, she does not and cannot know his many aliases or his travel destinations. Thus this border is very different from the one posited by Anzaldúa, in that it recognizes that refugees need to be protected from borders. Moreover, Mosquito is happy to be on the borders of some traditions; she enjoys the "freedom of the road" and escapes the dominant narratives of gender, race, and domesticity, while still recognizing that those same roads are dangerous for refugees. The very truck that provides her freedom becomes a place of refuge for people like Maria. Mosquito declares that the only community she is responsible for is "the community of me, myself and I" (607). However, she agrees with John Henry when he says that "Freedom ain't just responsibility for yourself. You've gotta be responsible to and for others too" (107). Mosquito is indeed responsible for more than herself—she takes responsibility for the refugees and even wants to be included by doing the strategy work for them. Monkey Bread says to her that Mosquito "is the freest woman she knows" (587). But it is important perhaps that she be the "freest" woman in order to help those very people whose freedom is at risk if they are caught by the border patrol.

As someone on the borders of dominant experiences, and someone who has cultural connections to the old Underground Railroad (in fact she was named after Sojourner Truth), Mosquito is sympathetic to the refugees' needs for a safe dwelling. However, it is also important that she be part of the dominant culture—at least to have official documentation showing that she is a U.S. citizen, in order to transport refugees who do not have theirs. She relates that even though she is a U.S. citizen, she is asked to show documentation (597) because she travels on the roads that are restricted by border patrols. Thus, to say the least, Mosquito's borders are not a cause for celebration. Rather, they stress that borders are and can be dangerous.

By the end of the novel, Mosquito is taking classes to become a hidden agenda conspiracy specialist who reads and deciphers letters the Sanctuary movement receives from various people who might be asking for help but cannot do so directly because others might be tampering with their mail. These are people that have been forced onto the borders by dominant groups. Mosquito ends her story by writing a code letter herself to Ray, in which she says that she has used everything she has learned in the hidden agenda conspiracy specialist class. She says, "[Y]'all only knows what I says. It be Ray that knows what I means" (611). In this way *Mosquito* is placing its reader on the borders of what we read in this novel the same way that the narrator herself is on the borders. And yet Mosquito's experiences on the border lend little support to the idea—popularized by much current scholarship—that living on cultural and physical borders provides a somehow unique and privileged perspective. As is well known, Anzaldúa suggests that despite a border existence that is marked as a painful space inhabited by those labeled as the "perverse," the "troublesome," and the "half-breed," the borderland is eventually reconstructed. It becomes a place of constant flux and allows its inhabitants to reinvent themselves while offering them both an empowering and desirable perspective. In/on Anzaldúa's borderlands, the "half breed" gets transformed into the more celebrated subject position of the mestiza, and the pain of nonbelonging is transformed into a universal belonging. In fact, a cultural view from the margins, edges, and borders comes to be celebrated, and the borders come to occupy an ironic center:

> As *mestiza* I have no country, my homeland cast me out, yet all countries are mine because I am every woman's sister or potential lover. (As a lesbian I have no race, my own people disclaim me; but I am all races because there is the queer of me in all races.) I am cultureless because, as a feminist, I challenge the collective cultural/religious male derived beliefs of Indo-Hispanics and Anglos; yet I am cultured because I am participating in the creation of yet another culture, a new story to explain the world and our participation in it, a new value system with images and symbols that connect us to each other and to the planet. (80-81)

Jones is obviously critical of this celebration by simply telling a story that shows that borders remain dangerous and oppressive for many people. Although Mosquito interacts with Mexicans, Chicanos, other Latin Americans, her story does not necessarily champion the cultural practices or assumptions that emerge out of being in/on Anzaldúa's borderlands. Anzaldúa's borders in which the pain of being on the borders is transformed to the borderlands in which "going outside the confines of the 'normal' " can be a positive is potentially appropriated in dangerous arguments that can advocate keeping those on cultural borders intact in their places without any opportunity for changing the social conditions of those who are oppressed. In reference to the notion of the cosmic race, Mosquito critiques the concept of the hybrid or the mestiza as a privileged position that bestows the special status of insider/outsider to its members. She says:

> Mexicans they's supposed to be the cosmic race. Like them Brazilians, they could call themselves the cosmic race. Like all that talk about multi-racism. We's just a cosmic race. 'Cept nobody wants to identify with the African in the cosmos. That's how I read that multi-racialism myself. Delgadina say them whites that's all for multi-racialism just want to use the multi-race as a buffer, you know. 'Cause somebody told them that in the next millennium the white people be the minority, so they wants as many people as they can to identify with them, rather than the other colored peoples. So now they's modifying their racial purity myth, 'cause its in their best interest, so's they can coopt the multi-racialists to play white....Then she say she don't know

whether they model be South Africa or Brazil. 'Cept Brazil ain't no racial paradise; they just let more people play white than in America. (27)

A cross-ethnic neo-slave narrative helps Jones to critique traditions as well as borders. It also helps to forge connections across ethnic and racial lines and challenges the ways in which border theory can and does lead to racial and ethnic enclaves. Moreover, as suggested earlier, the border can be just an enslaving as the racial enclosure.

Jones's attempt to thematize borders and yet move away from them itself counts as an interruption of the now virtually dominant conception that attributes to those who live on the border (specifically nonwhite people) with a perspective that perhaps whites don't have. For this can also suggest that African Americans, living on only one side of the border, cannot place themselves at the vantage point from which to narrate Chicano/a stories. In this manner, the dominant conception of borders can have the effect of circling back and creating the very ethnic enclaves and racial enclosures that Anzaldúa seems to reject when she suggests that she belongs to all nations since no nation belongs to her.

Mosquito in part is an effort to challenge *both* the racial enclosures that, in acts of explicit racism, forceably relegate people to living on the margins and borders *and* those seemingly antiracist celebrations of borders that in fact lead back to racial and ethnic enclaves. Therefore, we get an African American neo-slave narrative that, through a process of interruption, is deracialized and that thus can provide a standpoint from which to challenge Anzaldúa's border theory. As stated earlier, Jones's choice to move away from two dominant conceptions of identity—fixed and falsely "unfixed"—is a difficult task because the idea of the new Underground Railroad carries along with it historical realities that appear to be ethnically and racially exclusive. Narrating the new Underground Railroad is necessarily a burdensome task that, at the very least, requires readers of *Mosquito* to consider what the novel's reviewers call "failure" in concrete relation to its specific critical project.

Epilogue

As Tom LeClair, by way of the suggestive title of his review "Say What?" points out, Jones's novel discourages "plot and welcome[s] everything else. Jones refers to the history of blacks in Mexico and to that of her own family...; discusses languages that Mosquito doesn't speak but seems to understand; reports reminiscences from Mosquito's childhood in Kentucky...." But if Jones is to attempt a cross-ethnic recovery novel, then she must relate those histories of blacks in Mexico, juxtaposing her own histories with those of other peoples. The "failure" of the novel, then, has to be seen as a symptom of the difficulty of telling a cross-ethnic story outside racial enclosure.

What is it that Jones means to do when she writes a novel propelled by ideas and thoughts as opposed to plot lines? Perhaps it is to suggest that plot lines that immediately satisfy the reader's desires for suspense and closure may necessarily be burdened with suspect gender and racial politics. For example, addressing the reader, Mosquito says:

> I know there is those of you who wants to know more of various people in my story.... Some of you wants to know more about Maria.... Some of the men amongst you thinks that y'all would make more interesting men that the men in my story...and that it would be a better story if Ray had more of a role than Delgadina and that Ray would be even more interesting if I had him tell me more about him being a guerilla and all the different Macho types of things that he does when he goes there to Latin America....When Ray decides he wants to tell y'all his own story for hisself, he might tell y'all the type of complex and macho story that y'all mens can identify with true manhood. (600)

But we are not given Ray's story. Perhaps this suggests that the way to write a novel that manages to be rid of dubious racial and gender politics is to interrupt and even preempt the most desired plot lines — that the way to interrupt dominant discourses of race and ethnicity is to interrupt the plots that not only deliver expectations but often mask these very same discourses.

Notes

[1] Reviews of the novel *Mosquito* emphasize the difficulty encountered in reading this text. In "Going Underground" Greg Tate, who is largely sympathetic to *Mosquito*, states that the novel can be "called self-indulgent, if not incredibly demanding of even [Jones'] most sympathetic readers' time, tolerance, and intelligence." The question of its "failure" as a novel aside, however, such a reception suggests that *Mosquito* is delivering something unanticipated, something that frustrates the reader's expectations.

[2] Using empirical data Borjas states that "no study finds any evidence that immigrants and blacks are strong substitutes. In fact some studies report that blacks in [areas] with relatively large numbers of immigrants actually have slightly higher earnings than blacks in [areas] with relatively small immigrant populations" (225).

Works Cited

Anzaldúa, Gloria. *Borderlands, La Frontera: The New Mestiza*. San Francisco: aunt lute books, 1987.

Borjas, George. "The Impact of Immigrants on Employment Opportunities of Natives," in *The Immigration Reader: America in a Multidisciplinary Perspective*, ed. David Jacobson. Oxford: Blackwell Publishers, 217-230.

Douglass, Fredrick. *Autobiographies: Narrative of the life of Frederick Douglass, an American Slave, My Bondage and My Freedom, Life and times of Frederick Douglass*. New York: Library of America, 1994.

Jacobs, Harriet. *Incidents in the Life of a Slave Girl*. ed. Maria Child. Boston: Published for the author, 1861. Detroit: Negro History Press, 1969.

Johnson, Charles. *Middle Passage*. New York: Atheneum, 1990.

———. *Oxherding Tale*. Bloomington: Indiana University Press, 1982.

LeClair, Tom. "Say What?" *Salon.com*. Jan. 12, 1999. http://www.salon.com/books/sneaks/1999/01/12sneaks.html (Feb. 12, 2001).

———. *Mosquito*. Boston: Beacon Press, 1999.

Morrison, Toni. *Beloved*. New York: Knopf, 1987.

———. "Memory, Creation, and Writing." *Thought*. Dec. 1984, 385-390.

Rushdy, Ashraf. *Neo-Slave Narratives: Studies in the Social Logic of a Literary Form*. New York: Oxford University Press, 1999.

———. *Remembering Generations: Race and Family in Contemporary African American Fiction*. Chapel Hill: University of North Carolina Press, 2001.

Sekora, John. "'Mr. Editor, If You Please': Frederick Douglass, *My Bondage and My Freedom*, and the End of the Abolitionist Imprint." *Callaloo*. Summer 1994, 608-626.

Tate, Greg. "Going Underground," *Village Voice Literary Supplement*. February 1999. http://www.villagevoice.com/vls/160/tate.shtml (Feb 12, 2001).

Tuttle, Kate. "Blues Jam: Gayl Jones's Latest Novel Sinks Under the Weight of its Own Ideas," *The Boston Phoenix*. Feb. 11-18, 1999. http://www.bostonphoenix.com/archive/books/99/02/11/MOSQUITO.html (Feb. 12, 2001).

CHAPTER SEVEN

"Trouble in Mind": (Re)visioning Myth, Sexuality, and Race in Gayl Jones's *Corregidora*

Keith B. Mitchell

[W]ho then is this other to whom I am more attached than to myself, since at the heart of my most accepted identity with myself, it is he who agitates me?
—Jacques Lacan, *Écrits: A Selection*

Demeter, here's another one for your basket of mysteries.
—Rita Dove, "Blue Days"

Recently, many prominent scholars of African American literature have begun to explore the possibilities of reading African American texts in the context of psychoanalysis. Contemporary scholars such as Claudia Tate, Hortense Spillers, Patricia Waugh, and Jennifer Devrere Brody have more or less successfully employed psychoanalysis in close readings of African American literary texts. According to Claudia Tate, "Psychoanalysis can tell us much about the complicated social workings of race in the United States and the representation of these workings in the literature of African Americans" (*Psychoanalysis and Black Novels*, 5). In her assessment of the important potentiality of psychoanalysis in reading African Diasporic literature, I agree. However, I also want to emphasize that folklore and myth are, and always have been, strong cultural signifiers in African Diasporic literature. Gayl Jones, the author of numerous works, which include novels, poetry, plays, and literary theory, is no stranger to the importance of psychoanalysis and mythology as ways of reading African Diasporic literature. This essay will explore how Jones interweaves psychoanalysis and myth, and in particular the Greek myth of Demeter and her daughter Kore-Persephone, to deconstruct hegemonic notions of sexuality and race in one of the most controversial texts in the African American literary canon: Gayl Jones's *Corregidora* (1975).

While much has been written about *Corregidora* in the context of African American racialized, historical experiences—especially black women's experiences—what is startling is that so little has been written about *Corregidora* in light of Gayl Jones's obvious interest in psychoanalysis. For instance, one need only read the stories in her collection *The White Rat: Short Stories* (1977), a collection written before but published after *Corregidora*, to realize Gayl Jones's early interest in the inner workings of the human psyche. Jones is particularly interested in how these inner workings are related to African American racial and sexual trauma, and survival, and the history from which they stem. On the other hand, one need only read her long narrative poems *The Hermit Woman* (1983) and *Song for Anninho* (1981) to clearly see Jones's strong interest in myth, again, to understand and to come to terms with the inner and outer workings of African/African American racialized and sexualized Diasporic trauma. Toni Morrison, who edited *Corregidora*, states in an interview with Robert B. Stepto that *Corregidora* carries "the weight of history working itself out in the life of one, two or three people: I mean a large idea brought down small, and at home, which gives it a universality and a particularity which makes it extraordinary" (*Conversations*, 29).[1] Morrison implies that *Corrigedora* can be simultaneously read in terms of myth *and* psychoanalysis.

Corregidora's opening scene, which the protagonist Ursa Corregidora relates to the reader, sets the stage for a dual psychoanalytic and mythopoeic reading of Jones's novel. First, I will proffer a psychoanalytic reading of the opening scene and then show how it can also be read mythopoeically.

Ursa Corregidora, a blues singer at the ironically named Happy's Café, tells how her husband, Mutt Thomas, in a state of drunken jealously, has pushed her down a flight of stairs, an action which forces Ursa to have a hysterectomy—her womb completely removed. She recalls:

> I didn't see him at first because he was standing back in the shadows behind the door. I didn't see him until he'd grabbed me around my waist and I was struggling to get loose.
>
> "I don't like those mens messing with you," he said.
>
> "Don't nobody mess with me."
>
> "Mess with they eyes."
>
> That was when I fell.
>
> The doctors in the hospital said my womb would have to come out. Mutt and me didn't stay together after that. I wouldn't even let him in the hospital to see me when I knew what was happening. (*Corregidora*, 4)[2]

Feminist theorists, such as Laura Mulvey, have written much about the relationship between the power of the gaze and patriarchal mastery. Although Laura Mulvey's groundbreaking psychoanalytic text *Visual and Other Pleasures* (1985) deals primarily with cinema, her ideas, in terms of power and the male gaze, are certainly applicable to literary texts: "Traditionally, the woman displayed has functioned on two levels: as erotic object for the characters within the story, and as erotic object for the spectator...the woman as object.... She is isolated, glamorous, on display sexualized" (Mulvey, 62-64). That Ursa is a blues singer at Happy's Café puts her in a position of being looked at, constantly gazed upon by men. Moreover, Ursa is a very beautiful and sensuous woman, whose songs and extraordinary stage presence makes her an object of desire for her mostly male audiences. Their interest in her, real or imagined, makes Mutt extremely jealous. He feels that Ursa encourages the men to lust after her, and to teach her a lesson, he (accidentally) pushes her down the flight of stairs.

After the accident, Mutt is barred from Happy's Café. However, he becomes even more obsessed with Ursa, constantly spying on her through the café's window. In effect, Mutt uses a strategy of discipline and punishment that Michel Foucault describes as "panoptic":

> The Panopticon uses a technique of subjection that induces a permanent state of visibility constituted by the architecture of the "panoptic" building. It found its most intense expression in the prison, where inmates were aware of being placed under constant surveillance through their own observation of a centrally located observation tower. Whether the observation tower was actually "occupied" or not made no difference; it was the unverifiable

probability of surveillance that induced the "automatic" function of this kind of disciplinary power. (*Michel Foucault: An Introduction*, 59)

Mutt, like all the men in the novel, symbolizes disciplinary, patriarchal power. He symbolizes, like a prison guard or a slave master, Foucault's observation tower, or what Jacques Lacan calls the "phallic signifier." Mutt is constantly on the watch for Ursa's possible involvement with other men. Ursa, recounting her confrontation with Mutt, says, "While I was singing the first few songs I could see Mutt peeking in, looking drunk and evil. Then I didn't see him and thought he'd gone on home to sleep it off" (*Corregidora*, 3). Mutt seeks to control Ursa through constant surveillance in order to remind her that she belongs to him. In this regard, as his wife, Mutt thinks of Ursa as his property. "Surveillance," Michel Foucault reminds us, "becomes a decisive economic operator both as an internal part of the production machinery and as a specific mechanism in the disciplinary powers" (*Discipline and Punish*, 175). Surveillance, need we be reminded, was also an integral facet of the slave system. Mutt's actions challenge Ursa's mastery over her body and her voice, just as a slave master would summarily exercise power over his female chattel.

Happy's Café's primarily male audience's gaze, also associated with phallic power, threatens Mutt's seeming control over Ursa. When she, "mess with they eyes," Mutt feels a slippage of sexual and economic power over Ursa as other men watch her nightly performances and "mess with they eyes" (*Corregidora*, 3). He wants to keep Ursa his and his alone by keeping her away from other men. Thus Ursa finds herself in a double bind: She is a very beautiful woman, a blues singer by profession and desire; she cannot help but be the object of other men (and women's) gazes, their desire. Moreover, singing the blues helps Ursa to tell *her* own story as well as to (re)generate the horrors of her family's story.

As a blues singer, Ursa is in intimate dialogue with her audience. The songs she sings for them are meant to touch them emotionally, make them feel their pain and hers as well. Through her performance, Ursa asserts a kind of power over her audience. She becomes the object of their desire. However, the psychoanalytical caveat is that as a woman her power is mediated in the novel primarily through men. In speaking of women and power, Jacques Lacan notes:

> She retains her position as the object of the other's desire only through artifice, appearance, or dissimulation. Illusion, travesty, make-up, the veil, become the techniques she relies upon to both cover over and make visible her "essential assets." They are her means of seducing or enticing the other, of becoming a love-object for him. By securing her "deficiency" by these means, she also secures a mode of access to the phallic. Ironically, in this aim of becoming the object of the other's desire, she becomes the site of a rupture, phallic and castrated, idealized and debased, devoted to the masquerade (an excess) and a deficiency. (Grosz, 132)

After Ursa performs one night, Mutt tells her to "take that damned mascara off. It makes you look like a bitch" (*Corregidora*, 154). Whereas before, Ursa's masquerade—her gowns and makeup—was part of what first attracted Mutt to her, now he sees it as abject. However, Ursa notes that her blues performances "help explain what I can't explain," the why and how of her personal feelings (*Corregidora*, 56). Nonetheless, her performances also act as a screen, for, while the blues help to tell her story, they also conceal the deeper horrors of her matrilineal burden. Mutt refuses to understand Ursa's needs and desires. And in outrage spurred by figurative impotence, he pushes her down the stairs.

What is perhaps most interesting in this opening scene is that Ursa does not immediately say that Mutt *pushed* her. She says she fell. Jones's specific employment of the word "fell" has vast implications in interpreting Mutt's and the novel's other characters' relationships with Ursa. Ursa's statement implies a dual "fall": physical and psychical. The result of having her womb removed motivates her maternal/matralineal fall from grace. She also seemingly falls out of love with Mutt. And finally, at least for a while, her doctor orders her not to perform, which precipitates a spiritual fall. For a while, she has to stop singing the blues at Happy's Café to recuperate from her hysterectomy. Now, because she can no longer "make generations," she cannot fulfill her matrilineal obligation to pass on her family's story of loss and death to her *own* children. In the wake of her trauma, Ursa must try to understand and redefine herself in light of her wounded body and psyche.

The theme of the wounded female body takes on a mythic status from the onset of the novel. In the novel's violent opening scene, Gayl Jones's re(visions) the Greek Demeter/Kore-Persphone myth. In the Demeter/Kore-Persephone myth, Kore also falls from grace. She is abducted from the fields of Eleusinia and raped by Hades, Zeus's brother. She becomes Queen of the Underworld. By abducting Kore and taking her underground, Hades also prevents her from being seen. Amazingly, the myth also reveals that Zeus, the epitome of phallic power, allows Hades to do this to his niece with his blessing. With her marriage to Hades, King of the Dead, Kore, too, does not bear children. Her position as Demeter's daughter and Hades's wife makes her both a child of light and darkness, life in death. So, too, Corregidora is a child of both light and darkness. She is her mother's daughter conceived with a black man out of, if not quite love, most definitely familial obligation. But Ursa also acknowledges that she has the blood of Old Man Corregidora, the "mad Portuguese" (*Corregidora*, 10), coursing through her veins:

> I'd always thought I was different. *Their* daughter, but somehow different. Maybe less Corregidora. I don't know. But when I saw that picture, I knew I had it. What my mother and my mother's mother before her had. The mulatto women...." (*Corregidora*, 60)

Ursa accepts her ontological status as a child of light and darkness. She is the ancestral by-product of the intermingling of black and white "blood."

Tellingly, early in the novel, Tadpole truncates Ursa's name and calls her "Ursa Corre" (*Corregidora*, 8).[3] Returning to the Demeter/Kore-Persephone myth, in Greek mythology, Kore is the equivalent name for Persephone and means "small child." As Carl Jung explains:

> The figure responding to the Kore [as archetype] in a woman is generally a double one, i.e., a mother and a maiden, which is to say she appears now as the one, now as the other....The maiden is often described as not altogether human in the usual sense; she is either unknown or peculiar in origin, or she looks strange or undergoes strange experiences, from which one is forced to infer the maiden's extraordinary myth-like nature.... The psyche pre-existent to consciousness (e.g., in the child) participates in the maternal psyche on the one hand, while on the other it reaches across to the daughter psyche. We would therefore say that every mother contains her daughter in herself and every daughter her mother, and that every woman extends backwards into her mother and forwards into her daughter. This participation and intermingling give rise to that particular uncertainty as regards time: a woman lives earlier as a mother, later as a daughter. The conscious experience of these ties produce the feeling that her life is spread

out over generations—the first step towards the immediate experience of being outside time, which brings with it a feeling of immortality. The individual's life is elevated into a type, indeed it becomes the archetype of woman's fate in general. (*Archetypes and the Collective Unconscious*, 184-185)[4]

Ursa, as racialized archetype, undergoes lived experiences particular, not to every woman's life, but most certainly, in a historical context, to black women's lives. Regardless of time, place, or social condition, every black woman has experienced black and white male patriarchal oppression.

The stories passed down to Ursa by the women in her family are horrific tales of trauma that affect Ursa as an adult. Although Ursa's grandmother is the only female in the family who is a physical victim of incest by Old Man Corregidora, Ursa's great-grandmother, grandmother, and mother, and Ursa herself, are all victims of its traumatic reverberations. Ursa tells Tadpole McCormick, her boss and eventual lover:

> Corregidora. Old Man Corregidora, the Portuguese slave breeder and whoremonger. (Is that what they call them?) He fucked his own whores and fathered his own breed. They did the fucking and had to bring him the money they made. My grandmother was his daughter, but he was fucking her too. She said when they did away with slavery down there they burned all the slavery papers so it would be like they never had it. (*Corregidora*, 9)

Tadpole is so struck by the story that he finds it incredulous. He asks Ursa, "Who told you all 'at?" (*Corregidora*, 9) His mind cannot fathom such evil could and did happen during slavery. Ursa calmly tells him:

> My great-grandmama told my grandmama the part she lived through that my grandmama didn't live through and my grandmama told my mama what they both lived through and my mama told me what they all lived through and we were suppose to pass it down like that from generation to generation so we'd never forget. Even though they'd burned everything to play like it didn't never happen. (*Corregidora*, 9)

Similarly, Ursa Corregidora relates a childhood incident in which *she* questions the veracity of her Great Gram's story:

> "You telling the truth, Gram?"
>
> She slapped me.

"When I'm telling you something don't you ever ask if I'm lying. Because they didn't want to leave no evidence of what they done—so it couldn't be held against them. And I'm leaving evidence. And you got to leave evidence too. And your children got to leave evidence. And when it come time to hold up the evidence, we got to have evidence to hold up. That's why they burned all the papers, so there wouldn't be no evidence to hold up against them."

I was five years old then. (*Corregidora*, 14)

Great Gram's violent reaction to Ursa's questioning teaches Ursa what Great Gram believes is a valuable lesson in epistemic credibility. Historically, whites have attempted to discredit people of color, which is why Gayl Jones, through Great Gram's testimony, explicitly implies it is essential that black people believe in the truth/s of their own experiences. The dominant culture has shaped the world in its own image and reality through the manipulation of history. Linda Alcoff speaks to epistemological manipulation when she validates the importance, especially to discredited people, of testimonial knowledge. Alcoff explains that

> for too long it has been the case that epistemology has based its analyses of knowledge on atypical scenarios of direct perception by an individual; whereas if one is aiming for a general account of knowledge one would think the more typical case of belief generation should be taken as the paradigm, that is knowledge based on one form or another on the testimony of others.... Such knowledge raises different sorts of epistemological questions than direct perception, questions not about perceptual reliability or perceptual memory but about trust and the bases of interpersonal judgment, credibility and epistemic reliability. (*Women of Color and Philosophy*, 236)

Ursa Corregidora's orally recounting family history, from memory, is supposed to be the vehicle in which her particular family's horrific subterranean history, that is, unofficial history, is to be remembered. The stories have been told so often that they become mythic in stature, larger than the experiences of the Corregidora women. Again, Jones alludes to the Greek myth of Demeter and her daughter Kore-Persephone. In the novel, we learn that Great Gram was taken out of the field as a prepubescent girl and raped by Old Man Corregidora, a Portuguese slave trader. He made her a prostitute and virtually a prisoner in his brothel. Old Man Corregidora's brutality and cruelty, like Mutt Thomas's, deeply affect Ursa. Great Gram's and Ursa's stories mirror one another.

After Queen Isabella banished slavery in Brazil, Great Gram escaped and stole a picture of Old Man Corregidora before fleeing to Louisiana. She stole the picture because she wanted evidence, the need to know and to believe that what happened to her actually occurred. She has something tangible so that "whenever evil come I wanted something to point to and say, 'That's what evil looks like'" (*Corregidora*, 12). The Corregidora women's contestation with evil parallels the Demeter/Kore-Persephone myth. The god Hades as a representation of evil is much more complicated than the Judeo-Christian Satan. He abducts Kore from the Eleusinian fields and takes her down to the Underworld to be his queen. Although lost for days, Kore-Persephone refuses to eat any food Hades offers her, but eventually hunger/desire overcomes her resistance. She eats three pomegranate seeds, an act that forever binds her to Hades and condemns her to live in the Underworld as his queen for three months of the year. Her mother, Demeter, is so inconsolable that the land remains barren until the time she can be with her daughter again.

According to many feminist readings, the Demeter/Kore-Persephone myth exemplifies patriarchal arrogance and brutality against women. Similarly in *Corregidora*, Ursa's brutal physical and psychological experiences with Mutt Thomas have left her barren: physically unable to produce children and psychically bereft of maternal love and care. In fact, I would argue that all of the major male characters in the novel, who unequivocally hate and love the Corregidora women, are archetypal, racialized simulations of the god of the Underworld. In a dream-conversation with Mutt, Ursa says:

> But it's all your fault all my seeds are wounded forever. No warm ones, only bruised ones. No seeds. Let me in between your legs. It ain't a pussy down there, it's a whole world. Talking about *his* pussy.... The center of a woman's being. Is it? No seeds. Is that what snaps away my music, a harp string broken, guitar string, string of my banjo belly. Strain in my voice. (*Corregidora*, 47)

The men in the novel are unable to see women as human beings with feelings. The women struggle to feel emotions other than hate and frustration. Ursa never declares her love to either Mutt or Tadpole, who both reduce women's entire being to their genitalia. Sexual dominance is the focal point of everything that matters to them. Similarly, in the Greek myth, the god Hades demonstrates unrestrained lust for Kore-Persephone's sex. Once Kore becomes Persephone, Queen of the Dead, she, too, forfeits her seeds. Mutt tells Ursa that her sex is a "whole world" (*Corregidora*, 47). But after her fall, that world is barren. To make up for the loss, Ursa connects to her mother and the other Corregidora women through the blues. In this choral space, at least for a time, Ursa leaves that barren world. The blues, as a connection to her maternal ancestors, allows her momentarily to feel. For example, when Ursa feels recuperated enough to return to work, Cat urges her to sing. She aptly chooses the blues song "Trouble in Mind." The lyrics to "Trouble in Mind" reflect a newfound hope: "Trouble in mind/Oh yes, I'm blue, but I refuse to be blue always/The sun is gonna shine in my backdoor someday" (Richard M. Jones, Lyrics). Similarly, when Kore-Persephone leaves the Underworld, her return to her mother, Demeter, is a cause for celebration, unabashed elation reflected in the Earth's return to life. This ritual movement from death to life is a time for rejoicing.

However, in *Corregidora*, storytelling as an oral quasiritual also has devastating effects on Ursa. She has heard the matrilineal stories so often that exactly what happened to each of the Corregidora women becomes questionable but in the long run does not really matter. Ursa relates that when she (Ursa) was a little girl, "Great-Gram sat in the rocker. I was on her lap. She told the same story over and over again.... It was if the words were helping her, as if the words repeated again and again could be a substitute for memory, were somehow more than memory..." (*Corregidora*, 11). As Linda Alcoff observes, mnemonic epistemology, otherwise discredited by official written history, is a legitimate form of truth telling. Ritualized telling counters the hegemonic discourses of official history. However, ironically, the Corregidora women's histories have formed a linguistic chain to which Ursa is bound. These stories carry the full weight of Ursa's matrilineal family history, and it is Ursa's familial obligation to carry the burden. She has no choice because these stories are a part of individual and collective memory.[5]

Indeed, after her hysterectomy, Ursa tells Tad she feels "as if part of my life's already marked out for me—the barren part" (*Corregidora*, 6). Again, looking at the structure of this sentence, Ursa seems to be saying two things: her life has already been marked out or *planned* for her through discursive obligation, fate, and destiny. One could also read the statement as Ursa's saying that part of her life has already been marked out or *erased* for her because of her hysterectomy. That is, Ursa's obligation inhibits her from full self-actualization. Unlike her ancestors, she can no longer "make generations." Without her womb, Ursa feels useless. She questions her womanhood, a ghost that haunts Ursa throughout the text.

Sigmund Freud discusses the womb in relation to what he calls *unheimlich* or "the uncanny." He defines the uncanny as "undoubtedly [belonging] to all that is terrible—to that arouses dread and creeping horror" (*Collected Papers*, 368). According to Freud, womb fantasies fall into the category of the uncanny. Moreover, "the uncanny," as Freud theorized, "is that class of the frightening which leads back to what is of old and long familiar" (*The Uncanny*, 120). The matrilineal *fabula* that burden Ursa are old and certainly familiar, and they frighten her:

> At that time [Mutt] had his cousin take a picture of me and him, and I kept staring at the picture.... I got so embarrassed because it was me I was looking at, not *us*. I handed him back the picture and he put it on the mirror. But when he wasn't there I'd come by the bureau and just look at it. I'd never look when Mutt was home. But I knew why I was looking. Because I realized for the first time what all those other women had. I'd always thought I was different. *Their* daughter, but somehow different. I don't know. But when I saw that picture, I knew I had it. What my mother and my mother's mother before her had. The mulatto women. Great Gram was the coffee-bean woman, but the rest of us.... But I *am* different now, I was thinking. I have everything they had, except the generations. I can't make generations. And even if I had my womb, even if the first baby had come—what would I have done then? Would I have kept it up? Would I have been like *her*, or *them*. (*Corregidora*, 60)

Old Man Corregidora and his malevolent legacy still haunt her. Mutt's behavior towards Ursa patterns him as Old Man Corregidora's double. A conversation with Mutt mirrors the very words Old Man Corregidora tells Ursa's Great Gram. Mutt tells Ursa: "Your pussy's a little gold piece, ain't it Urs? My little gold piece." She responds,

"Yes" (*Corregidora*, 60). Jones is very careful in paralleling contemporary forms of black women's oppression with similar past historical moments. In fact, Jones makes it clear that there is not much difference between oppression of contemporary black women and their historical counterparts.[6]

For example, neither Ursa's mother, grandmother, nor great-grandmother marries. However, Ursa and Mutt "were married in December 1947" (*Corregidora*, 3). Approximately five months later, Ursa's accident occurs. Jones specifies the official date of Ursa's marriage to Mutt to distinguish Ursa's situation from her maternal ancestors. That is, Ursa and Mutt undergo the juridical process that makes them husband and wife, an option denied to Great Gram and which Ursa's grandmother and mother repudiate. However, Mutt's treatment of Ursa shows the reader that official documents mean very little when it comes to protecting black women from abusive men. As Mutt's actions reveal, like Old Man Corregidora, he can relate to women only through violence and oppression. In fact, Jones discursively links Mutt *to* Old Man Corregidora by having them behave similarly in speech and deed.

At the beginning of the novel, Mutt is described as "looking drunk and evil" (*Corregidora*, 4). Ursa's Great Gram describes Old Man Corregidora as the embodiment of evil. A photograph she steals before escaping to New Orleans depicts Old Man Corregidora as a grotesque monster:

> They said he had a stroke or something what turned his foot outside.... It did something to his neck too, because he always go around like he was looking for something that wasn't there. I stole [the photograph] because I said whenever afterward when evil come I wanted something to point to and say, "That's what evil looks like." (*Corregidora*, 12)

The stolen photograph is a talisman to ward off evil, but it is also a link to the past, which perpetuates the trauma through memory. For the Corregidora women, the photograph becomes a fetish. "More broadly," as Jennifer Blessing points out, "the fetish is a sort of charm that wards off evil that is enlisted to prevent the feared outcomes" (Rrose is a Rrose is a Rrose, 59). "A photograph is both a pseudo-presence and a token of absence" (Susan Sontag, *On Photography*, 16). Moreover, according to Roland Barthes, the photograph is intimately connected to death. Margaret Iverson's reading of Barthes' *Camera Lucida* is interesting in the context of *Corregidora*: "The nature of the [photography] as an indexical imprint of the object means that any photographed object or person has a ghostly presence, an uncanniness that might be likened to the return of the dead" (450). Thus, a symbolic relationship is established between Old Man Corregidora, Mutt, and Tadpole as archetype and the Greek god of the Underworld, Hades. In their self-contained kingdoms they are connected to violence and death. The Corregidora women are either physically and psychically abused, like Kore-Persephone.

One of the most interesting features of *Corregidora* is its complex treatment of incest, especially in its relationship to slavery and psychoanalysis: "For Lacan," Anne McClintock observes, "the universal (that is male) shift towards the father that engenders the Symbolic is inaugurated by the father's prohibition against incest." Lacan follows Freud and Levi-Strauss (who follow nineteenth-century anthropologists) in their contention that it was "the past of primordial law...that castration should be the punishment for incest" (*Imperial Leather*, 196).

Regarding Freudian and Lacanian psychoanalytic theory in the context of a slaveocracy, one can see how Gayl Jones challenges the oedipal construct and its notion of the family romance, especially in its prohibition of incest. In a plantation system, slaves are not regarded as human beings; they are property of the master. Therefore, whatever unnaturalness occurs in terms of human relations does not apply to slaves. Whatever occurs between the master and his female chattel transcends religious and juridical laws. On his plantation, Old Man Corregidora is the Law. Moreover, his actions are condoned by a patriarchal system invested in the trading of human flesh.

Inasmuch as Mutt's and Tadpole's respective marriages to Ursa, therefore, they are representatives of the Law. In an outburst of jealous anger, Mutt threatens to put up Ursa for auction as if he were her slavemaster. Jones, however, discursively subverts mastery/the Law through symbolic castration. Memories of castration return to haunt Ursa in a crucial flashback scene between Great Gram and Old Man Corregidora, as retold by Ursa's grandmother:

> Mama ran off cause he would have killed her. I don't know what she did. She never did tell me what she did.... He would have killed her though, if

> she hadn't gone.... But he never said nothing about what she did to him. What is it a woman can do to a man that make him hate her so bad he wont to kill her one minute and keep thinking about her and can't get her out of his mind the next. (*Corregidora*, 173)

This brings us to the most controversial scene in the text, when, after twenty years, despite their volatile history, Mutt and Ursa are reunited. As Ursa performs oral sex on Mutt, she thinks about Great Gram and,

> What it was a woman could do to a man that make him hate her so bad he wont to kill her one minute and keep thinking about her and can't get her out of his mind the next? In a split second of hate and love I knew what it was, and I think he might have know too. A moment of pleasure and excruciating pain at the same time, a moment of broken skin but not sexlessness, a moment just before sexlessness, a moment that stops just before sexlessness, a moment that stops just before it breaks the skin: "I could kill you." (*Corregidora*, 184)

For a number of reasons, this scene is probably the most difficult in the entire novel to interpret, mainly, I think, because the scene is very ambiguous in terms of who is speaking/thinking as oral sex is performed. For this scene conflates Great Gram's sexual encounter with Old Man Corregidora and Ursa and Mutt's sexual liaison at the end of the novel. In this singular narrative moment, history is compressed and Ursa operates psychologically and mythically outside of Time. The reader does not know whether it is Great Gram speaking and thinking or Ursa. Nor can we assuredly say who the "he" refers to in this scene, Old Man or Mutt. And finally, who is speaking or thinking, "I could kill you" — Great Gram /Old Man Corregidora, or Ursa/ Mutt as s/he realizes the distinct possibility of revenge through physical and psychological castration? She (Great Gram/Ursa) could cut off *his* (Old Man Corregidora's/Mutt's) power to make generations. And to complicate further our epistemic equilibrium, this particular scene echoes the moment in mythological Time in which Kore swallows the three pomegranate seeds that forever bind her to Hades as she becomes Persephone, Queen of the Dead. Paralleling Kore-Peresphone's act of desire, Ursa Corre states: "[Mutt] came and I swallowed" (*Corregidora*, 185). Like Kore-Persephone, Ursa Corre literally swallows Mutt's seed, thus forever cementing the bond of hate and love that exists between them.

Through a virtuoso postmodern performance, in writing *Corregidora*, Gayl Jones deftly uses psychoanalysis and myth to interrogate questions of power, sexuality, and race. *Corregidora* is a testament to Gayl Jones's unprecedented abilities as a writer. For over two decades after its publication, the novel continues to create enormous controversy, debate, and wonder.

Notes

[1] I want to suggest here that Morrison speaks to a Jungian understanding of politics and history. According to C. G. Jung, "When we look at human history, we see only what happens on the surface, and even this is distorted in the faded mirror of tradition. But what has really been happening eludes the inquiring eye of the historian, for the true historical event lies deeply buried...The great events of world history are, at bottom, profoundly unimportant. In the last analysis, the essential thing is the life of the individual. This alone makes history, here alone do the great transformations first take place, and the whole future, and the whole history of the world, ultimately springs as a giant summation from these hidden sources in individuals. In our private and most subjective lives we are not only the passive witnesses of our age, and its sufferers, but also its makers. We make our own epoch" (*Politics* 45).

[2] Mutt's attacking Ursa from the shadows has a number of important mythological and psychoanalytic implications. The god Hades is the King of shadows. In fact, part of his arsenal is a magic helmet that enables him to be cloaked in shadow to avoid detection. In Jungian psychoanalytic theory, the Shadow is an important archetype.

[3] Corre and Korê are homophones. Moreover, in Spanish slang *correr* means to orgasm or to come, which is ironic because sexually Ursa Corregidora can do neither.

[4] According to Robert Ellwood, "The psychology of C. G. Jung rests on psychic biography. Biography in this case means the narrative of the subject's inner life, above all as it is expressed in dreams and fantasies. For from the Jungian perspective, the real life of an individual, as of the world is inward" (*Politics* 37). One of the problems with looking at myth, archetype and the collective unconscious is that Jung looks at these notions as ontological phenomena. I want to suggest that they be understood as discursive phenomena. One sees this manifest in *Corregidora* with the persistent interruption of dream and fantasy sequences marked by italicization, in the narrative. Moreover, Ursa as archetype represents black women's oppression throughout history. Also, Ursa's archetypal existence outside of Time manifests in the cyclical nature of Ursa's leaving Mutt after her fall but returning to him at the novel's end. I would argue that Jones plays upon the Demeter/Korê-Persephone myth because Ursa leaves Mutt and through various encounters in the novel actively seeks out answers to

her existence. The fact that she returns to Mutt of her own free will and as a woman who is sure of herself tacitly indicates that Ursa has psychologically grown in her absence from him.

[5] One could go so far as to say that the Corregidora women's memories are part of a collective unconscious. "By collective unconscious Jung...meant mental contents shared with others, either the entire human race or a subdivision of it, such as a culture or nationality. These memories are preconscious and, "Being preconscious, those powerful forces could express themselves only in camouflage, usually through emotions bearing symbolic archetypal form: a culture's particular version of the Father, the Mother, the Hero, the Shadow. In traditional society, these images were best found in folkloric myths and symbols (*Politics* 44).

[6] Note that Jones names all of the characters that want to exploit Ursa after animals that are considered in *Kristevian* psychoanalytic terms abject. For example, a mutt is a mixed breed of dog whose parentage can only be conjectured. Tadpole symbolizes slimy creatures that are betwixt a land dwelling animal (a frog) and a water creature. The character Jeffrine, the young lesbian who tries to sexually molest Ursa Corregidora, suggests someone who is neither male nor female, neither fish nor fowl. Finally, Cat Lawson, Ursa's friend, is named after a creature that throughout Western history is associated with the abject. Moreover, her last name Law/son implies her relationship to patriarchal practices of sexually exploiting and controlling women as she does with Jeffrine and as she tries to do with Ursa.

Works Cited

Alcoff, Linda. "On Judging Epistemic Credibility." *Women of Color and Philosophy*. Ed. Naomi Zack. Malden, MA, and Oxford: Blackwell Publishers Inc, 2000. 235-262.

Barker, Philip. *Michel Foucault: An Introduction*. Edinburgh: Edinburgh University Press, 2000.

Barthes, Roland. *Camera Lucida*. Trans. Richard Howard. New York: Hill and Wang, 1982.

Blessing, Jennifer. *Rrose is a Rrose is a Rrose: Gender Performance in Photography*. New York: Guggenheim Museum, 1997.

Dove, Rita. *Mother Love: Poems*. New York: W. W. Norton, 1995.

Ellwood, Robert. *The Politics of Myth: A Study of C. G. Jung, Mircea Eliade, and Joseph Campbell*. New York: State University of New York Press, 1999.

Evans, Dylan. *An Introductory Dictionary of Lacanian Psychoanalysis*. New York and London: Routledge, 1996.

Foucault, Michel. *Discipline and Punish*. Trans. Alan Sheridan. New York: Vintage Books. 1995.

Freud, Sigmund. *Collected Papers*. Vol. 4. Trans. Joan Riviere. New York: Basic Books, Inc., 1938.

Grosz. Elizabeth. *Jacques Lacan: A Feminist Introduction*. New York: Routledge, 1990.

Hopcke, Robert H. *A Guided Tour of the Collected Works of C. G. Jung*. Boston and London: Shambala, 1999.

Iverson, Margaret. "What Is A Photograph?" *Art History* 17.3 (Sept. 1994): 450.

Jones, Gayl. *Corregidora*. New York: Random House, 1975.

———. *Eva's Man*. New York: Random House, 1976.

———. *Hermit Woman*. Detroit: Lotus Press, 1983.

———. *Song for Anninho*. Detroit: Lotus Press, 1981.

———. *White Rat: Short Stories*. New York: Random House, 1977.

———. *Xarque and Other Poems*. Detroit: Lotus Press, 1985.

Jones, Richard M. "Trouble in Mind." MCA, Inc., 1926.

Jung, Carl. *Archetypes and the Collective Unconscious*. New Brunswick, NJ: Princeton University Press, 1969. 968.

Kester, Gunilla-Theander. "The Forbidden Fruit and Female Disorderly Eating: Three Versions of Eve." *Disorderly Eaters: Texts in Self-Empowerment*. Eds. Lillian Furst and Peter W. Graham. University Park: Pennsylvania State University Press, 242-244.

Kristeva, Julia. *Powers of Horror: An Essay on Abjection*. Trans. Leon S. Roudiez. New York: Columbia University Press, 1982.

Lacan, Jacques. *Écrits: A Selection*. New York: Norton, 1977.

McClintock, Anne. *Imperial Leather*. New York and London: Routledge, 1995.

Morrison, Toni. *Conversations with Toni Morrison*. Jackson: University Press of Mississippi, 1994.

Mulvey, Laura. *Visual and Other Pleasures*. Basingstoke: Macmillan, 1989.

Sontag, Susan. *On Photography*. New York: Farrar, Strauss and Giroux, 1978.

Tate, Claudia. *Psychoanlaysis and Black Novels*. New York: Oxford University Press, 1998.

CHAPTER EIGHT

Prison Narratives, Narrative Prisons: Incarcerated Women Reading Gayl Jones's *Eva's Man*

Megan Sweeney

> I couldn't, I mean really, I couldn't put a name on Eva.
> —Shelly, North Carolina Correctional Institution for Women

> Eva bein' Eva, I said, man, we went through some hell, didn't we girl! You know, comin' up and stuff.
> —Audrey, North Carolina Correctional Institution for Women

> If she still hadn't have killed him, she still didn't stand a chance because she's a female.... She was fried one way or another.
> —Tanya, North Carolina Correctional Institution for Women

Although the pathologized and criminalized figure of the African American woman haunts public debate about welfare reform, single-parent families, and the war on drugs, explicit discussions of black women as agents of crime remain relatively scarce in academic and popular narratives. For instance, in a well-known criminology collection called *Crime*, welfare-dependent African American mothers implicitly represent the source—in James Q. Wilson's words—of "thirty thousand more young muggers, killers, and thieves than we have now," (Wilson 1995, 507), yet the collection offers no analysis of African American women's involvement in crime. The figure of the black female criminal functions as shorthand for "associations that work best when not fully or explicitly articulated" (Daniels 1997, 583); featuring African American women lawbreakers forces a narrative reckoning with their typical role as cultural decoy, as a means for rendering invisible the routine social violences of the U.S. political-economic system. Compounding African American women's hypervisible/invisible status is their relative absence even in progressive scholarship about women and crime.[1] With the exception of crucial efforts by critical race feminists, scholars, and activists such as Beth Richie, Kimberlé Williams Crenshaw, Angela Davis, Joy James, and members of Incite! Women of Color Against Violence, the prison abolition movement has tended to focus on African American men as victims of the racist criminal justice system, while discussions of sexual violence against women have tended to elide, or e-race, the experiences of women of color.[2] When it comes to representations of agents and objects of crime, then, the old adage still rings true: all the women are white, and all the blacks are men.[3]

Twenty-eight years after its publication, Gayl Jones's *Eva's Man* thus continues to occupy a rare position in featuring an African American woman who has sustained and committed acts of violence. Jones's novel offers the first-person fictional account of Eva Medina Canada, a woman who is incarcerated in a prison psychiatric hospital for poisoning and castrating Davis Carter, an acquaintance with whom she spent four days in a hotel. In her circular, repetitious, almost affectless narrative, Eva chronicles her sense of continual exposure to sexual harassment from multiple figures—primarily men—including her cousin, her mother's boyfriend, a plant foreman, and a man whom she stabbed in the hand for grabbing her between the legs. Although she emphasizes Davis Carter's attempts to exert sexual and emotional control over her during their four-day encounter in the hotel, Eva complicates her narrative by simultaneously foregrounding her feelings of sexual entrapment and sexual desire, and by maintaining silence when others harass her or demand that she explain her violent acts.

As part of a larger project focusing on imprisoned women's readings of texts about women and crime, I led a group discussion of *Eva's Man* with prisoners incarcerated in the North Carolina Correctional Institution for Women.[4] This essay explores some of the knowledges and insights that emerged in the women's readings of Jones's novel. The featured readers are African American, white, and Native American, and they range in age from 22 to 47. Some of the women had less than an eighth-grade education before coming to prison, while others had college degrees; many have earned their GED or an associate's degree while in prison. The women's prison sentences vary from three years for drug-trafficking, to life imprisonment for first-degree murder.[5] I am a white, middle-class woman, and I was 34 years old and working on my Ph.D. in Literature when I conducted this study.

Scholarship about *Eva's Man* often foregrounds the novel's refusal to posit a definitive explanation or evaluation of Eva's crime. Discussing how *Eva's Man* leaves the reader in a position of non-mastery, Madhu Dubey asserts that it "offers no possibility of a looking, a reading that can respect the integrity of the feminine object." Acts of looking and interpretation in the text are "invariably acts of masculine power," Dubey contends, because lawyers, the police, journalists, and the general public continually "assault Eva's integrity" with their sexist, stereotypical readings (Dubey 1994, 103). I want to argue that *Eva's Man* does gesture toward a method of reading that respects the integrity of the feminine object. While the media and curious onlookers attach "the easiest answer they [can] get" to Eva's crime (Jones 1976, 4)—reading her as a whore, as crazy, or as the victim of a deceitful lover—and while male characters rely on the easiest answer they can get in continually reading sexual availability in women's eyes, Eva begins her story by foregrounding a counter-method of reading.

Describing her encounter with Davis's wife, who comes to see her in jail, Eva explains:

> [Davis's wife] didn't say anything. She just stood there outside the cell and stared at me, and I stared back. The only thing I kept wondering is how did he treat *her*. Because it looked like he made her worse than he made me. I mean, if she was as bad-off on the inside as she looked on the outside. She must've stood there for fifteen minutes, and then left. She didn't have anything at all in her eyes—not hate not nothing. Or whatever she did have, I couldn't see it. When she left, I wondered what she saw in mine. (Jones 1976, 4).

Rather than illustrating the impossibility of interpretation, this encounter highlights a method of reading that privileges silence as an act of attentive listening, forestalls mastery and the immediate imposition of certain meaning, and draws attention to instances when existing explanations fail. Although Eva wonders whether Davis's wife is "as bad-off on the inside as she looked on the outside," she refuses to honor assumptions based on immediate appearances; respecting the integrity of the feminine object, she ultimately concedes that she cannot read the woman's eyes. Furthermore, this counter-method of reading attends to the reciprocal nature of looking and listening, as evident when Eva wonders what Davis's wife saw in her eyes. By fostering receptivity to the uncanny ways in which an encounter with the Other can render you strange unto yourself—changing you and refashioning the social relations in which you are located,[6] Eva's reading method expands possible horizons of visibility. It foregrounds the act of remaining receptive—through a potentially transformative mode of listening—as fundamental for illuminating forms of visibility and knowledge routinely occluded by dominant methods of reading and interpretation.

This notion of reading seems particularly useful for clearing away some of the self-evidences currently clouding horizons of theoretical visibility about African American women, crime, violence, and victimization. I am attempting to further such a project in this essay by featuring some incarcerated women's readings of *Eva's Man*. While the featured readers produce no standard "imprisoned woman's reading," all of the women approach Jones's novel as a realist text and value most its ability to capture aspects of their own lived experiences. June Jordan's 1976 review criticizes *Eva's Man* as "a monotone lamentation of one woman...who is nobody I have ever known," and as a font of "sinister misinformation about women—about women, in general, about black women in particular, and especially about young black girls forced to deal with the sexual, molesting violations of their minds and bodies by their fathers, their mothers' boyfriends, their cousins and uncles" (Jordan 1976, 37). For the readers featured in this essay, however, "the sexual, molesting violations" of which Jordan speaks are matters of fact, not "sinister information." All of the women speak of sustaining violence at the hands of men, and all speak of coming dangerously close to killing a violent male partner.[7] As they discuss Jones's novel—continually clarifying what they believe it is missing—the incarcerated readers seem to be engaged in complex, sometimes contradictory efforts to find themselves in, and to distance themselves from, Eva's story.

Drawing on their acts of critical reading and on their own prison narratives, I explore, in the following pages, how the imprisoned readers variously reproduce, resist, and rework existing discourses about women, crime, and violence. I want to highlight how women use *Eva's Man* as a tool for understanding more fully the relationship between sexual violence, race, class, gender, and crime; for coming to terms with the many roles that silence has played in their lives; and for situating themselves in relation to discourses about victimization and resistance. I hope to underscore the difficulty, and the fundamental necessity, of engaging in such a project of transformative listening as a means to open up new possibilities for seeing the "black female criminal." Such a project involves "not being afraid of what is happening to [us]" as women's powerfully affecting testimonies call us to abandon the hygienic certainty and comforting familiarity of "know-it-all criticism" and common-sense scripts (Gordon 1997, 205, 203).

Seeing Anew "The Abuse Excuse"

As our group discussion of *Eva's Man* was coming to a close, a 33-year-old African American woman named Shelly told me, "If you find any more books by Gayl Jones, you better just put 'em in the trash."[8] Shelly's comment captures the general sense of frustration that the incarcerated women experienced in reading *Eva's Man*. Like many readers and critics, the women expressed impatience and discomfort with the text's blurred distinctions between fact and fantasy and with its refusal to provide an explanation or final judgment of Eva's crime.[9] As a 41-year-old white woman named Rae articulates, *Eva's Man* gives "no rhyme or reason" for Eva's crime or for "why she is the way she is. It leaves you guessing." Rae shares the women's overall preference for true crime books, which clearly depict criminal protagonists as "either crazy, greedy, stupid, or very smart."

The incarcerated women's discomfort with Jones's protean portrait of Eva seems to stem, in part, from their first-hand experience with a justice system that leaves little room for accommodating ambiguity or complex and partial notions of agency, responsibility, guilt, and innocence. Moreover, the women seem to feel a pressing need to make sense of Eva's story as they struggle to come to terms with the violences that they have committed and sustained themselves. Notably, each of the readers makes sexual, physical, and/or emotional abuse her central consideration in trying to lend sense to Eva's crime. In contemporary U.S. culture, the connection between abuse and crime tends to function as an empty trope, a shorthand script for the notion that "broken homes" and breaches of "family values" spawn criminals. Rather than fleshing out the complex ways in which abuse affects people's abilities to lead safe and healthy lives, and rather than drawing attention to abuse as a systemic defect of the existing family norm, dominant popular and legal discourses dismiss efforts to consider lawbreakers' experiences of victimization as attempts to invoke "the abuse excuse" (Dershowitz 1994, 4) or as matters of "social awareness" to which courts "must be absolutely blind" (*Wuornos v. State* 1994, 1012).[10] The incarcerated readers' efforts to link abuse and crime do not stem, however, from desires to excuse their own or Eva's crimes; rather, they stem from the women's hard-won and painful efforts to understand their own lived experiences.

On the one hand, Patty—a 37-year-old Cherokee—dissociates herself from Eva as an unflattering representation of a female criminal. "This isn't giving a good message about us at all!" she laments, arguing that if "a common housewife" were to read *Eva's Man*, she "would just be appalled" by Eva and assume "she needs to be locked away forever." Patty attempts to solidify her distance from Eva by insisting that Eva was mentally incapable of standing trial and that she suffers from multiple personality disorder. On the other hand, Patty appreciates Jones's effort to understand what Eva "or any of us" may have gone through before committing a crime, because "not many people in society want to take that time." Although she finds no "drastic" evidence of physical or sexual abuse in Eva's narrative, Patty reads between the lines and feels a strong sense of connection with her pain: "I have compassion for her because I can see, I can hear …she's hurting tremendously." Commenting on Eva's repeated reference to breast milk turning into blood, Patty suggests: "To me it was like that was her life, that [Davis Carter] was just sucking the life from her. I don't know how he was doing it, but he was."

When Eva is arrested for killing Davis, the police captain asks the detective handling her case, "She got any marks on her?" Sue, a 31-year-old white woman, directly responds to this passage in trying to make sense of Eva's crime. "You don't have to have marks," she insists, referring to her own experiences of intense emotional abuse. Jill, a 40-year-old white woman who killed her abusive husband, likewise accounts for Eva's crime by describing how her own emotions were "beaten and beaten and beaten." Explains Jill: "That's what I remember, is what was said, instead of like physical abuse. Those bad thoughts never go away for me."

Eva's murder of Davis comes as no surprise to Maria, a 23-year-old white woman, or to Audrey, a 43-year-old African American woman, both of whom read Eva's repetitive emphasis on incidents of sexual harassment as painfully close to their own experiences. "I don't think there was anything bad about her and I don't think she was crazy," says Maria. "I just think that she kept all that stuff bottled up inside of her 'til she couldn't take it no more and she just went off on that man.... It's like they took and took and took from her, so she took from him." Audrey echoes Maria's emphasis on the reality, the seriality, and the cultural invisibility of others' violence toward Eva: "I was wondering why that couldn't be a true book.... She done took so much, she took so much, she took so much, why didn't anybody reach out to help this person? ...I think it's just basically giving you just a real taste of what reality is, because this is usually what it is, you know."

Maria especially values *Eva's Man* because it captures how memories of past traumatic events keep resurfacing and affecting one's actions in the present. Drawing connections between her own acts of first-degree murder and arson and her multiple experiences of sexual and emotional abuse, Maria explains that she likes how Jones's novel moves back and forth between past and present. "It's not like...something happened years ago and it's dead and gone and boom, I just killed somebody because of it," she clarifies. If a man approaches Eva and says something "that just clicks a memory, she goes back to something in her childhood, or something that happened a week ago. It just shows how those things connect to each other really well."

Given her own sense of imprisonment—before coming to prison—in patterns of violence and memories of trauma, Maria believes that prison serves as a refuge for Eva. Relating her experience to Eva's, she explains: "I know when I first went to jail…that's like the first time I did feel like peace of mind because I got away from all of my relatives and you know, the different men that was doing things. …So then all I had to do once I was locked up is just deal with what was in my mind and then go forth on it." Jill concurs that Eva was "really free" in prison for the first time in her life. "No man could get to her, and I think she loved that probably. She probably thought it was bliss!"

Audrey articulates her deep identification with Eva's cumulative experience of violation by addressing her directly: "Man, we went through some hell, didn't we girl!" Audrey reached her own breaking point after withstanding years of life-threatening violence from her husband, which caused her to miscarry one child, almost lose another, and lose her teeth and some of her fingers. One night, when a woman she barely knew came to her house and accused her of stealing her man, Audrey beat the woman to death with a brick. Her rage, as she understands it, had little to do with that particular incident and everything to do with her accumulated fury against her husband: "At the time, I didn't know what I was doing.… I guess some of that anger that I always kept packed down, packed down, it just exploded. And I hate it was her.… If I had to do time, I wish I was doin' it for him, 'cause he's the one that really, really did me like he did, and hurt me like he have."

Just as Eva's life story of "ordinary" violence remains culturally invisible until she refuses the role of sacrificial victim and becomes the agent of sacrifice, the imprisoned women's readings of *Eva's Man* bring visibility to the systemic, socially sanctioned forms of violence against women that courts of law and public opinion continue to occlude. Refusing a strictly private accounting and public disavowal of Eva's crime—refusing to remain "absolutely blind" to matters of "social awareness"—the incarcerated women summon us to see how cumulative experiences of violence can cause women to become violent themselves.

Giving Silence "Shape and Name"[11]

As Eva tells her tale, she conveys a profound sense of being imprisoned in others' misreadings and misprisions, their refusals to hear and concomitant demands that she speak. "I said nothing," she writes over and over, in response to Davis's insistent "I want to know you inside out" (Jones 1976, 45), to her psychiatrist's continual demands for explanation, and to countless others' plaguing refrain, "How did it feel?"[12] Nevertheless, Eva concedes that the "past is still as hard on [her] as the present" (Jones 1976, 5), and her narrative stands as her attempt to tell her story, in her own terms, and on her own time. In their individual and group discussions of *Eva's Man*, the incarcerated women likewise emphasize their experiences of being silenced in their families, in their communities, and in the justice system, and many underscore the difficulty—and the ongoing necessity—of giving voice to their experiences.

Although such emphases on silence and coming to voice may sound like feminist clichés, the incarcerated women's testimony highlights how recent feminist critiques of speakouts about victimization insufficiently attend to the experiences of socially marginalized women. In a well-known version of these arguments, Renee Heberle argues that public testimony about women's sexual victimization confers a monolithic reality onto "an otherwise phantasmatic, illegitimate, and therefore fragile edifice of masculinist dominance" (Heberle 1996, 63).[13] Although she wants to avoid "totalizing interpretations of the 'reality' of sexual violence" (73), Heberle's own argument decontextualizes the situation of the speakout, posits a generic deliverer and recipient of testimony, reinforces conceptualizations of victimization and agency as mutually exclusive, and characterizes narratives of victimization as one-dimensional tales which produce a homogeneous set of political effects. In arguing that she is "considering the political effects of speaking out about sexual violence rather than denying its therapeutic and cathartic effects" (68), Heberle excludes from consideration women for whom the therapeutic and political effects of speaking out cannot be separated, women—like those featured in this essay—who hunger to learn that they are not alone, that their experiences form part of a wider structural pattern, and that their personal traumas point to trouble at the level of the system. Articulating their experiences can serve as an essential first step toward performing a critical ontology of themselves—coming to know where they live in order to begin the patient work of creating a space of movement and artistry within the structures of domination that so profoundly shape them as subjects. Furthermore, Heberle's claim that speakouts merely tell society what it already knows glosses over the willful ignorance at work in our social disavowal of some victims' pain, and it occludes the need for continued efforts to understand the astonishingly high percentage of incarcerated women who have sustained sexual violence as children and/or adults.

By alternately inhabiting and refusing Eva's silences, the incarcerated readers draw crucial attention to the overlapping ways in which personal silence, cultural silencing, and social disenfranchisement continue to shape women's experiences of victimization. Eva's failure to tell her parents about men's attempts to molest her struck a powerful chord with many of the readers. Although critic Melvin Dixon faults Eva for "rebelling against language" and imprisoning herself in silence (Dixon 1984, 246, 254), the imprisoned readers emphasize the cultural refusal to hear accounts of molestation. Rae and Arlene agree that Eva "may have felt that she was better off by not saying anything," since people would merely accuse her of lying about her situation, especially about her uncle's sexual advances. Sue says that she "can understand the silence part" of *Eva's Man* because she has only recently told anybody about being molested by her brother: "If there ain't no communication goin' on in the house, you keep things bottled up inside." Patty—who was molested by her uncle with her mother's knowledge, and who participated in killing the man who molested her own daughter—speaks volumes when she says of Eva: "She was like a child that was seen and not heard."

The relationship between Eva's silence and the cultural silencing of women's experiences of sexual violation surfaces particularly powerfully in the reading response of Melissa, a 27-year-old Native American woman. Having been molested by her brother, several cousins, uncles, and her mother's boyfriend, Melissa surmises that men must have greater freedom than women to voice their victimization: "When men sittin' around gettin' drunk...they might be like, 'You know, man, when I was little, what my uncle come and did to me?'...Then all the men can sit and relate to that." Women, on the other hand,

> have these things happen to them, and they just bury 'em. You know, I mean we're not allowed to talk about 'em, we're not allowed to deal with 'em, and we're fragile anyway, so all that builds up and then more experiences happen and happen and happen, you know what I'm saying? I think that's something just...womenhood come up with. "Oh, don't worry about it baby, it's all right."...I mean, okay, why not worry, 'cause it's botherin' me?

For many of the readers, the accumulation of violences and silences to which Melissa refers helps to explain why Eva refused to defend her actions after murdering Davis Carter, just as she refused to defend herself at age 17 after knifing a man who was harassing her. Nicole, a 22-year-old African American woman, echoes Janelle Wilcox's claim that Eva's silence "functions as a metaphor for the unhearing audience that confronts her.... What can a bitch-cunt-hussy-whore say that will counter what is inscribed in the dominant male discourse?" (Wilcox 1996, 80). Taking on Eva's voice, Nicole states: "Why talk? They ain't gonna believe me. They got their set of stories." This "set of stories," the readers repeatedly insist, systematically silences the factors motivating women's violent crimes. Jill emphasizes how unusual it was for Eva's future husband to ask, "You hurt somebody, or somebody hurt you?" (Jones 1976, 105). In her own case, she explains, "they didn't ask me what he had done to me but saw what I did to him and thought...there was no reason. And there's always a reason." Audrey offers: "You try explaining yourself on the inside of yourself because nobody else wants to hear." In Eva's case, she continues, "It's just like...she bit his thing off 'cause she was crazy, she's a savage. But what was going on in the house 'til it got to that point?"

The synergistic effect of multiple sources of silencing, beginning with the failure to see and to hear "what was going on in the house," occupies a central place in Shelly's reading response. Despite other readers' protests that Tyrone—the boyfriend of Eva's mother—merely placed Eva's hand on his penis, Shelly insists that he was having sex with Eva and that Eva's mother allowed the sexual abuse to continue. Although she did not cite the passage, Shelly's insistence may stem, in part, from the fantasy sequence in which Eva dreams that Tyrone "jams himself up inside [her]" (Jones 1976, 124). However, Shelly's attempt to fill in the silences of Eva's narrative by naming the molestation that others fail to see might also be read as a creative act of resistant reading, an attempt to come to terms with her own mother's refusal to recognize that she was being molested by her stepfather.

Shelly goes on to explain how silence "in the house" can contribute to, and compound, a woman's sense of social disenfranchisement:

> I guess this is another reason why a lot of black women, you know, silence. And now I kinda, can kinda relate to Eva, because when my stepfather was doin' the things he was doing and I was tellin' my mom...she didn't go anywhere. She didn't pack our stuff up and leave him, you know, she was still there and he was continuing to do the things that he did.... And I mean, I was young...I had nowhere else to go, didn't know any better. So in Eva's situation that was some of the stuff that was goin' on too, so when she got older, she probably felt like, well, why say anything? No one's gonna do anything.

Shelly's sense that "no one's gonna do anything" was painfully corroborated when she was raped two times in her early twenties. She tried to press charges after the first rape, which was committed by a man who also set fire to his mother's house. However, "he was given more attention and time for this fire that he set than for what he did to me," Shelly explains, "and I'm probably not even the only one that he had did it to." Searching for the means to understand the social disenfranchisement that this cultural silencing both stems from and exacerbates, Shelly states: "He got time for the arson and not for the rape, and once that happens to so many black girls, you know, they see that happen, they be like, well, why should I even go downtown? They're not gonna do anything about it." Calling to mind the refrain that Eva continually hears: "If you don't want a man to speak to you, you ought to stay in the house" (Jones 1976, 153), Shelly adds that both white people and "upper class" black people assume "she was probably a prostitute anyway" when a poor black woman tries to press charges against her rapist. Because of her lived experience of the silencing forces at work from "the house" to "downtown"—which dictate that "when a black girl get[s] raped, it's just swept to the side"—Shelly maintained complete silence the second time that she was raped.

Although the incarcerated readers unanimously share Eva's sense of not being heard, some nevertheless feel frustrated with Eva's self-imposed silences, which counter their developing understanding that healing requires bearing witness to painful experiences. Sue, who has recently broken her childhood silence about molestation, argues that it "isn't right" for Eva to remain silent, and she insists that Eva "get a backbone." Patty faults Eva for assuming that "people have already judged her" and argues that she "will always be haunted" unless she lets others know "what they made her feel like...the anger, the hurt, the bitterness." Drawing a connection between Eva's hauntings and her own need to reckon with her estranged mother, Patty reminds herself: "If I'm gonna grow, then I need to face these hauntings of my own."

Other readers view *Eva's Man* itself as a form of bearing witness that can teach women "to deal with whatever childhood stuff they've got" and to "seek help or just leave" before reaching the point of violence. Conjuring up the deep sense of shame that surrounds women who have been engulfed in violence, Audrey explains: "If you go through so much stuff in life it's sometimes you don't even want to talk about it because you afraid you won't be accepted.... Like you would be the only one that has a dark cloud following over you only, and the rain is falling." Stories like Eva's help to reduce the isolation and fear of stigmatization, she suggests, since "they're going through the same thing, and maybe you could look at it and say, well they're handling theirs."

Tanya, a 31-year-old African American woman, perhaps best captures the role that a literary text such as *Eva's Man* can play in the difficult work of breaking outwardly imposed and self-imposed silences about victimization. "I would highly recommend *Eva's Man*, for real," Tanya says, echoing Audrey's view that "somebody might have gone through the same thing Eva went through." Her own narrative parallels Eva's in conveying her sense of continual exposure to sexual assault. After recounting how she survived numerous rape attempts by male and female acquaintances, Tanya describes being caught in an expanding web of violence and silence that led her to drive the getaway car for a series of robberies that her boyfriend committed. When she was five months pregnant, for instance, her boyfriend started punching her in the stomach for allegedly lying to him. "If he hit me in my face," Tanya reasoned at the time, "he would leave bruises and that way I would be able to show somebody what he's doing." He did not leave bruises, however, and Tanya maintained silence about that incident as well as several others. Far from claiming "the abuse excuse" in order to avoid taking responsibility for her actions, she describes her silence about her escalating problems as an attempt to protect others: "I would take in my own burden, you know, to keep everyone else from suffering.... Nobody knew, and my parents for real still don't really know the full extent of what all happened."

Tanya's experience of being trapped in silence was exacerbated when she went to court. "My lawyers didn't even want to hear anything I had to say," she explains. "They were just like, sign the paper and take this [plea].... No one wanted to hear, okay, well he put a gun just aside my head, or he made me do it, because if he hadn't done that, you know, I wouldn't have gone." In summarizing her sense of Eva's silences, Tanya could just as well be speaking of herself: "I mean, regardless if she did open her mouth, she didn't stand a chance.... If she still hadn't have killed [Davis], she still didn't stand a chance because she's a female. He could have beat her 'til she was halfway dead, she still didn't stand a chance. She was fried one way or another."

Although Tanya fully understands Eva's silences, she nonetheless cautions against the danger of succumbing to silence and encourages Eva, and herself, to undertake the difficult task of bearing witness. "They done Eva dirty so long the woman won't even talk. I know what it's like not to talk to people, I really do. And I still find myself doin' it," Tanya explains. "But don't sit in your room so long that after a while no one will listen to you.... There's no sense shuttin' yourself from the world." As part of her own efforts to give voice to her experiences, Tanya has spoken with her parents about *Eva's Man*. She explained to them that Eva's story "might sound twisted, but it makes all the sense in the world, you know, because everything's not A, B, and C. There's a motive behind whatever. It might not mean anything to you, but it means a world to the other person." Modeling the method of reading that Eva demonstrates, Tanya offers a reminder that no easy formula, and no readily identifiable single cause, can capture the accumulation of lived experiences that lead so many women to prison: "everything's not A, B, and C." Her reading calls us to abandon "know-it-all criticism," common-sense scripts, and narrow legal notions of reasonableness in order to begin *hearing* the kinds of stories that remain culturally inaudible yet make "all the sense in the world" to women who end up in prison. As Tanya and the other readers struggle to give silence shape and name—filling Eva's silences with their own narratives, and wrestling with the dominant "set of stories" in order to bring clarity and visibility to their experiences—they powerfully demonstrate that bearing witness to individual manifestations of the communal problem of sexual violence is difficult and decidedly unfinished business.

"You Ain't Natural": Resituating Resistance

Since its publication, *Eva's Man* has confounded critical attempts to situate Eva within existing discourses about victimization and resistance. While the terms of public debate often force black women to identify along ungendered lines of race or along de-raced lines of gender, Eva flouts both black nationalist and many feminist definitions of victimization and resistance.[14] She challenges the violated madonna stereotype, fails to comply with the stylized sentimentality often demanded of "proper" female victims, and occupies the position of both object and agent of sacrifice. What will "such perverse ambivalence contribute," June Jordan asks, "to the understanding of black girls in need of rescue and protection?" (Jordan 1976, 37).

As the incarcerated readers struggle to situate Eva and themselves in relation to dominant narratives about victimization and agency, they suggest an implicit response to Jordan's question: narratives that accommodate ambivalence grant imprisoned women what Avery Gordon calls "the right to complex personhood." Complex personhood, Gordon explains, means that people are beset by contradiction; they are neither mere victims nor superhuman agents, they "recognize and misrecognize" themselves and others, and they variously "get stuck in the symptoms of their troubles" and "transform themselves." Furthermore, complex personhood means "that the stories people tell about themselves, about their troubles, about their social worlds, and about their society's problems are entangled and weave between what is immediately available as a story and what their imaginations are reaching toward" (Gordon 1997, 4). By highlighting how the readers recognize and misrecognize themselves in Jones's ambivalent portrait of Eva—drawing on available stories and reaching for those that do not yet exist—I want to attend to the aporias and spaces of tension in and among available stories about sexual victimization and resistance. In particular, I want to foreground some of the contradictions and self-imposed silences that result as African American women attempt to reconcile their own experiences with dominant narratives about black women's resistance.

In order to minimize the tensions between Eva's expressions of sexual desire and sexual violation, some of the incarcerated readers deem her a whore. Nicole reasons: "She went home with [Davis] the first day, and she done laid down in the bed...and he done told her all that disgusting stuff, how menstruation smells. And she still wanted to stay there and lay down and laugh about it!" Patty agrees that Eva "could be brought to submission real easy. If I walk up to you and say, 'Oh, I see it in your eyes you want me,' and then BAM!, we're in the motel, I mean, come on!" Other readers wrestle more with Jones's "real puzzling " juxtapositions of sexual victimization and sexual desire. In working to understand why Eva "didn't want to do nothing" with Davis or Tyrone but then started "having sexual feelings," Melissa seems to be seeking greater understanding of her extended sexual relationship with her cousin. "I guess I really started feeling a lot of guilt," she explains; while her friends were always talking about their boyfriends, "with me, it was always my cousin."

At another level, the readers' overall discomfort with Jones's juxtapositions of sexual desire and sexual violation highlights the extent to which communities and courts simplify—even excise—women's sexual desire in adjudicating questions of victimization and resistance. "You ain't natural," Davis accuses Eva, because her sexuality is not bounded by either a romantic or an economic contract (Jones 1976, 120).[15] Eva "ain't natural," moreover, because she de-naturalizes the desexualized image of a "proper" female victim of sexual violence. By infusing her portrait of Eva's sexual victimization with an emphasis on female sexual desire—including non-monogamous heterosexual and lesbian forms of desire—Jones demonstrates the possibility of linking the struggle against sexual violence with the struggle to expand sexual possibilities for women.[16] With its concluding scene of a sexual encounter between Eva and her cell mate, Elvira—in which Elvira says, "Tell me when it feels sweet, Eva," and Eva responds, "Now" (Jones 1976, 177)—the novel suggests that Eva's ability to speak her own sexual pleasure is a crucial aspect of her resistant agency, of her arrival in the present and her availability to a different future. As Sue says: "Where before it was like, just lay down, spread my legs and let him do it, I think this time Eva actually had a chance to voice what she thought. It was givin' her a chance to experience and find somethin' she liked."

When assessing Eva's agency and capacity for resistance, some of the incarcerated women ask the question most often raised in legal and cultural assessments of battered women's agency: Why didn't she leave? As Shelly comments, Davis Carter was not "keeping [Eva] hostage." Other women respond to this question by highlighting the grave danger of separation assault as well as some of the reasons why women have a sense of restricted agency. Maria refers to her own experiences in suggesting that Eva was suffering from "a guilt trip" with Davis because she was unaccustomed to men "being nice" to her. She was "in her own prison, within herself," Maria argues, regardless of whether she "physically could get away." Calling to mind the violent conditioning that left her psychologically shackled to her own boyfriend's demands, Tanya asserts that Eva is like a dog who refrains from urinating in the house for days, despite great need, because he knows that otherwise "you gonna beat him up" when you return.

The limitations of existing narratives about black female resistance to sexual violence emerge most clearly in comparing the reading responses of two African American readers, Audrey and Shelly. Whereas Audrey closely identifies with Eva as a model of violent resistance—which she came to see as the only way out of her own abusive situation, Shelly disdains Eva for failing to "fight back" immediately, for allowing herself to be victimized in the first place.

As Audrey tries to explain why Eva stayed in the hotel room with Davis, she emphasizes her own contradictory desires to protect herself from, and to sustain her relationship with, her extremely abusive husband. On the one hand, Audrey graphically depicts how utterly dismissed she felt when seeking legal protection from her husband:

> You go downtown, you got black eyes, you know, lip bleedin', and one of your teeth is like to rock out. They say, 'Oh well, take her by the hospital,' they don't want to even face her...one of your eyeballs is springin' out, and they're not even gonna talk to this man who done knocked it out.... Oh, he probably have to give you the little ice pack for your head, you know, might even sew your eye back in, but don't take him to jail!

On the other hand, Audrey expresses a deep sense of shame over her own lack of resolve to put an end to the relationship. She laments returning to her husband after seeking a restraining order, and she chastises herself for trying to protect him even after he severely beat her when she was five months pregnant: "My brother was wearin' his ass out and I'm sittin' there hollering like a fool, 'Leave him alone!' ...I was sick."

Audrey's admiration for Eva, who reached a point of refusal earlier than she did herself, seems evident when she describes what Davis's wife might have been thinking when she met Eva after the murder: "If I had had the nerve to do what you did, then I wouldn't have went through all of this." Audrey describes her own final resolve, "I wasn't gonna be hit no more," with considerable pride: "One night...I didn't even try to wake him up. I said, 'I'm gonna kill you, you black son of a bitch,' and I had the meat cleaver and it come down. He was grabbin' for it, and these fingers fell off in my bed, all three of 'em, and he went out that damn window, took the window stash and everything. 'Cause I had took enough, took enough, took enough." Deeply identifying with Eva, who likewise "took so much, took so much, took so much," Audrey explains that she, too, was deemed "crazy" by her community when she turned to violent resistance "because they don't think women supposed to have the nerve to strike back at the men." Furthermore, Audrey shares Eva's embrace of the Queen Bee, the novel's quasi-mythical castrating woman who allegedly causes the death of all men who love her. Citing her ability to remain "in control" and "do her own thing," Audrey literally shouts her admiration for the Queen Bee: "Queen Bee! Ooooooo, ooooooo, I wouldn't mind being her! Ohhhhh! I don't think I'd have wanted the mens to die though, but if she did kill 'em, I mean that's too bad!" Audrey's reading of *Eva's Man* thus points to her strong desire for a sense of gender solidarity with black women, while at the same time highlighting the need to develop strategies that adequately protect black women without fueling the racist criminal justice system's massive incarceration of black men.

Audrey's hearty admiration for Eva's resistance sharply contrasts with Shelly's disdain for Eva's passivity. Eva defies Shelly's conviction that black women, unlike white women, will not tolerate abuse. Capturing the almost unanimous, cross-racial sentiment that emerged in the group discussion of *Eva's Man*, Shelly asserts that a white woman "will take that abuse and take that abuse 'til she really can't take it no more" because "that's the way she's raised, to stay there and try to work it out." She argues that black women, by contrast, are "very seldomly" victims of abuse because they say, "I watched my mom get beat all her life, I'm not fittin' to get beat," or they say, "You not gonna beat me 'cause my daddy been beatin' me. I took too many beatings. I'm gonna fight you back or bust you down." When I asked whether black women always fight back, Shelly responded, "The majority. Now you have some that stays there and constantly get beat over and over and over again. But it's not many." While she empathizes with the victimization that Eva endured as a child, Shelly disdains her for mimicking white female passivity as an adult, when "she knew better than to let this man take advantage of her." Eva, who "took so much," defies Shelly's conviction that black women "won't take it" and prompts her to state: "I couldn't, I mean really, I couldn't put a name on Eva."[17]

At the same time, however, Shelly seems to be struggling to "put a name" on herself within the racialized and polarized terms of the victim/agent script, which offers few possibilities for acknowledging without shame that she, too, remained in a physically abusive relationship with her son's father.[18] On one level, Shelly seems to be speaking not from past experience, but from an intense desire for a different future, when she states: "The first time you hit a black woman, she's gonna hurt you badly and leave 'cause she's not gonna let it happen again." Embracing this narrative—which does not reflect her own experience—may function for Shelly as a sort of rhetorical willing-into-existence of that which does not yet fully exist: consistent communal valuing of black womanhood, and black women's immediate ability to recognize and to leave abusive situations.

On another level, however, Shelly's embrace of the culturally dominant narrative of heroic black female resistance leads to a form of self-silencing; she disavows in herself the vulnerability, ambivalence, and "stupidity" that she disdains in women, like Eva, who remain in situations of violence. When Shelly argues that a black woman stays in an abusive relationship "because that's what she want[s]," she seems to be seeking possibilities for naming her own experience with as little stigma as possible, by attributing more agency to black women—who want to stay—than to white women—who "know no better." Yet even this formulation disavows the pain that African American women like Shelly endure in abusive relationships; it occludes the multifaceted reasons why women remain in situations of abuse, and it renders invisible the less obvious and more partial acts of resilience and resistance that women perform in trying to make abusive relationships work. Shelly thus participates in a pattern whereby women of color's desire to maintain a sense of agency leads them to disavow the extent and the seriousness of their violent treatment, thereby reinforcing the societal denial of women of color's sexual victimization.[19]

Although Shelly disdains Eva's passive victimization, she simultaneously critiques black women such as Eva who "kill [a man] the first time…when she could have walked away." Shelly has abandoned her vow to kill any man that touches her without permission because she is "not lookin' to come back to prison." Actively forming her resolve to avoid violent resistance, she asserts, "Depending on how bad he hurt me, I would probably walk away. I would go and get the police and, knowing all the things that I know now—'cause I'm more educated than what I was when I came in here—somethin' would be done. Where one authority won't, the next one will." Shelly's new-found determination to find justice within the system, and her faith that "somethin' would be done," stand in sharp contrast to her earlier sense that black women remain silent about sexual victimization because "no one's gonna do anything." A sense of individual empowerment and renewed faith in the system will not suffice, however, to eradicate the large-scale communal problem of sexual violence. Such a task requires eliminating the imprisoning narratives and patterns of social organization that perpetuate sexual violence by occluding its prevalence and its structural underpinnings. Furthermore, eradicating sexual violence requires rendering visible the systemic nature of sexual violence in prisons themselves as well as the ways in which prisons siphon off resources that could far more effectively reduce violence by promoting economic, educational, racial, and gender equality.

As Shelly and other readers search for forms of resistance that will not lead to incarceration, they provide an important counter-narrative to unnuanced feminist calls for "fighting back." In a widely cited version of such an argument, Sharon Marcus advocates "a politics of fantasy and representation" that privileges images of women "fighting back," but her call for representations of women's resistance quickly slides into a call for physical forms of "fighting back." Critiquing anti-rape manuals that advise against resistance, and urging women to exercise their "will, agency, and capacity for violence," Marcus argues: "Simply by fighting back, we cease to be grammatically correct feminine subjects and thus become much less legible as rape targets" (Marcus 1992, 397, 396). Although she clarifies that "we should not be required to resist to prove our innocence at some later judicial date," Marcus concludes, "We should do so to serve our own immediate interests.... Clearly it is preferable to have stopped a rape attempt ourselves than to have our raped selves vindicated in court" (392).

It is the normative status of "we," of "our immediate interests," and of "clearly" that seems most troubling in juxtaposing Marcus's claim with incarcerated women's reflections about "fighting back." Her argument insufficiently contextualizes various women's parameters for exercising agency, given the multiple forms of victimization they may be negotiating. As the imprisoned readers repeatedly emphasize, the issue of fighting back is complicated by the fact that, in the words of Tanya, "The ones closest to you is the main ones...that mistreat you." For some women, preserving their chances for housing, financial support, or employment takes precedence over "fighting back." Other women who have endured years of rape by family members emphasize that fighting back is not something they can simply will themselves to do. As Maria explains, "Even now, still, I get in that little shell where it's like I just can't do anything."

Furthermore, Marcus's claim that the "grammatically correct mirror of gender" reflects back to women "images which conflate female victimization and female value" (393), and her call to imagine the female body as "a potential object of fear and agent of violence" (399) reveal her argument's grounding in a notion of white, middle-class femininity. The incarcerated readers—whose reflections have rarely appeared in the "grammatically correct mirror of gender," and whose race, class, and sexuality are all too often read as indicators of violent tendencies—necessarily view the issue of fighting back through the lenses of their race and class positionings. The pervasive cultural myth that black women will always "fight you back or bust you down" stands in tension with the women's first-hand knowledge that women of color, lower-class women, and lesbians face disproportionate punishments for aggressive behavior. As the readers repeatedly emphasize, the costs of "fighting back" in states such as North Carolina are particularly high, given the state's restrictive definition of self-defense. Sakina, a 35-year-old African American woman convicted of killing her rapist, captures some of these tensions when she states: "I promised myself that a man would never do what my father done to me. But once we start tryin' to defend ourself, it's like we back in slavery. This place right here's a slavery place.... So it's no winnin' or losin' point here."

Tamia, a 24-year-old African American woman, likewise emphasizes the inextricable links between interpersonal violence and state violence. Describing the many imprisoned women who have murdered their husbands or boyfriends, Tamia states:

> Think about all those broken bones that these women done had, all the black eyes, I mean, all the bruises and stuff, and how many times we done went to the police for help, help, help, and nobody does anything. But as soon as we get to the point where it's a life or death situation, either he dies or I die, and I end up killing him first, I get sentenced to life in prison. Okay, where's the justice in that?

Arlene fears that fighting back will lead to an entire generation of African American women spending their lives in prison. "The generation that's coming up after me, I see 'em fightin' back more," she explains. "They're not takin' it.... It's good in one way, but then in the end, it seems like the woman gets the worst. Seven times out of ten, she winds up in a place like this because she had tried to defend herself." Although Arlene says that she is "not one to take licks," her urgent message for younger women is, "Don't come here. Don't come here."

Poor, working-class, and racially marginalized women face what Angela Davis calls "surplus punishment," given the "pandemic of private punishment" and the soaring numbers of women being sent to prison, where sexualized violence "is effectively sanctioned as a routine aspect of the landscape of punishment" (Davis 1998, 344-345, 350). With their firsthand knowledge of surplus punishment, the incarcerated readers offer a powerful reminder that calls for a politics of fantasy about women's violent resistance must be contextualized in relation to the historical and material contexts in which variously situated women do and do not fight back. It is only by fully acknowledging these contexts that such a politics can be productive in pushing the boundaries of women's current social positioning.

Due to the immediacy of state violence in their lives, the incarcerated readers collectively highlight a source of resistance routinely overlooked in discussions of victimization, agency, and violence: women's efforts to interrupt cycles of violence by educating themselves, their violent partners, and/or their children about alternatives to perpetrating and enduring violence. Explaining her resolve to leave her husband after nine years of abuse, Arlene recalls how she and her siblings would be "cryin', beatin' on the door" in their attempts to save their mother from their father's violence. "I wasn't goin' through it," she finally decided, "and I wasn't havin' my son go through it." She describes her subsequent twenty-year relationship with another man as a long, often painful process—which included a six-month prison term for her partner—of teaching him an alternative to "that fight thing." He eventually "got the message," Arlene explains. "Keep your hands to yourself so I don't wind up comin' to prison for killin' you!" She has also tried to teach her sons to keep their hands to themselves, reminding them, "This woman is somebody's child, somebody's daughter, and think about if you have kids, if you want somebody abusing your children."

For Audrey, who witnessed her father stab her mother in the head nine times during a routine incidence of abuse, violence has been the controlling feature of her life narrative. She defiantly declares, however, "The cycle stops with me," and she proudly recounts her daughter's rewriting of a life script potentially filled with violence: "Let me tell you what my daughter did.... She brought that boy['s] clothes home to that boy's mama, sure did, took that boy's stuff and told her, 'Miss [X], I don't want your son no more.' Said, 'Here go his stuff. You can go get him, 'cause I tried to tell him to come off, but he [wouldn't and he] ain't livin' with me no more.'"

In their attempts to grapple with questions of victimization, agency, and violence, both the incarcerated readers and *Eva's Man* itself thus perform crucial work in contributing to, and underscoring the need for, theorizations of resistant agency that accommodate the complexity of women's lives: the tangled interplay of sexual desires and desires for protection from violence; the manifold reasons why women of all races sometimes remain in situations of violence; the many forms that resistance can take in the midst of victimization; and the difficulty of finding adequate means to resist violence without contributing to its vicious cycle.

Prison Narratives, Narrative Prisons

Shelly's statement, "I couldn't put a name on Eva," calls to mind Eva's reading of Davis's wife and captures how Jones's uncanny portrait provides opportunities for rendering strange our foregone conclusions, for fostering receptivity to new ways of seeing what remains occluded in reified patterns of thinking about women, crime, and violence. In exploring incarcerated women's complex processes of identifying and dis-identifying with Eva, I have argued that their readings generate fundamentally important insights about the complex personhood of women in prison. First, in their attempts to contextualize Eva's violence in relation to cumulative experiences of interpersonal and social violence, the imprisoned women underscore our ongoing, pressing need to develop cultural and legal frameworks that remain absolutely attentive, rather than "absolutely blind," to the systemic, socially sanctioned forms of violence that lead women to become violent themselves.

Second, the incarcerated women's insistent emphases on the many ways in which their own and Eva's stories of victimization have been silenced, and their active, resilient efforts to give shape and name to these experiences, counter-balance theorists' increasing tendency—given the risk of reifying female victimhood—to underaddress questions of victimization. Drawing attention to the profound ways in which gender, sexuality, race, and class impact the social disavowal or legitimization of victimization, the imprisoned readers highlight socially marginalized women's continuing need to bear witness to, and to reckon with, their experiences of victimization. Moreover, the readers demand a far more substantive cultural and legal response to the subjective manifestations of social and structural forms of wounding.

Third, in struggling to parse out Eva's status as object and subject of violence, the incarcerated women both emphasize the need for, and help to cultivate, narratives that can attend simultaneously to variously situated women's sexual desires and pleasures, to their acts of resistant agency and resilience, and to their profound experiences of victimization. Furthermore, in foregrounding how extra-legal forms of "fighting back" all too often lead poor women and women of color to the violent space of the prison, the imprisoned women issue a powerful call for feminists to keep state violence at the forefront of our theoretical consciousness.

In generating these insights, the incarcerated readers and *Eva's Man* itself also draw attention to the role that fictional representation can play in challenging reductive legal frameworks for reading lawbreaking women's experiences. In Renee Heberle's view, the movement against sexual violence should find alternatives to its dependence on the legal system, rather than "normalizing strategies of representation that fit the needs of the legal system." For instance, Heberle argues, feminist efforts to move away from depictions of women as victims "will not help" in the legal context since "the law needs victims in order to render justice" (Heberle 1996, 74). The incarcerated readers nonetheless serve as flesh-and-blood representatives of the concrete material effects that ensue from legal representations of victimization, violence, and agency. In the words of Toni Morrison, the oppressive language of the legal system "does more than represent violence; it is violence; does more than represent the limits of knowledge; it limits knowledge" (Morrison 1993). Generating more complex, compassionate, and accurate representations of women whose lives are encircled by violence thus seems crucial for challenging the descriptive thinness and epistemological violence of dominant legal narratives. By attending to incarcerated women's readings of *Eva's Man*—by "looking to the bottom" and "adopting the perspective of those who have seen and felt the falsity of the liberal promise"— feminists can help to redefine the elements of justice and translate women's concrete experiences into forms that courts of law and public opinion might recognize (Matsuda 1995, 63). Likewise, by grappling with the "perverse ambivalence" of *Eva's Man*, we can begin to free our theoretical and legal imaginations from the narrative prisons that circumscribe current thinking about lawbreaking women.

If we allow these prison narratives to haunt us, as Avery Gordon suggests, "in the name of a will to heal" (Gordon 1997, 57), we might begin to *see anew* women involved in crime. By illuminating how individual trauma and violence relate to trouble at the level of the system, and by reminding us that things "could have been and can be otherwise," the incarcerated women's readings of *Eva's Man* call us to halt our escalating efforts to render social problems invisible by disappearing the damaged, dispossessed, and dispensable behind prison walls.

Notes

[1] Although African American women represent the most rapidly expanding group of prison inmates, crime statistics are typically broken down by race or by sex, but not by both, and it remains difficult to find basic statistical information about black women's participation in crime. The Bureau of Justice Statistics began to provide data broken down by gender and race in 1992, but the Uniform Crime Reports still do not provide such data.

[2] See, for example, Crenshaw 1995, Richie 1996, Davis 1997, Davis 1998, and James 2000. Since its inception in 2000, Incite! Women of Color against Violence has sponsored a yearly conference and numerous initiatives designed to end violence against women of color and their communities. For trenchant analyses of the frequent elision of black women in cultural and legal debate about violence against women, see Crenshaw 1992 and Williams 1997.

[3] This formulation was made famous in the 1982 anthology edited by Gloria T. Hull, Patricia Bell Scott, and Barbara Smith, *All the Women Are White, and All The Blacks Are Men, But Some of Us Are Brave: Black Women's Studies*.

[4] This larger project explores seventeen incarcerated women's readings of a range of texts about women and crime—from "true crime" books to Toni Morrison's *Paradise*—as sources of theoretical intervention into current debates about gender, crime, violence, and punishment. I solicited interviewees for the project by posting fliers in the housing units of the North Carolina Correctional Institution for Women, which invited women to participate in group discussions and individual interviews about books relating to women and crime. Each interviewee participated in six group discussions, an individual life history interview, and two individual interviews focusing on their practices of reading true crime books.

[5] The breakdown of criminal charges is as follows: 6 second-degree murder, 3 drug sales, 2 armed robbery, 1 first-degree murder and arson and conspiracy, and 1 attempted child molestation.

[6] My reading here is informed by Avery Gordon's discussion of haunting in *Ghostly Matters: Haunting and the Sociological Imagination*.

[7] Three of the interviewees were involved in the death of an abusive spouse or sexually violent acquaintance, and five have seriously injured their partners during episodes of abuse.

[8] I use pseudonymous first names in referring to the incarcerated women in order to preserve the interviewees' anonymity and to suggest the informality of the book club setting. Several of the women chose their own pseudonyms at the beginning of the study. In transcribing the prisoners' testimony, I used spellings that convey as precisely as possible the particular cadence of women's speech. I side with scholars who argue that the political importance of representing subjects' speech as accurately as possible outweighs the risk of emphasizing non-standard or grammatically incorrect aspects of their speech.

[9] During an interview with Claudia Tate, Jones emphasizes Eva's strategic elusiveness: "The question the listener would continually hear would be: how much of Eva's story is true, and how much is deliberately not true, that is, how much of a game is she playing with her listeners, psychiatrists, and others?" (Jones 1983, 91).

[10] In his appellate opinion supporting the death sentence of Aileen Wuornos—a woman executed by the state of Florida in 2002—Florida Supreme Court Justice Gerald Kogan stated: "Some might characterize trials such as Wuornos' as social awareness cases, because Wuornos herself unquestionably has been victimized throughout her life.... Nevertheless, 'social awareness' does not dispose of the strictly legal issues, beyond which this Court must be absolutely blind."

[11] I take my subheading from Carole Maso's novel, *Defiance*, in which the protagonist writes: "How to purge the horror. Not possible. At best to give it shape and name" (Maso 1998, 125).

[12] Jones states in a 1982 interview that, ideally, Eva wouldn't even have talked to the psychiatrist, but their interactions were necessary for the plot of the novel (qtd. in Wilcox 1996, 72).

[13] Heberle is building on Sharon Marcus's argument that "the need to define rape and to assert its existence can distract us from plotting its vanishing point." See Marcus 1992, 399.

[14] See Dubey 1994 for further discussion of the text's flouting of feminist and black nationalist aesthetic demands.

[15] See also Hengehold 2000.

[16] Legal theorist Katherine M. Franke notes that women's right to enjoy their own body is entirely absent from feminist legal arguments about violence against women. See Franke 2001.

[17] Shelly's inability to classify Eva calls to mind the closing line of June Jordan's review of *Eva's Man*: "Who is she?" (Jordan 1976, 37), as well as Davis's question to Eva, "Who are you? Where did you come from?" (Jones 1976, 20).

[18] See Ammons 1995.

[19] Black women are far less likely than white women to report rapes and to seek support services and counseling. See Minow 1993.

Works Cited

Ammons, Linda. 1995. "Mules, Madonnas, Babies, Bathwater, Racial Imagery and Stereotypes: The African-American Woman and the Battered Woman Syndrome." *Wisconsin Law Review* 5: 1003-1080.

Crenshaw, Kimberlé Williams. 1992. "Whose Story is it, Anyway? Feminist and Antiracist Appropriations of Anita Hill." *Race-ing Justice, En-gendering Power: Essays on Anita Hill, Clarence Thomas, and the Construction of Social Reality*. Ed. Toni Morrison. New York: Pantheon Books. 402-440.

———. 1995. "Mapping the Margins: Intersectionality, Identity Politics, and Violence Against Women of Color." *Critical Race Theory: The Key Writings That Formed the Movement*. Ed. Kimberle Crenshaw, Neil Gotanda, Gary Peller, and Kendall Thomas. New York: The New York Press. 357-383.

Daniels, Cynthia. 1997. "Between Fathers and Fetuses: The Social Construction of Male Reproduction and the Politics of Fetal Harm." *Signs: Journal of Women in Culture and Society* 22.3 (Spring): 570-616.

Davis, Angela. 1997. "Race and Criminalization." *The House That Race Built*. Ed. Wahneema Lubiano. New York: Vintage Books. 264-279.

———. 1998. "Public Imprisonment and Private Violence: Reflections on the Hidden Punishment of Women." *New England Journal on Criminal and Civil Confinement* 24 (Summer): 339-351.

Dershowitz, Alan M. 1994. *The Abuse Excuse and Other Cop-Outs, Sob Stories, and Evasions of Responsibility*. Boston: Little, Brown and Company.

Dixon, Melvin. 1984. "Singing a Deep Song: Language as Evidence in the Novels of Gayl Jones." *Black Women Writers: A Critical Evaluation*. Ed. Mari Evans. Garden City, NY: Anchor Press.

Dubey, Madhu. 1994. "Don't You Explain Me." *Black Women Novelists and the Nationalist Aesthetic*. Bloomington: Indiana University Press. 89-105.

Franke, Katherine M. 2001. "Theorizing Yes: An Essay on Feminism, Law, and Desire." *The Columbia Law Review* 101 (Jan.): 181-208.

Gordon, Avery. 1997. *Ghostly Matters: Haunting and the Sociological Imagination*. Minneapolis: University of Minnesota Press.

Heberle, Renee. 1996. "Deconstructive Strategies and the Movement Against Sexual Violence." *Hypatia: A Journal of Feminist Philosophy* 11.4 (Fall): 63-76.

Hengehold, Laura. 2000. "Remapping the Event: Institutional Discourses and the Trauma of Rape." *Signs: Journal of Women in Culture and Society* 26.1 (Autumn): 189-214.

Hull, Gloria T, Patricia Bell Scott, and Barbara Smith, eds. 1982. *All the Women Are White, and All The Blacks Are Men, but Some of Us Are Brave: Black Women's Studies*. Old Westbury, NY: Feminist Press.

James, Joy, ed. 2000. *States of Confinement: Policing, Detention and Prisons*. New York: St. Martin's Press.

Jones, Gayl. 1976. *Eva's Man*. Boston: Beacon Press.

———. 1983. "Gayl Jones." Interview by Claudia Tate. *Black Women Writers at Work*. Ed. Claudia Tate. New York: Continuum. 89-99.

Jordan, June. 1976. "All About Eva." *New York Times Book Review* 16 May: 37.

Marcus, Sharon. 1992. "Fighting Bodies, Fighting Words: A Theory and Politics of Rape Prevention." *Feminists Theorize the Political*. Ed. Judith Butler and Joan W. Scott. New York: Routledge. 385-403.

Maso, Carole. 1998. *Defiance*. New York: Penguin Books.

Matsuda, Mari. 1995. "Looking to the Bottom: Critical Legal Studies and Reparations." *Critical Race Theory: The Key Writings That Formed the Movement*. Ed. Kimberlé Crenshaw, Neil Gotanda, Gary Peller, and Kendall Thomas. New York: The New Press. 63-79.

Minow, Martha. 1993. "Surviving Victim Talk." *UCLA Law Review* 40 (August): 1411-1445.

Morrison, Toni. 1993. The Nobel Lecture in Literature. The Nobel Foundation, Stockholm. 7 Dec.

Richie, Beth. 1996. *Compelled to Crime: The Gender Entrapment of Battered Black Women*. New York: Routledge.

Wilcox, Janelle. 1996. "Resistant Silence, Resistant Subject: (Re)Reading Gayl Jones's *Eva's Man*." *Genders* 23 (30 June): 72-87.

Williams, Patricia. 1997. "American Kabuki." *Birth of a Nation'hood: Gaze, Script, and Spectacle in the O.J. Simpson Case*. Ed. Toni Morrison and Claudia Brodsky Lacour. New York: Pantheon Books. 273-292.

Wilson, James Q. 1995. "Crime and Public Policy." *Crime: Twenty-eight Leading Experts Look at the Most Pressing Problem of Our Time*. Ed. James Q. Wilson and Joan Petersilia. San Francisco: Institute for Contemporary Studies.

Wuornos v. State. 1994. 644 So.2d 1000 (Fla.).

CHAPTER NINE

Unsilencing Lesbianism in the Early Fiction of Gayl Jones

Thomas Fahy

> There have also been more responses to the sexuality, or the "neurotic sensuality" in [my] books, than to the lesbianism. I don't recall the lesbianism entering into any critical discussions except as an overall part of the sexual picture.
> —Gayl Jones in an interview with Claudia Tate (1979)

> In contrast, an author like Gayl Jones, who has not been associated with or seemingly influenced by the feminist movement, has portrayed Lesbians quite negatively.
> —Barbara Smith, *Wild Women in the Whirlwind* (1990)

Black feminist criticism has not always lived up to its claim to examine the various ways race, gender, and sexuality intersect to oppress black women.[1] As Valerie Smith notes in "Black Feminist Theory and the Representation of the 'Other,'"

> No doubt because it has remained marginal, what has been primarily a heterosexual, Afro-American-centered feminist discourse has been concerned with refining its own mode of inquiry, perhaps at the expense of annexing itself to the experiences of "others" such as lesbians and other women of color. (50)

Yet the impact of this ambiguous and sometimes exclusionary relationship to lesbianism has not fully been evaluated. Critical discussions of Gayl Jones's fiction, in particular, reveal a conspicuous silence about same-sex desire. This can arguably be attributed to Jones's heterosexuality, her complex portrayal of black women's sexuality, and the fact that her first publications, which coincided with the formation of black feminist criticism, got caught in a crossfire of anxieties about the image and place of lesbianism in this critical discourse.

Focusing on works by Barbara Smith and Ann Allen Shockley, critics who were central in establishing the terms of lesbian-informed readings in black feminist discourse, this essay begins by arguing that early black feminist criticism discouraged queer readings of Gayl Jones. Since the publication of this scholarship, critics have neglected the queer dimensions of her fiction[2]—despite Jones's remarks about this omission in a 1979 interview with Claudia Tate: "I don't recall the lesbianism entering into any critical discussions" (146). Even though lesbianism does not appear in her most recent novels, *The Healing* and *Mosquito*, it unquestionably shapes the identities of her female characters in earlier works. As a way of redressing this silence about the queer elements of Jones's narratives, I will examine the discourses of same-sex desire in *White Rat*, *Eva's Man*, and *Corregidora*. The women in these works are restricted, in part, by a society that impedes homosexual articulation; as a result, they try to find solutions for the problem of speech through storytelling, sexualized talk, song, and meaningful silences. Because speech and silence have different meanings at different times, they can express a wide range of sexual experiences, and this spectrum of possibilities is cultivated by women conflicted about their own desires. In this way, Jones contributes to a black lesbian political project by both giving voice to sexual identities that have been stifled by heterosexism and challenging her readers (and some of her characters) to question a dichotomous understanding of sexuality.

"Alternative to Loneliness": Women Who Love Women in *White Rat*

Considered one of the foundational works in black feminism, Barbara Smith's "Toward a Black Feminist Criticism" highlights the ways various oppressions, including homophobia, intersect and devalue the work of black women in the twentieth century.[3] Her essay also offers a reading of Toni Morrison's *Sula* that empowers lesbian perspectives by making woman-identified readings (and arts) an integral part of black feminist discourse. When revisiting this project in a later work, "The Truth That Never Hurts: Black Lesbians in Fiction in the 1980s," Smith examines the slowly growing acceptance of lesbian writings in public and academic circles but questions the contributions of heterosexual critics: "Black feminist critics who are Lesbians can usually be counted upon to approach Black women's and Black Lesbian writing non-homophobically. Non-Lesbian Black feminist critics are not as dependable [...and those] who are homophobic [...] ignore Lesbian existence entirely" (239). By questioning the contributions of non-lesbian critics, Smith reinforces an essentialist binary that enables her to reject certain depictions of lesbianism, and this can lead to simplified or summary conclusions.

Smith's reading of Gayl Jones's works offers a useful example of this problem. After specifically criticizing Jones for "[portraying] Lesbians quite negatively" (217), Smith calls for positive representations of black lesbians in literature:

> By positive I do not mean characters without problems, contradictions, or flaws, mere uplift literature for Lesbians, but, instead, writing that is sufficiently sensitive and complex, which places Black Lesbian experience and struggles squarely within the realm of recognizable human experience and concerns. (222)

Yet the phrase "recognizable human experience" begs the question: recognizable for whom? In other words, Smith claims to embrace characters with problems and flaws, yet dismisses Jones for having exactly these types of characters. Arguably, this exclusion comes from the fact that Jones's characters are messy. They often feel conflicted about homosexual desire or vacillate between heterosexuality and homosexuality. But Jones's message is exactly that—people are messy. Suffering and uncertainty transform us. They change our perception of the world and ask us to question society, sexuality, and the self. As I will show, Jones intentionally embraces this "mess" in order to suggest greater possibilities for sexual desire. This strategy is also overlooked by critic Ann Allen Shockley, who offers a dismissive and simplistic reading of Jones in "The Black Lesbian in American Literature: An Overview." She ignores the character of Cat in *Corregidora* and the fact that *Eva's Man* culminates in a sexual act between two women. She also disregards the short fiction "Persona" in one sentence: "The story is murky and extremely subtle, as if the author was afraid to touch it with a heavy pen" (139). Once again, this response seems to be motivated by Jones's refusal to produce both "positive" images of lesbians and characters who can easily be identified as either lesbian or heterosexual.

The complexity of Jones's characters is nowhere more evident than in their struggles with language. Numerous stories in *White Rat*, a collection of short fiction published in 1977, depict black women who search for ways to express same-sex desire. The pressures of heteronormativity—which Cathy Cohen defines as "those localized practices and those centralized institutions which legitimize and privilege heterosexuality and heterosexual relationships as fundamental and 'natural' within society" (440)—force many of these women to communicate in a discourse of silence. In "The Women," a coming-of-age story about a girl, Winnie, who struggles with her own sexuality in light of her mother's lesbian relationships, women have to choose between a language that demeans homosexuality and silence. Gertrude, Winnie's mother, refers to her ex-lovers as "bitch's whores," and Winnie calls her friend Retta a "queer donut" after she expresses desire for other girls. She specifically responds to her own ambiguous desires by vituperating homosexuality: "I ain' going to be like my mama when I grow up. I ain' goin' to be a bitch's whore" (43). Clearly, Gertrude's relationships with women, as well as her failed marriage, offer Winnie a problematic model of sexuality. As Keith Byerman explains in *Fingering the Jagged Grain: Tradition and Form in Recent Black Fiction*,

> All the mother's relationships go through cycles of devotion and hostility [...and when Winnie] accidentally sees her mother passionately kissing another woman [...] it forces on her a full awareness of her mother's behavior which, combined with the derogatory comments about lesbians she has heard from her girlfriends and their parents, leads her to a renunciation of such a life for herself. (175)

Furthermore, she makes this renunciation even though her sexual experience in the story is limited to one childhood episode, when she and Retta masturbate each other in bed: "'You doin' it. ' 'Cept we dif'rent. We *little* girls. When you get titties you ain't suppose to let a girl do it. That mean you queer. I an't goin' be queer' " (41). This passage presents heterosexuality as a learned behavior and homosexuality as a natural one—something that can be done in secret until adulthood. This experimentation is acceptable, in part, because society does not think that children have sexual desires; but ultimately, since Winnie doesn't have a language that validates same-sex desire (only a language to demean it), she degrades it publicly. In other words, this rejection of lesbianism occurs on a linguistic level, for if no positive discourse exists, then she must reject it: "I ain't goin' be queer" (41).

Believing she has no other alternative, Winnie feels forced into heterosexual relationships, and later in her life, she becomes silent. When she meets Garland, he describes her unusual behavior in terms that play with the dual meanings of "queer" (homosexual and strange): "Don't talk to boys. Don't talk to girls neither. You kinda funny, but don't know what kind of funny" (45). She is caught between two sexual polarities that have been constructed by the available discourse—one socially acceptable, the other deviant. Similarly, when Retta's mother attributes the homosexual behavior she has witnessed at her job to an unnatural, gender-segregated environment, Gertrude remains silent:

> "You know women hugging on each other. Guess when you in a sit'ation where you ain't got nothing else, like them prisons too you hear about, you get that way. But it just ain't right. I don't think it's right. Do you think it's right?"
>
> My mama don't say nothing. (39)

This silence denies the type of social validation that typically privileges heterosexuality and prevents Retta's mother from labeling different sexual identities as either "right" or "wrong." In this example and throughout these stories, lesbians often choose silence because language is used against them ("it just ain't right."). As a result, silent physical affection becomes a safe form of communication, and Jones uses this to suggest that some communication between women, especially lesbians, exists beyond words. Fanny Bean, for example, "would smile at me but never speak" (30). And Winnie's experience with the girls who smoke in the bathroom is one of silent understanding and communication: "Me and milk coffee, who say her name was Shirley [...] didn't say anything to each other, just sat on the fence and watched the people that passed by. Then when the bell rang we went different ways to our lockers to get our books" (47).

Though silence offers some degree of resistance for both Gertrude and Winnie, Jones also recognizes its limitations and is critical of silence that simply reinforces assumed dichotomies between heterosexual and queer. The value of silence for lesbians is limited because it is not a discourse that can change socially constructed attitudes about lesbianism. As Cheryl Clarke explains in "Lesbianism: an Act of Resistance": "I, for one, identify a woman as a lesbian who says she is. Lesbianism is a recognition, an awakening" (128). "Women" suggests the same need for an active recognition and articulation of lesbian identity. The silence and mystery surrounding Gertrude's sexuality has fostered only distrust and revulsion in her daughter. What Winnie doesn't understand (because this point is actively suppressed) is that a wider range of sexual identities exists and that acknowledging lesbianism should not require a rejection of heterosexuality.

Jones further criticizes such rigid categories by questioning the notion of natural desire in "Persona." This story, whose title refers to the mask of heterosexuality that lesbian women feel pressured to wear, presents the failure of silence to help black lesbians break free from the categories that restrict them. Miss King, the narrator, is a teacher at a female college who not only prevents herself from expressing sexual attraction for other women but also acquiesces to the school's attempts to stifle such desires in others: "At the freshman lecture the psychiatrist told them they would experience sexual ambiguity here. [...] But it was natural [...] most would feel it, attachments to each other, the process of growing up. They'd break away. Many young girls thought they were...worried about their sexuality but [...]. Things would even out" (86). In effect, this introductory lecture preempts any discussion about sexuality by using scientific authority to persuade the incoming class that lesbian desire is a natural, but temporary, feeling. Since it will "even out," these women are being "taught" to disregard homosexuality as a lasting possibility. Once again, Jones shows us how confused the language of "natural" desire is; like Retta's and Winnie's conversation in "Women," this lecture calls the category of "natural" into question. In these settings, heterosexuality seems to be completely *un*natural—it is something these women feel pressured to accept.

Jones also links this idea of natural desire to silence, suggesting that the latter allows homosexuality to remain invisible. Miss King achieves this invisibility, in part, by preventing herself from speaking. Throughout the story, she thinks, "I started to say something but didn't" (91). Even though she wants to "say something" (91), she never does, and she even prevents other women from doing the same. When Jean Gant suggests that the school do away with the freshman lecture, Miss King sits in silence, implying that she too equates the natural with the heterosexual. In another example, as Susan begins to talk about the hardships of her personal life, King deflects the topic: " 'Yeah, the classes are okay. Hers is anyway. Academically, I don't have any complaints, but…Maybe you'll learn to like it here. The first year anyplace takes adjustments. Even if you were at a coeducational college' " (89-90). The narrator's reference to a coeducational college mimics the attitudes and beliefs of the earlier lecture, dismissing the girl's concerns about her own sexual desires. Miss King's discomfort with and inability to talk about her sexuality are further reflected in the characteristics she attributes to another student, Gretta: "silent," "uncomfortable," and having knees "so close together." These descriptions represent her own inability to access other women and speak about desire.[4]

Silence, as this story illustrates, also reveals the need lesbian women have for acknowledgment—a need to be seen and recognized—and Jones suggests that finding a voice is a crucial first step. The text closes several years later with an image of the narrator forcing Susan (her current lover) to look at her: "I stared at her. She looked as if she didn't see me. I put my hand in her short hair and made her look at me" (94). For Miss King, this act of looking communicates her unspoken need to be recognized and constitutes a silent rejection of heteronormativity. Susan, however, goes one step further and speaks some of her desires, offering a partial model for lesbian expression. Her sexual relationship with the narrator is characterized by verbal openness, and the story suggests that Susan has come to terms with her lesbianism through language. In many ways, her ability to articulate sexual desire for another woman has enabled her to recognize her own desires.

"Pretending the Floor Was the Ceiling": Unspoken Desire in *Eva's Man*

Most of the relationships in Eva's (the protagonist's) life are defined by violence, alienation, or self-loathing, with one exception—her great-grandmother's love for a gypsy named Medina. After kissing Medina's palm, Great Grandmother tells her husband that they will never have sex again because she doesn't love him: "She said she never knew how he was going to love her now" (50).[5] For Eva, who has been imprisoned for the murder and castration of her lover Davis, Great Grandmother's passion for Medina is the only positive model she has for expressing desire and achieving love. Yet, as seems fitting in the context of Eva's refusal to speak to police and psychiatrists, the love between Great Grandmother and Medina never occurs through language. This silent model for homosexual expression may be positive, but Eva's attempts to mimic it fail, in part, because she has been imprisoned by heteronormativity. Throughout the text, Eva is held captive by different spaces—a hotel room with Davis and a cell with Elvira—that represent opposing sexual identities. This binary between heterosexual and homosexual is so rigid that it pressures Eva into silence about her own sexual ambivalence. It doesn't enable her to use the story of Great Grandmother's love as a starting point for exploring her own ambiguous desires.

Eva sees other women trapped by heteronormativity, and they too suppress the language of same-sex desire to adhere to social norms. When Eva and her mother visit Billie and Charlotte, for example, Charlotte confides in Eva that "Mama keeps asking me when am I going to get a man. [...] I don't want a man" (89). This statement is the furthest Charlotte can go in expressing her attraction to other women, and her quiet resistance to marriage only exacerbates her mother's pressure on her to "make generations." The pressure to procreate is also, according to Madhu Dubey, a nod to the heterosexual imperatives of Black Nationalist discourse. Black Nationalist ideologies, she observes, "defined black feminine identity within a heterosexual and reproductive frame that reinscribed the white U.S. bourgeois ideology they set out to subvert" (13). Charlotte is clearly a victim of these ideologies, and, in effect, this pressure prevents her from expressing sexual desire for other women. She can only act upon her desire in secret:

> She touched my waist and said that I had a little waist. She kept her hand on my waist. [...] She pulled a mat from the corner and lay down on it. 'There's room for two people.'[...] Charlotte took my finger and put it in her mouth. She said she was showing me what the little girl did. I pulled my finger out. (90, 99)

At the same time, however, Eva doesn't fully embrace heterosexual norms, often using silence to respond to questions about her attitude toward men. For example, she repeatedly reminds Alfonso, who questions her about the men in the bar, that she is self-sufficient:

"I'm not looking for nobody."

"Yes you are. You lookin for the meat and gravy, only I ain't the right meat and gravy."

"I didn't say I was looking. [...] I said nothing." (72-73)

Eva uses gender-neutral terms and silence to describe sexual interest, suggesting some level of sexual ambivalence. To escape the pressures of making generations and being in an actively heterosexual relationship, she marries James Hunn, whom she perceives as a father-figure. At one point, Moses Tripp says to her "The onliest reason you married the nigger was because he was safe. [...] You wouldn't've married me. [...] I ain't safe" (165). Tripp charges her with being afraid to marry a "real" man, but this safety is not necessarily a successful alternative to lesbianism. It does not mitigate her struggles with heterosexuality, as illustrated by the descriptions of her passionless and precarious sex life with James: "When James first laid me down in the bed, he kept saying over and over again that things was all right. I couldn't tell whether he was telling himself or me. I screamed up at him, 'Why didn't you kill *her* then!'" (164). She has no language for desire, and what she uses is flawed and out-of-place. The pronoun "her" remains unclear in the text but could refer to herself or her genitals. In any case, these words clearly reflect a violent resistance to heterosexual sex, not pleasure.

In addition to this type of flawed language, the women throughout Jones's texts also limit their own sexual possibilities by using violent language learned from men. Eva's fragmented identity can be attributed, in part, to the ways that she has appropriated other men's language and stories. When she first fends off the advances of Moses Tripp, she thinks "I didn't give a shit what his name was, I was thinking in the kind of language Alfonso would use" (97). This type of male discourse typically links violence and sex throughout the novel, and Eva buys into this, in part, because silence doesn't protect her from the aggressiveness of others. Eva, therefore, resorts to violence when silence fails, assaulting both the doctor who wants her to explain her actions and Elvira, who wants her as a lover. After Elvira tells Eva, "We got some in here, you know, that's that kind. Cause if you wont someone to stroke it for you, there's them that will," Eva thinks: "Stuff a sausage up her ass. [...] Finger up her raw ass" (154-155). These violent images of sexual violation suggest that Eva inextricably links sex and violence. With both men and women, she feels sex is something forced on her, and this prevents her from articulating either heterosexual or homosexual desire.

Though Eva's silences empower her throughout much of the story—"by controlling what she will and will not tell, [Eva] maintains her autonomy. Her silences are also ways of maintaining this autonomy"[6]—her attempts to find a language for desire do not work. When she decides to have a sexual experience with Elvira at the end of the novel, she explains: "I leaned back, squeezing her face between my legs, and told her, 'Now'" (177). To some extent, choosing to have sex with another woman has given her the power to speak. At the same time, the command "Now" is an assertion of power, not desire. Once again language fails her. Throughout the story, Eva seems incapable of (and uninterested in) being emotionally tied to anyone, and defensive aggression replaces her desire. If we see this willingness to have a lesbian encounter as reflecting her own inclination, then it is her need to see relationships as antagonistic that keeps her from experiencing it. In other words, this final scene represents Eva's impulse to have the kind of intimacy enjoyed by her great-grandmother, while marking her failure to achieve it within the masculine language that she uses to keep the world at bay.

"They Never Let You Live It Down": Ursa's Homophobia

Throughout *Corregidora*, Jones explores several discourses that reinforce as well as undermine homophobia: 1) storytelling, 2) silence, 3) homophobic language, 4) sexualized talk, and 5) the blues. The novel begins with Ursa, a blues singer, being attacked by her drunken husband. The assault kills her unborn child and leaves her barren. Subsequently, Tadpole McCormick, the owner of Happy's Café, and Cat Lawson, the neighborhood hairdresser and Ursa's friend, begin taking care of Ursa. Cat, "a smooth-complexioned [...] and young-looking" woman (14), first appears as an affectionate mother figure who cooks Ursa meals, gives her a place to stay for several days, and offers good, but painfully honest, advice about her relationship with Tad. Ursa suddenly ends their friendship and refuses to speak to her, however, when she discovers that Cat is a lesbian who is sexually attracted to her. This rejection eventually forces Cat out of the community, transforming her into a debilitated and isolated figure who literally vanishes from the narrative.[7]

Like Billie in *Eva's Man*, the Corregidora women pass on a history by "making generations" (having children), yet the pressure to do so essentially removes sexual desire and pleasure. Ursa's mother, for example, uses Martin to get pregnant: "she wanted only the memory to keep for her own but not his fussy body, not the man himself. Almost as if she'd gone out to get that man to have me and then didn't need him, because they'd been telling her so often what she should do" (101). Since sex is solely a means for procreation,[8] it negates her own sexual desires. Ursa also feels emotionally stagnant because her family has "squeezed Corregidora into [her]" (103). When Tad asks her what she wants, for example, she responds: "What all us Corregidora women want. Have been taught to want. To make generations" (22). Her own desires and thoughts have been subsumed by the matriarchy of her family and the history of slavery; they have transformed sex into an act without feeling for the sole purpose of creating a living historical record.

Jones specifically links Ursa's stifled desires with Cat Lawson's lesbianism to criticize the way society has conditioned lesbian women to abnegate their own sexual desires. As illustrated by Ursa's rejection of Cat and her violent reaction to Jeffy, her use of homophobic discourse reflects Ursa's own inability to escape the heterosexual/homosexual binary that "making generations" has imprinted on her psyche. Ursa's alignment with heterosexual imperatives, like her desire to "make generations," has led her to destroy Cat.

Because of the social stigma associated with homosexuality, Cat is forced to adopt a discourse of silence. She is afraid to talk about homosexuality because of the ways society responds to it: "'They say Jeffy's daddy, something was wrong with him.'" Ursa also labels homosexuality a sickness: "'You ask me, something must be wrong with all of 'em'" (43). Earlier in the novel, she can ignore Cat's ambiguous references to lesbianism—"'That'd make you go through more, not having a man.' [...] I went on as if I hadn't heard it" (44-45)—but once Cat's sexuality is explicitly revealed, Ursa feels threatened:

> [Cat]: "You don't know what it's like to feel foolish all day in a white woman's kitchen and then have to come home and feel foolish in the bed at night with your man. I wouldn't mind the other so much if I didn't have to feel like a fool in the bed with my man. [...]"
>
> She wanted me to tell her that I knew what it was like, but I wouldn't tell her. Yes, I know what it feels like. [...] She was waiting for an embrace I refused to give. [...] I wouldn't look up at her. (64-66)

Eve Sedgwick explains that this type of reaction to "coming out" is not uncommon: "The double-edged potential for injury in the scene of gay coming out [...] results partly from the fact that the erotic identity of the person who receives the disclosure is apt also to be implicated in, hence perturbed by it" (81). To some extent, Ursa rejects Cat to prevent the community from making any possible association between them. She would rather deal with gossip about her and Tad than risk being labeled a lesbian. Fully aware of the social stigmas associated with coming out, Cat finally has to ask Ursa to remain quiet: "they never let you live it down" (66). She soon moves and never appears in the novel again. When Ursa hears about her at the end of the text, Cat has "[let] herself look her age" (176) and been deformed by an industrial accident. This accident reinforces her isolation by de-feminizing her—leaving her bald and disfigured.

Moreover, because the women in *Corregidora* use male language to talk about sex, they lack an effective discourse for desire. On one level, Ursa and Cat use "male" discourse in a way that exposes language as an inadequate medium for female expressions of sexual desire. It is defined by sexually explicit, often derogatory language and the language of possession.[9] Ursa's mother, for example, describes the sinister quality of male language: "I kept expecting him to be like the other mens was, and say real evil, 'You got a mouth, ain't you bitch? I know you can talk' " (114). More explicitly, Ursa tells Mutt that her language during sex came from him: "You taught me what Corregidora taught Great Gram. He taught her to use the kind of words she did. [...] 'You fucking me, bastard' " (76). This language clearly puts women in a passive role. "A man always says I want to fuck, a woman always has to say I want to get fucked" (89). Having no agency in this equation, women are given no room to articulate desire. This passive linguistic construction of fucking and being fucked, therefore, inhibits the possibility of other sexual identities because it does not enable women to have agency.

To move beyond the limitations of heterosexist language, the discourse of music offers a possibility for same-sex desire. The blues is often an art form that articulates oppression and suffering. As Ursa explains, the blues "helps me explain what I can't explain" (56). It gives voice to silenced desires—desires subsumed by male discourses: "[My Mama] listened, but it was a quiet kind of listening one has when they already know, or maybe just when it's a song they've sung themselves, but with different lyrics" (182). Music provides an unspoken connection between Ursa and her mother, and, as Cat suggests, this type of connection can exist between heterosexual and lesbian women. When describing how Ursa's voice changed after the assault, she says:

> "Maybe even moved more, because [your voice] sounds like you been through something. Before it was beautiful too, but you sound like you been through more now. [...] Like Ma, for instance, after all the alcohol and men, the strain made it better, because you could tell what she'd been through. [...]"

"Well, I don't have to worry about the men, I said."

"That'd make you go through more, not having a man," she said, and looked as if she'd wished she hadn't said it. (44)

The reference to the lesbian blues singer Ma Rainey and Cat's own unvoiced lesbianism subtly suggests that the blues is a medium where the tension between heterosexuality and homosexuality can be expressed. In "It Jus Be's Dat Way Sometime: The Sexual Politics of Women's Blues," Hazel Carby argues that the discourse of the blues empowers black women, and she looks at blues singers' ability to offer a response to black women's sexuality that is not restricted by middle class limitations. Carby specifically discusses Ma Rainey's "Prove It On Me Blues" as "an assertion and affirmation of lesbianism. [...It] vacillates between the subversive hidden activity of women loving women with a public declaration of lesbianism" (18). The power the blues has to communicate women's desires has the potential to give lesbianism a voice through song. Through artists like Ma Rainey, Bessie Smith, and Ethel Waters, lesbianism becomes a public discourse that gives lesbian identity space in a heterosexual society. Jones seems to make this connection between Ma and Cat as a call to action for lesbian women to find an art for expression.

Concluding Remarks

Throughout Gayl Jones's fiction in the 1970s, heterosexual/homosexual binary is expressed through silence and various forms of speech. By integrating the silenced voices of same-sex desire into her works, Jones explores various discourses that can empower and limit black lesbians. She shows that the suppression of these desires (by heterosexism and homophobia) does not make them go away; it only isolates individuals and further fractures the black communities in her texts. After reevaluating some of the early criticism that problematically situated Jones as hostile to lesbianism, it is clear that her work needs to be reconsidered from queer perspectives. Jones's fiction confronts some of the complicated problems that surround coming out and lesbian desire. Homophobia and heterosexism are ugly prejudices, and her fiction vividly exposes this ugliness. Even if we don't want to look, the persistence of these prejudices today suggests that we still need to.

Notes

[1] In *Black Feminist Thought*, Patricia Hill Collins argues for the importance of developing a theory of language that empowers black women to resist a multiplicity of oppressions. She goes on to say that "black feminist thought affirms and rearticulates a consciousness that already exists. More important, this rearticulated consciousness empowers African-American women and stimulates resistance" (31-32). In another example, Mae Henderson describes these intersecting oppressions as a "simultaneity of discourse"—"a mode of reading which examines the ways in which the perspectives of race and gender, and their interrelationships, structure the discourse of black women writers" (258). Also see Mary Helen Washington's introduction to *Black-Eyed Susans*, the preface and first chapter of Deborah McDowell's *"The Changing Same": Black Women's Literature, Criticism, and Theory*, and the first chapter of Hazel Carby's *Reconstructing Womanhood*.

[2] Jones scholarship has been broad, focusing on issues such as folk song (Claudia Tate and Melvin Dixon), discourse—particularly the tension between speech and silence (Mae Henderson, Janelle Wilcox, and Biman Basu), external and internal crises involving questions of sanity and heterosexual romance (Jerry Ward, Carol Davidson, Keith Byerman), sexuality (Ashraf H. A. Rashdy, Deborah Horvitz), and maternal bonds (Madhu Dubey, Corinne Blackmer). A number of these critics have also contextualized Jones in the Black Aesthetic and Black Nationalist movements. But queer readings have been noticeably absent (or have been addressed only in passing) in Jones criticism of the past twenty-five years.

[3] For more recent scholarship on homosexuality in black communities and black arts, see bell hooks's "Homophobia in Black Communities" in *The Greatest Taboo: Homosexuality in Black Communities* (2001) and Siobhan B. Somerville's *Queering the Color Line: Race and the Invention of Homosexuality in American Culture* (2000).

[4] In her forward to *White Rat*, Mae Henderson also asserts that "both formal discourse and personal dialogue in 'Persona' are punctuated by recurrent mid-sentence breaks and ellipses. Thus, the narrative strategy itself represents the suppression of both the narrator's discourse and her desire" (xvii).

[5] Throughout Jones's work, touch is a very important part of female sexuality. Some theorists, such as Irigaray and Merleau-Ponty, have linked touch with women and vision with men. Yet Cathryn Vasseleu complicates this argument in *Textures of Light: Vision and Touch in Irigaray, Levinas and Merleau-Ponty* by arguing that "Irigaray demonstrates [...] that touch is conceived of in terms of vision" (17). In other words, "Irigaray has a regard for the indeterminacy of touch which invites a reconsideration of the constitution of vision" (17).

[6] Gayl Jones in an interview with Claudia Tate (146-147).

[7] In fact, lesbian women have a tendency to disappear in African-American fiction. Consider, for example, the two lesbians in Gloria Naylor's *The Women of Brewster Place* and Clare in Nella Larsen's *Passing*.

[8] In another example, Great Gram tells Ursa, at the age of five, that she was forced to sleep with both Corregidora and his wife for several years. When Ursa asks her if she is telling the truth, Great Gram slaps her and explains the need for making generations—"to leave evidence of the past" (14). For Ursa this story places both heterosexual and homosexual relationships in the context of the coercive and brutal history of slavery. Corinne Blackmer has commented to me that this moment is "the genesis or 'primal scene' of [Ursa's] subsequent ambivalent relations with black lesbians as an adult: she cannot separate her grandmother's disavowal of lesbian pleasure from the seductive fashion in which the Corregidora legacy is 'imprinted' on her body and psyche."

[9] In "Angry Arts: Silence, Speech, and Song in Gayl Jones's *Corregidora*," Amy Gottfried argues that this possession occurs because "a woman is wholly defined by her vagina and her womb" (560).

Works Cited

Basu, Biman. "Public and Private Discourses and the Black Female Subject: Gayl Jones' *Eva's Man*." *Callaloo* 19.1 (1996): 193-208.

Bell, Derrick. "The Race Charged Relationship of Black Men and Black Women." *Constructing Masculinity*. Ed. Maurice Berger, Brian Wallis, and Simon Watson. New York: Routledge, 1995. 193-210.

Blackmer, Corrine E. "I Hold Time in the Palm of My Hand: Maternal Abjection and Temporal Revelation in Gayl Jones's *Eva's Man*." Forthcoming.

Bowen, Angela. "Completing the Kente: Enabling the Presence of Out Black Lesbians in Academia." *The New Lesbian Studies: Into the Twenty-First Century*. Ed. Bonnie Zimmerman and Toni A. H. McNaron. New York: The Feminist Press, 1996. 223-228.

Byerman, Keith E. *Fingering the Jagged Grain: Tradition and Form in Recent Black Fiction*. Athens: The University of Georgia Press, 1985.

Carby, Hazel. "It Jus Be's Dat Way Sometime: The Sexual Politics of Women's Blues." *Radical America*. Vol. 20. Somerville: Alternative Education Project, 1986. 8-22.

Christian, Barbara. *Black Feminist Criticism: Perspectives on Black Women Writers*. New York: Pergamon Press, 1985.

Clarke, Cheryl. "Lesbianism: an Act of Resistance." *This Bridge Called My Back: Writings By Radical Women of Color*. Ed. Cherríe Moraga. Watertown, MA: Persephone Press, 1981.

———. "The Failure to Transform: Homophobia in the Black Community." *Home Girls: A Black Feminist Anthology*. Ed. Barbara Smith. New York: Kitchen Table/Women of Color Press, 1983.

Cohen, Cathy J. "Punks, Bulldaggers, and Welfare Queens: The Radical Potential of Queer Politics?" *GLQ: A Journal of Lesbian and Gay Studies.* Volume 3 (1997): 437-465.

Dixon, Melvin. "Singing a Deep Song: Language as Evidence in the Novels of Gayl Jones." *Black Women Writers (1950-1980): A Critical Evaluation.* Ed. Mari Evans. New York: Anchor Books, 1984.

Dubey, Madhu. "Gayl Jones and the Matrilineal Metaphor of Tradition." *Signs: A Journal of Women in Culture and Society.* 20.2 (1995): 245-267.

———. *Black Women Novelists and the Nationalist Aesthetic.* Bloomington: Indiana University Press, 1994.

Foucault, Michel. *Mental Illness and Psychology.* 1954. Trans. Alan Sheridan. Berkeley: University of California Press, 1987.

Gottfried, Amy S. "Angry Arts: Silence, Speech, and Song in Gayl Jones's *Corregidora.*" *African American Review* 28.4 (1994): 559-570.

Henderson, Mae G. Foreword. *White Rat.* By Gayl Jones. Boston: Northeastern University Press, 1991.

Holland, Sharon P. " 'From This Moment Forth, We are Black Lesbians': Querying Feminism and Transgressing Whiteness in Consolidated's *Business of Punishment.*" *Beyond the Bindary: Reconstructing Cultural Identity in a Multicultural Context.* Ed. Timothy B. Powell. New Bruswick, NJ: Rutgers University Press, 1999. 139-162.

hooks, bell. "Homophobia in Black Communities." *The Greatest Taboo: Homosexuality in Black Communities.* Ed. Delroy Constantine-Simms. Los Angeles: Alyson Books, 2001. 67-73.

Hull, Gloria T. *Color, Sex, and Poetry: Three Women Writers of the Harlem Renaissance.* Bloomington: Indiana University Press, 1987.

Jones, Gayl. *Corregidora.* 2nd ed. Boston: Beacon Press, 1986.

———. *Eva's Man.* 2nd ed. Boston: Beacon Press, 1987.

———. *White Rat: Short Stories.* New York: Random House, 1977.

McDowell, Deborah E. *"The Changing Same.": Black Women's Literature, Criticism, and Theory.* Bloomington: Indiana University Press, 1995.

Mercer, Kobena. *Welcome to the Jungle: New Positions in Black Cultural Studies.* New York: Routledge, 1994.

Ross, Marlon B. "Camping the Dirty Dozens: The Queer Resources of Black Nationalist Invective." *Callaloo* 23.1 (2000): 290-312.

Sedgwick, Eve Kosofsky. *Epistemology of the Closet.* Berkeley: University of California Press, 1990.

Shockley, Ann Allen. "The Black Lesbian in American Literature: An Overview." *Conditions: five.* Ed. Lorraine Bethel and Barbara Smith. 1979. 133-142.

Smith, Barbara. "Toward a Black Feminist Criticism." *All The Women Are White, All the Blacks Are Men, but Some of Us Are Brave.* Ed. Gloria T. Hull, Patricia Bell Scott, and Barbara Smith. Old Westbury, NY: Feminist Press, 1982. 157-175.

———. "The Truth That Never Hurts: Black Lesbians in Fiction in the 1980s." *Wild Women in the Whirlwind*. Ed. Brayton McLaughlin. New Brunswick, NJ: Rutgers University Press, 1990.

Somerville, Siobhan B. *Queering the Color Line: Race and the Invention of Homosexuality in American Culture*. Durham, NC: Duke University Press, 2000.

Springer, Kimberly, ed. *Still Lifting, Still Climbing: African American Women's Contemporary Activism*. New York: New York University Press, 1999.

Tate, Claudia C. "Interview With Gayl Jones." *Black American Literature Forum* 13 (1979): 142-148.

Vasseleu, Cathryn. *Textures of Light: Vision and Touch in Irigaray, Levinas, and Merleau-Ponty*. New York: Routledge, 1998.

Ward, Jerry. "Escape from Trublem: The Fiction of Gayl Jones." *Black Women Writers (1950-1980): A Critical Evaluation*. Ed. Mari Evans. Garden City, NY: Anchor Press, 1984. 249-257.

Wilcox, Janelle. "Resistant Silence, Resistant Subject: (Re)Reading Gayl Jones's *Eva's Man*." *Bodies of Writing, Bodies in Performance*. Ed. Thomas Foster, Carol Siegel, and Ellen E. Berry. New York: New York University Press, 1996. 72-96.

Zimmerman, Bonnie. *The Safe Sea of Women: Lesbian Fiction 1969-1989*. Boston: Beacon Press, 1990.

CHAPTER TEN

Things Deserving Echoes: Gayl Jones's Liberating Poetry

Howard Rambsy II

The majority of criticism concerning Jones's works focuses on her novels and short stories; however, more thorough investigations of her poetry reveal an alternative and complimentary view of Jones as a contributor to the paradigms of African American and American literature. Along with viewing Jones's work within literary traditions, the oral and aural qualities of her poetry demand that we listen as we read. By paying close attention to the blending of oral and literary traditions within her work, we might gain a greater appreciation of Gayl Jones as a writer/storyteller.

Jones's volumes of poetry *Song For Anninho* (1981), *The Hermit-Woman* (1983), *Xarque and Other Poems* (1985), and her poems published in literary magazines provide first-person narratives from a range of characters, especially black women, and explore relationships between women and men, as well as between daughters, mothers, and grandmothers. Jones exhibits a range of possibilities as a writer/storyteller as she represents narratives about magical and mysterious women and seventeenth- and eighteenth-century Brazilian culture and history, in particular, the experiences of enslaved black peoples. Gayl Jones's poetry serves as a useful site for considering the multiple voices and voicings of women and for producing historical narratives—narratives which complement and counter dominant narratives. Such liberating poetry deserves echoes (resoundings, responses, and repetition).

In her book of criticism *Liberating Voices: Oral Tradition in African American Literature,* Jones "explores the technical effects" of African American writers developing their literature by "transforming," if not slightly departing from, "European and European American traditions." In the process, they incorporate "their own distinctive oral and aural forms" into black-authored writings.[1] By examining poems, short stories, and novels by African American writers, Jones analyzes the ways these writers used the blues and jazz forms, spirituals, folktales, and "a whole spectrum of oral references" which "not only [held] forth artistic possibilities, but also [implied] aesthetic, thematic, and social dimensions" (1). Since the oral forms are written, *read,* or re/presented in words, black literature "must oblige itself to visual and auditory magic" (13). The framework for "hearing" black oral forms in literature provided in *Liberating Voices* proves useful for approaching the *magic* of Jones's own texts.

Along with taking into account the use of "black" forms such as the blues and African American oral traditions, we might also consider what I will call the "black sites" or "African American sites" of production where texts are transmitted. Critic Biman Basu has explained that Jones is "keenly aware of the difficulty of such a text [as *Eva's Man*] being positively received in the African-American community."[2] Consequently, the paucity of criticism—positive or negative—in regards to Jones's poetry makes it difficult to assess the reception of her poems from *any* community. However, unlike with her novels and short stories and except for her book of poetry *Song For Anninho* published by Beacon press, institutions within "the African-American community" published Jones's poetry. Situating Jones's poetry within African American and American literary and oral traditions as well as viewing her work in terms of black feminist discourse remain important. Nonetheless, taking into account African American sites of production (which include spaces and places where works are published) might contribute to our expanding appreciation of the body of Jones's works.

To consider black sites means to acknowledge the sense of audience and modes of production as it relates to a network of African

American expressive forms such as music, literature, and oral traditions as well as the inter- and intrarelatedness of these forms to themselves and each other. Along with major determining factors such as race, gender, and class, a sense of place and perspective shape or influence cultural productions as well. That is to say, the social locations where cultural works are produced are significant. Of course, black expressive forms are not exclusively and "purely" black nor do they consist of a static or monolithic blackness. The aesthetics that make up the black aesthetics found in literature, music, and dance, for instance, include varying and shifting degrees of African, African American, Eurocentric, and Asian influences. However, the groupings of black people by choice and force in certain geographical or institutional sites under particular circumstances and conditions at specific historical moments play a significant role in the development of distinctive features and functional roles of African American cultural expressions. The ritualized activities that occur at some black churches, for example, serve as a case in point.

The singing, sermons, music, call-and-response, dancing, and testimonials (testifying) are dependent on each other for a typical service. Notwithstanding the forms of hierarchy that exist in churches in general, an actual service might be seen as a moving, democratic, and even liberating event for participants and observers to the extent that many black voices are heard and other forms of free expressions are encouraged. The collective expressions within a black church provide African Americans with an alternative site for the production of historical narratives and ways of communicating and theorizing about their experiences and places in the history of the United States. The activities and expressions that go on in black churches led Ralph Ellison to explain that, "if I went back into the church, I would go back into a shouting Negro church. I am a fairly sophisticated man, but I think that more would be communicated to me through that form [and site?] of communion than through some other."[3] I emphasize the idea of sites of production so that we do not overlook the interplay of black expressive forms/forums with themselves and each other as in the case of a black church service and also so we do not, as historian Michel-Rolph Trouillot explained, "grossly underestimate the size, the relevance, and the complexity of the overlapping sites where history is produced, notably outside of academia."[4] The sites where black-to-black communications occur influence what is expressed and how it is expressed. That is to say, sites including churches, juke-joints, dance clubs, African American publishing institutions (presses, newspapers, magazines, etc.), barber shops and hair salons, formal and informal discussion groups, and, more recently, websites and listservers on the Internet contribute to the development of black expressive forms as well as to distinct African American ways of knowing and showing. So while not as public, visible, or powerful as publishing institutions such as *The New York Times*, Beacon Press, and *PMLA*, black literary sites of production such as *The Mississippi Link* newspaper, Lotus Press, and *Callaloo*, for instance, are not merely private, invisible, or powerless. Rather, such sites have histories, goals, values, and audiences that affect how writings by and about black lives and cultures are presented and ultimately received.

Taking black sites into account is important especially since "place" or social location help determine whose voices are heard and whose are not. In order to hear more of the voices and voicings of black women, we might turn to sites within communities of African Americans where black women have a relatively more significant listening audience as singers, writers, healers, testifiers, fortune tellers, and storytellers. That the voices of black women are heard in the sometimes small and private quarters of African American communities then does not mean that public institutions should be let off the hook for their roles in silencing, censoring, and censuring African American women.[5] Nonetheless, within African American sites of production, we might consider how black women creative intellectuals such as poets, storytellers, painters, and singers create and develop what bell hooks calls "spaces of radical openness":

> without such spaces we would not survive. Our living depends on our ability to conceptualize alternatives, often improvised. Theorizing about this experience aesthetically, critically is an agenda for radical cultural practice....For me this space of radical openness is a margin—a profound edge. Locating oneself there is difficult yet necessary.[6]

Indeed, we might locate Gayl Jones's poetry somewhere in the spaces of "a profound edge." The poems of Jones's that I will examine appeared on the pages of black literary journals, and Lotus Press, an African American press, published the two volumes of poetry I will cover. That her works appear in these black sites allows us to "imagine" Gayl Jones the storyteller sharing stories with communities of African Americans. In these places of real and *imagined* communities we witness Jones developing "spaces of radical openness." And so while cognizant of the restraints from within that black women writers might face from black communities, Jones nonetheless dares to "take us to unseen territories." Her poems (or short short stories) seek to liberate us from static and monolithic ideas of blackness and non-extraordinary views of women.

In her volumes of poetry *The Hermit-Woman* and *Xarque and Other Poems* and in her poem "The Fur Station," Jones's focus on black people in Brazil complicates narratives within American and African American discourses that often overlook the existence and experiences of "black Americans" living outside of the Caribbean and the United States. Jones's preoccupation with seventeenth- and eighteenth-century Brazil, especially the experiences of black women, re/presents both a theory and practice of the possibilities of female creative expression and exploration. Also, the mythical, magical, and mysterious women of Jones's poetry suggest the value of histories or memories of impossibility within the matrix of black expressive culture. In the processes of reading Jones's poetry, we "see" and "hear" the workings of a writer/storyteller.

Structurally, many of Jones's poems are long narrative poems written in the first person with short lines. The narrative form of her poems is such that when reading her work aloud it becomes difficult to make easy distinctions between her work as long poems or short stories. On the one hand, Jones's poems—at least those discussed here—are not "autobiographical" in the sense that Jones preoccupies herself with writing personal narratives about her experiences living in Kentucky. On the other hand, her works are, in one sense, "autobiographical" to the extent that the author-narrators of the poems provide brief histories and personal narratives concerning their experiences. By "becoming" or taking on the voices of various ordinary and extraordinary women, Jones explores and re/presents a range of possibilities in her poetry.

The theme of exploration runs throughout Jones's *The Hermit-Woman*. In the title poem, the speaker informs her visitors that "I am an explorer too, / but I stay in one place, / and strangers come to me."[7] Visitors see the hermit woman sitting "at the edge / of a high mountain" and assume that she can answer questions, speak differently, or perform miracles. Yet, the hermit repeatedly tells her visitors that "I am any ordinary woman" and provides her thoughts but not necessarily direct answers to visitors' questions on what she has learned from living in solitude. She says, "In silence / one can either / take advantage of time, / or destroy it" and later "I awake from sleep. / I complain of idleness (my own). / I complain of silence / (when it's treacherous)" (11). Staying in one place and listening to strangers, the hermit has gained wisdom through self-exploration. Rather than provide direct answers to the questions of her visitors—a couple of lovers—the hermit tells them that she will prepare mushrooms to eat "while you answer / your own questions, / or just kiss again. / I'll come back / at the end of it / and listen" (11).

In "The Hermit-Woman," the wise old woman politely rejects her role and expectations as a wise old woman who can tell fortunes, give secrets about the power of love, or know the answers to all questions. Instead, what the hermit-woman of Jones's poem appears to value more so than giving answers to others is what she has acquired through her own self-explorations and by listening and observing her visitors. Jones suggests in "The Hermit-Woman" that fulfilling explorations are not achieved by young, adventurous lovers nor by those who travel across vast geographical distances; rather, by staying in one place and observing the seemingly minor details of her life, "any ordinary woman" might be "an explorer too." Jones further considers the possibilities of exploration in her poem "Wild Figs and Secret Places."

In this poem, also published in *The Hermit-Woman*, the female author-narrator is a healer, explorer, and seer (one who can view the past and future as well as the thoughts of various individuals), and she leads a male, foreign mapmaker on a journey through a New World. Early in her narrative, the author-narrator avoids identifying herself specifically or by name for the mapmaker and thus locates herself within a collective: "Who am I? / Who needs to know? / I am merely a human woman" (20). Contrary to ideas that suggest that groups should be led by exceptional men or women, Jones makes self-proclaimed ordinary women the focus of her poetry, ordinary women who have amazing capabilities. By resisting to clearly identify the women of her poetry by name and detailed physical descriptions, does Jones suggest that extraordinary women walk amongst those of us who are merely human? Or, is Jones making the point that those who appear and claim to be merely human women have extraordinary, often hidden gifts? What are those gifts? Exactly who and which women have them? "Who needs to know?"

In "Wild Figs and Secret Places," the author-narrator constantly expresses an ambivalence toward the past and memories: "I know the whole story / I already know it / So what is the use of repeating it?" (21), and:

> If I wanted
> I could live without memory
> It is only journeys forward that count
> Time is a hard kiss on the jaw
>
> I have been an adventuress in my day
> an adventuress of the body and spirit
> Sometimes I have worn bruises for lipstick. (20)

The author-narrator's adventuresome spirit perhaps leads her to distance herself from the past, from continuously repeating what has already been done. As she says, she prefers forward journeys. Nonetheless, throughout the narrative, instead of remembering the past, she seems to "know" the past—her own as well as others. She lives in the now-ness of the past, present, and future, and has left nothing unexplored: "This is a New World to you / but to me? / Hah! / There aren't any secret places any more" (23). Not only does she know the New World, her body has internalized it: "...you can see a map of the country / the whole territory / in the veins of my hands" (24). And still,

> There are parts of the map
> I will not show.
> There are places I will always keep secret.
> I will eat the tips of my fingers

> to keep them unknown and
> unvisited
>
> it is better. (24)

Here, the woman acknowledges that she will keep some of the New World's secrets to herself; she ensures that some places and spaces remain a mystery. Apparently, she knows that some visitors and foreigners might not respect and protect some people and places and thus critiques the dangers of colonization. For instance, she already has her "own" names for mountains and rivers in the New World, "but already / I can see new names on your tongue" (25). When one considers the extents to which foreign explorers have colonized and renamed various parts of the world, it is significant that the author-narrator of the poem decides to keep some places secret. Keeping places and people hidden, Jones's poem suggests, might be one method for resisting colonization.

Although the foreign mapmaker believes that it is impossible, the author-narrator wonders if he "can travel / in all directions / at one time" (26). The author-narrator's own abilities to transcend time and space with her imagination, to explore her own thoughts as well as those of the mapmaker, and to "anticipate you like a memory" reveal that she, and by extension the poem, can travel in multiple directions. The poem and narrator not only move in multiple directions, they also move at their own pace—shifting back and forth from the present events to anecdotes and side comments that do not necessarily relate to the flow of the narrative. By moving at her own pace, the author-narrator compels the mapmaker to follow and listen if he expects to learn and find his way in the New World. More importantly, Jones's poem suggests that readers must follow and listen if they are to understand this "merely human woman" in a New World and realize that even as they are listening, some places will be kept secret. And finally, since the author-narrator is a seer and moves in multiple directions at once, readers must ponder whether the entire story is taking place in the present, being remembered, or being predicted.

What Jones's poem keeps most secret is the identity and full understanding of the author-narrator. She resists easy or simple definitions and categorization: "I am not a magical woman /...No, I am my own woman, / and there aren't any places / where you can enter me with any ease" (23). She has not borne children because she has eaten a plant that has made her sterile: "Nevertheless, I am a woman / Yes" (24). She also observes that "you do not know / whether I am a young woman / or an old one," and "I want to forget I am a woman, / but I always remember" (27). And finally,

> In your country
> I see what they do
> with such women as me
> and so I do not
> probe further (27).

As these comments suggest, the author-narrator critiques various narrow definitions of women and is ambivalent about being seen as a woman because the views and treatment of women can be confining if not abusive. Realizing what it has meant to be a woman, she wants to "forget" those parts of being a woman in the New World, and by keeping herself mysterious and moving in multiple directions, the author-narrator attempts to allude being captured and possessed.

Although she says she is not a magical woman, what makes it even more difficult to pinpoint whom and what she is relates to her seemingly magical or unbelievable powers. She sees into the mapmaker's past as well as the events taking place in his country, and "you want to know how I / know your language" (28). Throughout the narrative, she reveals the seemingly impossible powers that her mind has not only to remember and predict but also to shape the course of events. For instance, when the mapmaker asks her "If I were a solider / how would you have killed me?" she responds simply, "By wanting to" (31). Unlike the mapmaker and colonizers who have traveled to various places and claimed territories often by force, the author-narrator prefers and values her use of mental powers to explore the contours of various people and distant places. And of course, the author-narrator's goals and powers are a re/presentation of Jones's project of creating, to apply bell hooks phrasing again, "a space for radical openness." If nowhere else but in the world of Jones's poem, the author-narrator defies the impossible.

Although "Wild Figs and Secret Places," when read aloud suggests some of the important qualities of Jones's work in terms of storytelling, the structure of the poem is such that readers gain a sense of how Jones's work performs on the page as well. When the author-narrator speaks directly to the mapmaker, her words are in quotations. Most of her narrative, however, does not appear within quotation marks and suggests that she is thinking out loud or sharing her thoughts with us—the readers. Seeing the story on the page then allows readers to appreciate how effortlessly the author-narrator moves back and forth from her own thoughts to dialogue with the mapmaker. Another aspect of the poem that must be "seen" on the page in order to be fully appreciated occurs as the author-narrator reads and presents the mapmaker's thoughts:

> *I have met a native woman,*
> *At first I thought she was*
> *one of those river monsters*
> *we have read about*
> *But then I realized*
> *she was a human being.* (29)

The author-narrator goes on to present the mapmaker's thoughts as he is thinking. Rather than say the above is what the mapmaker is thinking, the author-narrator (and Jones by extension) "shows" what and how he is thinking by italicizing his words and allowing him to intrude on the woman's story. She places his story within her story and controls when she will make his words visible. Presenting such shifts in voices and viewpoints might be difficult or confusing for a storyteller to perform out loud; however, on the page, Jones utilizes punctuation marks and italics to achieve various shifts without interrupting the flow and pace of the narrative. Or better yet, she utilizes various markings to control how people and events will be presented.

By merging the past, present, and future and by shifting voices and viewpoints throughout the narrative, Jones complicates linear versions of history. Her poem demonstrates that the story, the storyteller, and the listener or listeners can sometimes shape the history or histories that are being created and recreated. Like a number of Jones's poems, "Wild Figs and Secret Places" provides a useful and interesting guide for mapmakers and readers seeking to explore a New World. Along with critiquing the problems of colonialism and creating the figure of an unbelievable, merely human woman, Jones suggests that explorers might try to approach the uncertainties of New Worlds by attempting the impossible: traveling in multiple directions at once. Jones continues such varied movements in her next volume of poetry.

In the title poem of the volume *Xarque and Other Poems*, Jones offers a view of a series of narratives presented by the central character Euclida, a young woman who lives with her mother and works in a xarque (dried meat) factory in Recife, Brazil, in 1741. The poem presents stories within stories as Euclida listens to conversations, stories, and her mother Bonifacia "tell me mysteries."[8] At one level, Euclida's stories and the stories of other women presented throughout the poem highlight Jones's emphasis on the ways communities of women communicate and establish spaces to remember the past and/or create historical narratives. For instance, by listening to stories about her grandmother Almeyda, who "some say ... knew mysteries / and had powers from out of the world," Euclida gains a deeper sense of her own place in the world and her relationship to her relatives (13). She also asks her mother to "tell me about my father then," which Bonifacia does after she prefaces her comments with the statement: "Part Sudanese and part Angolan. / It's impossible to tell you / of that man and tell him rightly" (14). Stories, or as Euclida calls them "mysteries" in the poem function to entertain and inform people of who and whose they are, where they come from, and the events which brought them to where they are.

In terms of Jones's work as a site of historical production, "Xarque" re/presents the experiences of enslaved, African-descended peoples in Brazil, and it is also interesting to note that her poem draws on her previous works which focused on the experiences of African slaves who sought to found a settlement free from their Portuguese masters.[9] "Xarque" builds then, on the actual past of enslaved peoples in Brazil and the histories that Jones had recreated and created in her own previous writings. Jones extends the charge that black people should "know your history" as her writings reveal that she is not only attempting to know her history but also actively producing histories.

In "Xarque," rather than provide an overall critique of the practice of slavery, Jones focuses more attention on the private and significant histories of Euclida and how the "mysteries" she hears, sees, and tells connect her to her past and determine how she will deal with the present and future. Euclida learns that the Africans failed to mount a successful uprising and "massacre" of their white masters because "the Sudanese and the Bantu / couldn't decide who would lead" (38). As the slaves argued among themselves, the whites discovered their plans and dissolved the uprising. The slave men who attempted to escape "were executed, / and their heads exhibited in public" and the women were sent to Minas "because of the shortage of white women, / and where there's a necessity / there's a way" (39-40). "But I don't have to tell you more," the woman storyteller says to Elucida, "You don't need to know how I came here / Except that a fee was paid." The storyteller does conclude that "all this" occurred because "we couldn't decide / who'd supply the leader" (40).

The discussions of the failed uprisings throughout the poem suggest the significance of intraracial or intracultural differences among Africans. Even though white slave masters placed Africans under the category "black slave," Jones's poem demonstrates that Africans had a broader and more complex idea of what it meant to be African. They understood—which ironically accounts in part to their own demise—that outside white control, "the Black Experience" was not universal. Unlike distant African-descended blacks who might create a more generalized view of Africa, the Sudanese, Bantu, and Angolan peoples enslaved in Brazil were much too conscious of their ethnic and cultural backgrounds and identities to come to easy conclusions about what kind of African would be best suited to lead and represent the Africans. To the extent that Jones's poem highlights the differences and divisions between Africans and Africans or black people and black people, "Xarque" reminds us that racial unity is not necessarily the same as racial solidarity. In short, the black race, like any other race of people, is not always in agreement on who their race leader should be. Of course, that Africans failed to resolve their differences was especially significant since they were enslaved and mistreated, for the most part, because of their skin color rather than their ethnic and cultural differences. And the consequences, as Jones illustrates, for a failed black uprising was especially harsh: decapitation for men and physical (including sexual) servitude for women.

Although people throughout the poem explain to Elucida how and why the divisions and "prejudices among African races" presented problems for black progress and liberation, the women whom Elucida admires and converses with are most noticeable because of their different and *differenced* (varied) backgrounds as well as their multiethnic and transnational identities. Bonifacia's friend Tirana, for instance, is a "free woman," Sudanese, born in Madagascar and presently living in Brazil. For Elucida, "Just looking at her reminds me / of strange things and marvelous places, / though I've never been anywhere" (7). Like the other magical and mysterious women of Jones's work, Tirana represents wonderful possibilities for ordinary women within and outside of Jones's work (of course within the context of Jones's poetry the concept of "ordinary women" is slippery and loaded with meanings). That Tirana appears to be extraordinary and yet so connected with the collectivities of which include Bonifacia and the women who work in the xarque allows "a shy woman / who fears change," as Elucida describes herself, to listen to and be heard by a black woman who "boasts of never / having been a slave to a white person" (18) and tells stories of places where "the women walk about the streets / as freely as any man" (20). Initially, Elucida thinks that "Tirana" is "such a silly name" until she listens and learns from the woman that "Maybe it's silly. / But it's a name I gave myself." Elucida learns that tiranas are "songs that women sing / about love's tyranny" which "I've never heard men sing such songs. / I've never heard them. No" (8). Elucida explains that

> Tirana hunts birds.
> Tirana knows any bird by its sound.
> Tirana can touch the air,
> and know which direction to go in.
> Tirana reminds me of the forest,
> or the moon.
> Things that don't show off
> their secrets. (34)

In a racist and sexist society, there's no wonder that Elucida values the stories of and her connections with a magical and mysterious woman such as Tirana. Such women bring Elucida a view of far and distance places in the form of stories. The stories are important in that they are told from the personal perspective of women thus providing for a narrative that focuses specifically on the varied experiences of black women.

Moreover, that the narratives are expressed in personalized settings by and among women allows for even young shy women such as Elucida to interrupt Bonficia's and Tirana's stories to ask questions and make observations. Unlike typcial general and standardized versions of History which might rarely focus on the personal voices of black women, Jones's "Xarque" not only provides and exercises a space for black women but also makes "interruptions" integral to the flow of the story. The places and spaces where black women gather and tell stories and "mysteries" represent sites within the matrix of black culture, which I described earlier, where individuals might gather and produce interrupted, unbelievable, and yet meaningful narratives.

The importance of relationships between extraordinary and ordinary black women as well as between storytellers and their audience is illustrated in Elucida's comments that "I dream of wild figs / and my warrior grandmother. / But I am a shy woman" (7). Although for the moment she does not have access to certain kinds of freedoms, Elucida does have access to stories and dreams about her warrior grandmother and the liberating possibilities embodied by "wild figs." For people whose immediate and total liberation appear non-existent, access to histories—which among other ways might be presented in the forms of dreams, myths, and stories—become especially significant. Unlike their surroundings and bodies both of which they do not even own, black women such as Elucida, Bonficia, and Tirana do have significantly more control in creating and recreating the stories of their lives. Because so-called "real-life" and "real History" have so often excluded voices and considerations of black women, it's no strange coincidence that Jones's narratives and women develop much of their meaning and importance on seemingly unreal and unbelievable things. Therefore even those histories which sound untrue carry "truth" and meaning in their very existence. The existence of stories by black people and songs that only women sing provides evidence that such peoples even under oppressive conditions have survived. And if nothing else, stories about magical, mythical, and mysterious women give younger, shy ordinary women something to dream about. Nonetheless, the author-narrator of Jones's poem "Waiting for the Miracle," published in her volume of poetry *Xarque and Other Poems*, quietly addresses those who doubt the unbelievable.

The author-narrator of this poem is a female attendant who makes tea and writes down questions "and requests for miracles. / I guide people in" to see the saint Black Mary Jane (60). The author-narrator remembers

>the first vision
>of Mary Jane. Who wouldn't
>expect something wonderful?
>Black as night and hair
>as straight as angels'
>(as they used to say).
>One eye black as jet,
>the other gold as sun.
>Conditions for madness
>or the fantastic
>I chose the latter. (60)

The author-narrator explains that Mary Jane "gets visitors from around the world," and some of those people witnessed the saint performing various miracles:

>One saw Mary Jane
>standing in the air.
>Another saw her
>turn pretty.
>(I always thought
>she was pretty.
>Anyway, I was in the kitchen.
>I can't corroborate.)
>
>Another saw her at night,
>eating the moon like a pear. (62)

The author-narrator carefully distinguishes between the ways various people "saw" the saint performing miracles which suggests that the miracles could mean different things to individuals depending on their perspectives. Thus as shown above, the author-narrator feels it is necessary to interrupt and contradict her narrative about the miracle sightings in order to say why, from her perspective, Mary Jane could not "turn pretty." As usual in Jones's poetry, such interruptions or side interjections allow the author-narrator to control and personalize the story.

Even though some people said that they had seen the saint perform miracles, others doubted her powers and expressed such doubt to the author-narrator. "I don't believe. / All lies" and "Can she really change shapes?" a man asks. The author-narrator simply replies, "It has been said" (64). As she continues to satisfy the doubters, someone shouts, "The saint's in motion!," "The saint's in the air!," "Oh, it's true!," and "Oh, it's scary!" (65) The author-narrator hesitates to go observe at first: "I don't move. / I know what is not possible" (65). Finally,

> ...I rush to see too.
> But it is not the saint
> in the air.
> It is all the others.
> In the air, and spinning.
> The saint is the axis.
> The saint is sitting still,
> and laughing. (65)

In this poem, Jones seems to make at least two points about those who believe that the stories surrounding saints or magical and mysterious women who perform miracles are all lies. For one, her poem suggests that those people in positions to see and believe the saint's miracles can do so. Thus, those people living "along / the metal edge of society, / tramped in, / waiting for something, / waiting for *it*" have seen Mary Jane perform miracles. Perhaps, those in the mainstream of society lack the ability and patience to see. Secondly, even those who see the miracles the saint performs might not understand or actually recognize the miracles. In the poem, unbeknownst to them, the visitors are in the air and spinning not the saint. She is sitting still. At one level, the fact that some people misunderstand the saint's miracles and others do not believe her miracles serves to support the idea of such women's mysteriousness. Of course, in the poetry of Gayl Jones, there have been women more unbelievable and mysterious than Black Mary Jane.

In "The Fur Station" published in the now defunct literary magazine *First World*, Jones writes from the perspective of a male, a Brazilian animal hunter who has "all kinds of blood, / Scottish and Irish and

Portuguese and French and a / drop or two from a Zulu woman." The hunter sets traps for his prey and explains that "some animals, you know, are capable / of changing, of metamorphoses." In fact, the hunter once caught a bear that changed into a woman. After watching the woman struggle in the trap, he let her go "and had to defend myself against the bear again." The hunter concludes that the woman was "some adultress or adventuress...paying her debt" by living in the body of a bear. The hunter explains to listeners who might be skeptical of his story that "you can't answer everything with logic." Moreover, throughout the narrative, the hunter informs the listener or readers that he is "a pure Christian" and doesn't "believe in witchcraft, African or European." Even so, he has observed seemingly unbelievable things. But, as he explains, "how does one penetrate the tropics, without illusions? / Before I came here I lived off mistakes."[10] Perhaps, those illusions and "mistakes" that he lived through were similar to our myths, stories, histories, and everyday narratives—our narratives about John Henry and Stagolee, our narratives about Santa Claus and American dreams—narratives that are as magical, mythical and mysterious as the poetic narratives of Gayl Jones.

The work of a writer/storyteller such as Jones connects to a number of African American traditions all at the same time. Or as the author-narrator of "Wild Figs and Secrets Places" suggests, it seems possible for some explorers, perhaps poets, to travel in multiple directions at once. Therefore, Jones's work relates well to the longstanding traditions of African American storytelling and folklore and simultaneously locates itself among more contemporary works in African American literature. For instance, Jones's representations of ordinary yet extraordinary women are not unlike those women in Toni Morrison's *Song of Solomon* and *Beloved,* and the magical powers and shape-shifting capabilities of some of Jones's women are similar to those women in the novels of Octavia Butler, a black science fiction writer.

In the imaginary worlds of her poetry, Jones creates spaces and places of the seemingly impossible—spaces and places where the voices of black women control the production of histories of the past and future. In a real world where so many voices are silenced, so many histories forgotten, and so many ideas suppressed; the fantastic, unbelievable, and liberating worlds (and words) of Gayl Jones should be echoed. Or if nothing else, one hopes that within black speech and literary communities, she can at least get a witness.

Notes

[1] Gayl Jones, *Liberating Voices: Oral Tradition in African American Literature* (Cambridge, MA: Harvard University Press, 1991), 1.
[2] Biman Basu, "Public and Private Discourses and the Black Female Subject," *Callaloo* 19:1 (1996): 195.
[3] Ralph Ellison, "Remarks at The American Academy of Arts and Sciences Conference on the Negro American, 1965" in *New Black Voices: An Anthology of Contemporary Afro-American Literature*, ed. Abraham Chapman (New York: Mentor, 1972), 408.
[4] Michel-Rolph Trouillot, *Silencing the Past: Power and the Production of History* (Boston: Beacon Press, 1995), 19.
[5] As social theorist Patricia Hill Collins has pointed out, "naming oneself and defining ideas that count as truth are empowering acts," but "although important, private naming is not enough—truth must be publicly proclaimed." Patricia Hill Collins, *Fighting Words: Black Women and The Search For Justice* (Minneapolis: University of Minnesota Press, 1998), 237.
[6] bell hooks, *Race, Gender, and Cultural Politics* (Boston: South End Press, 1990), 149.
[7] Gayl Jones, *The Hermit-Woman* (Detroit: Lotus Press, 1983), 9. Subsequent references appear parenthetically in the text.
[8] Gayl Jones, *Xarque and Other Poems* (Detroit: Lotus Press, 1985), 13. Subsequent references appear parenthetically in the text.
[9] See Jones's *Song For Anninho* as well as excerpts "From Almeyda" in *Puerto del Sol* 14 (Fall 1975): 45-48. See also Gayl Jones "Almeyda," *Massachusetts Review* 18 (Winter 1977): 689-91.
[10] Gayl Jones, "The Fur Station," *First World* 2, No. 3 (1979), 23.

Works Cited

Basu, Biman. "Public and Private Discourses and the Black Female Subject." *Callaloo* 19: 1 (1996): 193-208.

Collins, Patricia Hill. *Fighting Words: Black Women and The Search For Justice*. Minneapolis: University of Minnesota Press, 1998.

Ellison, Ralph. " Remarks at The American Academy of Arts and Sciences Conference on the Negro American, 1965." *New Black Voices: An Anthology of Contemporary Afro-American Literature*. Ed. Abraham Chapman. New York: Mentor, 1972. 401-408.

Gottfried, Amy. "Angry Arts: Silence, Speech, and Song in Gayl Jones's *Corregidora*."

African American Review 28: 4 (Winter 1994): 559-570.

Henderson, Mae. G. "Foreword to the 1991 Edition." *White Rat: Short Stories* by Gayl Jones. Boston: Northeastern University Press, 1977. ix-xxvii.

hooks, bell. *Yearning: Race, Gender, and Cultural Politics.* Boston: South End Press, 1990.

Johnson, E. Patrick. "Wild Women Don't Get the Blues: A Blues Analysis of Gayl Jones' *Eva's Man*." *Obsidian II* 9:1 (Spring-Summer, 1994): 26-46.

Jones, Gayl. *Liberating Voices: Oral Tradition in African American Literature.* Cambridge, MA: Harvard University Press, 1991.

———. *Song For Anninho.* (1981 rpt.) Boston: Beacon Press, 2000.

———. *The Hermit-Woman.* Detroit: Lotus Press, 1983.

———. *Xarque and Other Poems.* Detroit: Lotus Press, 1985.

———. "The Fur Station." *First World* 2, No. 3 (1979), 23.

Trouillot, Michel-Rolph. *Silencing the Past: Power and the Production of History.* Boston: Beacon Press, 1995.

CHAPTER ELEVEN

Resistance, Reappropriation, and Reconciliation: The Blues and Flying Africans in Gayl Jones's *Song for Anninho*

Lovalerie King

Song for Anninho (1981) is Gayl Jones's tribute to the memory of Palmares, a seventeenth–century African state located in the Barriga Mountains between Alagôas and Pernambuco in Brazil.[1] Though it began as a *quilombo*—or what some scholars refer to as a *mocambo*, much like the *maroon* communities in the Caribbean and *outlyer* communities in the United States—at its zenith in the mid-1670s, Palmares is said to have boasted between twenty and thirty thousand inhabitants.[2] Its rulers were called Zumbis; the last was Zumbi Sueca. With the exception of about two decades' time during its almost one-hundred-year existence, Palmares was under almost perpetual assault from Dutch or Portuguese colonial forces. Government-sponsored forces would seek out and destroy the physical site of Palmares; surviving Palmareans would rebuild in a new location. Jones's long narrative poem compliments the contemporary cultural movement and excavation project that Abdias do Nascimento helped to organize on behalf of Brazilians of African descent worldwide.[3]

The long absence of factual written records from within the destroyed nation of Palmares means that historical narratives have been based on a factual record provided by invading colonial forces. Jones is left with the project of representing a Palmarean perspective through the commingling of history and folklore, including the oral history kept alive through Afro-Brazilian folk tradition. Thus, her long narrative poem about the final destruction of Palmares showcases her meticulous attention to Brazilian history, her knowledge and use of African and African American folk traditions, and her use of black women writers' revisionist strategies. The specific factual event that is the focus of this essay reveals Jones's use of the blues and the Myth of the Flying Africans to imagine the Palmarean version of a specific factual event: the collective deaths of some two hundred Palmareans during the final destruction of their nation.

Before proceeding with my discussion of Jones's recreation, her mythmaking via poetry, some attention to the factual record seems appropriate. Available information dates the origins of Africans in Brazil from around 1532. By 1580, there were at least ten thousand Africans in Brazil; and by 1630, the sugar plantation system in the region where Palmares flourished contained some one hundred and fifty *engenhos* (sugar mills). Africans were being imported at the rate of more than four thousand annually, and many of them escaped and sought refuge in the Barriga mountains, where they formed communities. Palmares was the largest, best organized and most enduring of these communities (Ennes 170).

Ernesto Ennes correctly acknowledges that some authors treat the history of Palmares as "no more than a tiresome revolt of slaves," and others treat it as "a strong and well-organized republic" (201). Regardless of treatment, the original inhabitants of Palmares were most likely Bantu speakers from Loanda in Angola. Arthur Ramos writes, for example, that the

> customs and usages of Palmares were modeled on those of Bantu origin with such changes and adaptations as the needs of a community in the new world required. On this, as well as many other points, our sources of information are inadequate. The *best data* are obtained from the accounts and chronicles of members of the expedition sent against the Negroes (Ramos, 65; emphasis mine).

In time, the ethnic makeup of Palmares would include Amerindians and members of other groups as they became integrated into Palmares society through various means. The word "Negro" did not only apply to blacks in this context; rather, it included some *pardos* or *gente do cor*, people "of color" not easily accepted "as either *pretos* or *brancos* ("whites"). It also applied to *crioulos* or those born in Brazil of African or mixed parentage, to *ladinos* or those who spoke Portuguese and usually espoused the Catholic faith, and the Africanos or those who were neither Portuguese–speaking nor native to Brazil" (Ramos 65). Some confusion surrounds the original date and location of Palmares. We can attribute discrepancies about its origins to inconsistencies among extant contemporaneous references, including Jesuit Father Pero Rodrigues's 1597 statement that "'foremost enemies of the colonizer are revolted Negroes from Guiné in some mountain areas, from where they raid and give much trouble'" (Kent 174). Another reference concerns a notation that around 1602, Pernambuco governor Diogo Botelho "learned from an Amerindian chief named Zorababé that there was a 'mocambo...of negroes from Guiné...in the palmares of river Itapicuro'" (Kent 174). To further confuse the matter of origin, R. K. Kent notes significantly that neither of the above references pertains to the site of what later became known as the Republic of Palmares. According to Kent, Rocha Pitta, "a contemporary of Palmares," claimed that Palmares was founded by "'forty Negroes from Guiné' who had abandoned plantations from Pôrto Calvo" (176). The problem writes Kent, is that for the period under discussion, "Guiné" is "not a fruitful geographical expression. It stood for anything between a limited section of West Africa and the entire continent" (176). Kent maintains that Palmares "was not regarded as an ordinary *mocambo*, or hideout. By 1612, it had a considerable reputation. It was an organization with which the *moradores* (local settlers) could not cope alone. The foundation of Palmares thus appears to have taken place in 1605–06, possibly earlier, but certainly not later" (175). Ramos suggests that although the "majority of Brazilian historians give 1630 as the beginning of the *quilombos* "that made up Palmares, evidence "seems to indicate...that prior to this time, bands of slaves had begun to settle in the region destined to become this community" (55–56). According to Nascimento, Palmares serves as a symbol of resistance to New World slavery dating from 1595, and the "saga of a hundred years' resistance to colonial siege by the Portuguese and the Dutch, from 1595 to 1696 is an example and a symbol to Pan Africanists the world over" (66).

Jones exploits confusion in the factual record to render her version of events, a revision that highlights African resistance to New World slavery. For despite the confusion surrounding an exact date of origin, it is clear that the legacy of African resistance to New World slavery is intricately connected to and interwoven into the historical record on Palmares.[4]

Jones's creative project serves as an alternative to linear historical narratives about Palmares, even as it engages those narratives to illuminate their relationship to fiction. Formal aspects of the poem support and propel the narrative and create the possibility for the type of work that Toni Morrison describes in "The Site of Memory." Morrison explains how she engages in "a kind of literary archeology," in which "on the basis of some information and a little bit of guesswork you journey to a site to see what remains were left behind and to reconstruct the world that these remains imply" (92).[5] Both authors use the technique of revealing history through memory. Morrison's most noteworthy work in this regard is *Beloved* (1987), and Jones, for whom Morrison has served as editor, often employs this technique. It seems that for Jones, as it had been for Morrison, the nature of the imaginative act is essential to the overarching objective of disclosing the interior lives of the subject people in intimate detail—from their own perspective. In *Song for Anninho*, the story comes to us via the memory of Almeyda, a traumatized survivor of the final assault on Palmares. Jones makes Almeyda's narrative official by bestowing upon her the name of certain colonial government officials.

As one of the subject people, Almeyda remembers and then "passes on" via a blues ethos her "official" version of events surrounding the history (Herstory) and destruction of Palmares. Almeyda has good reason to sing the blues.[6] She has lost her man, her home, her people, and in a most brutal fashion, her breasts. She clearly needs to heal, and that healing comes through ritual presided over by Zibatra, a conjure woman who appears on cue as if by magic. In keeping with the formal structure of the blues, Almeyda must come to terms with her loss and look toward the future. Jones's blues singer in *Song for Anninho* "possesses a healthy ability to remember the past" without becoming totally immersed in it and disabled by it (Rushdy 280).

The temporal setting for *Song for Anninho* is during the reign of Zumbi Sueca, a reign that began sometime after 1675 in what Pero Rodrigues has described as the third and final phase of the Republic.[7] By 1674 Palmares encompassed over sixty leagues. It was completely self-sustaining, with hundreds of houses, well-kept lands with complex irrigation systems, abundant vegetation, churches, smithies, and a fully functioning government and legislative system. Indeed, it seems that the point at which Palmares became least dependent on the surrounding plantations was also the point at which it became the greatest liability to the goals of the colonizers, who were loathe to allow an independent African state to exist in their midst.[8] The story begins on a mountaintop with 20-something Almeyda regaining consciousness. Zibatra, a conjure woman, attends her. A soldier from the invading forces has severed Almeyda's breasts, and Zibatra tells her that she found them floating like "two globes" in the river. The last thing Almeyda recalls is fleeing and being near the river with her husband, Anninho. Zibatra's herbs and incantations help to loosen Almeyda's memory so that the latter is able to recite her autobiography. Almeyda eventually gives voice to her pain and her joy, and in providing her own story, and serving as the collective "I" for those individual Palmareans lost to time and history, she also provides a chronicle of her people's final two decades.[9]

Jones presents her revisionist Herstory of Palmares in three parts. The first section (some 51 pages) recalls the story of Palmares and the battle during which protagonist Almeyda and her husband, Anninho, escape, and Almeyda suffers a traumatic injury. The relationship between Almeyda and Anninho dominates the second section of the poem (some 21 pages) as Almeyda reveals through dream and memory the nature of her relationship with Anninho in Palmares. Past, present, and future merge in section three, reuniting the two lovers (as well as the community) for all time.[10] The narrative, structured upon a series of opposites and oppositions, moves from physical loss to spiritual recovery. In her critical review of *Song for Anninho*, Trudier Harris points out that oppositional pairings in the poem include:

> man and woman, love and hate, war and peace, life and death, slavery and freedom, change and stasis, language and silence, hurt and health, seeing

(eyes) and seeing (knowledge, clairvoyance), and past and present (with their variations of past/future, present/future), and memory/reality. Some of the oppositions are controlled by time, and others go beyond it; that concept is also central to the poem. (Harris 107)

Other oppositional pairings include beginning/ending (A/Z, Almeyda and Zibatra), hardness/softness (tenderness, gentleness), and spiritual/material. *Song for Anninho* often refers to spiritual ways of being in relation to material/physical ways of being, and it is the spirit of the action or event that Jones wishes to render in her creative enterprise.

Though the general mood of the poem, and Jones's liberal use of repetition throughout her construction of the narrative, easily connect *Song for Anninho* to the folk form known as the blues, Jones relies on other aspects of folk tradition to complicate the historical record. According to Henry Glassie, the mission of folklore is to balance and complicate "history's linear tale of sequential triumphs by attention to real people—women at the loom, men on the battlefield—operating in terms of their own limited capacity to construct the future" (401). In other words, a basic difference between history and folklore resides in folklore's informative value in rendering the more intimate details of people's everyday lives.

The folk forms Jones uses to construct her Palmarean perspective reflect her knowledge of the Angolan-derived people under discussion. She makes liberal use of repetition, a technique appropriate both to the blues and to the telling and retelling (circularity) of folk myths and legends. Her archeological endeavor involves the careful, segment-by-segment (or fragment-by-fragment) extraction of the information from Almeyda's memory. Segments are stated and repeated (as with an oral history), and with each repetition, the original segment is signified upon, improvised and revised as the story comes closer to completion and the reader comes closer to understanding. Albert Lord writes that repetition is the structural characteristic most noticeable to Ovimbundu tales, pointing out that repetition "pervades almost all of the stories," and takes on several forms:

> As a phenomenon in oral literature, in products of verbal art, repetition always...had something of the magical about it...Repetition of incidents and repeated patterns of incidents are, moreover, characteristic compositional devices of oral style. The storyteller...needs a repertory not only of common

phrases but also of frequently recurring incidents and groups of incidents in order to rebuild any tale in its retelling or even to remember it as he listens to it for the first time...An act or incantation is performed a number of times until some result is obtained, a series of repetitions until something interrupts (assaults). (xiii)

Repeating a phrase here, or a passage there, is essential to mythmaking and storytelling, especially where a history must be passed on orally from person to person and from generation to generation. Repetition functions on this level in the poem because the protagonist (and, through her, the author) relates information that is essential to keeping alive the memory of a people, which includes the legacy of love and caring that conventional historical narratives subjugate.

Thus, repetition also functions in *Song for Anninho* as a way of signifying upon conventional linear histories derived from the factual record. Morrison is again helpful in providing a lens through which to examine historical representations of fact. She writes that the old saying "truth is stranger than fiction" may be "truer than we know, because it doesn't say that truth is truer than fiction; just that it's stranger, meaning that it's odd. It may be excessive, it may be more interesting, but the important thing is that it's random—and fiction is not random" (93). The crucial distinction, then, "is not the difference between fact and fiction, but the distinction between fact and truth. Because facts can exist without human intelligence, but truth cannot" (Morrison 93).

Jones illustrates this in reimagining what I call "the tale of the cliff" in *Song for Anninho*. According to the factual record, during the final assault on Palmares a number of Palmaristas reportedly jumped, were driven, or fell in confusion over a cliff.[11] Relying primarily on Ennes, Kent reports the event this way:

> The breakthrough occurred during the night of February 5-6, 1694. Some two hundred palmaristas fell or hurled themselves—the point has long been debated—"from a rock so high that they were broken to pieces.'"Hand-to-hand combat took another two hundred palmarista lives, and over five hundred 'of both sexes and all ages' were captured and sold outside Pernambuco. Zambi [Zumbi], taken alive and wounded, was decapitated on November 20, 1695. The head was exhibited in public "to kill the legend of his immortality." (187)

Kent is noncommittal about the nature of the plunge, noting the debate among scholars. Relying on "incomplete" documents contained in Arquivo Histórico Colonial, Ennes, on the other hand, characterizes the incident as antiheroic (in relationship to the Palmaristas):

> ...During the second watch of the night, between the fifth and sixth of February, suddenly and tumultuously [Zumby] with all his people and the equipment which could follow him through that space, made an exit. The sentinels of that post did not perceive them almost until the end. In the rearguard Zumby himself was leaving, and at that point he was shot twice. As it was dark, and all this was taking place at the edge of a cliff, many—matter of about two hundred—fell down the cliff. As many others were killed. Of both sexes and ages, five hundred and nineteen were taken prisoner. (209-210)

Ennes's second source is a February 18, 1694, letter from a colonial official to the Overseas Council:

> In this confusion, on that very night, the negroes, in despair, threw themselves against the stockade with which we had encircled their fortification.... A volley of muskets was fired on those who were already outside the encirclement, by which many were killed and so many were wounded that the blood which they shed as they withdrew served as a guide for the troops who followed them. They imprisoned many; and others began to gather again, but mistaking the way, a great part of them hurled themselves from a rock so high that they were broken to pieces. (210–211)

After reporting this particular perspective, Ennes underscores his intent by asserting that it was not by a voluntary effort that "two hundred negroes threw themselves from the top of the cliffs of the Serra do Barriga: it was due to the hastiness of their flight, to the disorder of the retreat, to a fear of violence of the invaders, to a dread of the attackers" (211). In short, according to Ennes, the Palmaristas lost their way in their own neighborhood, and responding like frightened, confused animals, fell over a cliff. In partial contradiction to the above assessment, Ennes also calls the cliff incident a strategic retreat brought on by "lack of organization," and he lambastes Oliveira Martins, Nina Rodrigues, Rocha Pombo, and others who have hailed the efforts of the Palmaristas as heroic. Still, he challenges any claim that Zumbi committed suicide, asserting that he died not "as a victim of the disaster, nor of these wounds, but at the hands of the Paulistas...twenty-two months later, November 20, 1695" (211).[12]

It seems quite possible that the factual record contains a date or dates representing conflations of several assaults, and/or that Zumbi was captured before the final assault on Palmares. Ennes offers no information about why Zumbi's death was delayed, but others suggest (as does Jones's poem) that he escaped and had to be recaptured. In another such interpretation, Ramos takes his account of the cliff incident from Oliviera Martins's "Black Troy," paraphrasing at first that as "the commanding officers of the attacking forces entered the fortified settlement, Zumbi and his principal subalterns took refuge on a rocky promontory. Preferring death to surrender, they threw themselves from the towering precipice" (73). Ramos concludes with a direct quote from Martins: "Valor mixed with brutal fury, it revealed a spectacle to our army which inspired the profoundest awe" (73).

The point here is that what stands as official history has been subjected to human interpretation, and in the process the "truth" has become somewhat obscured. Ramos's description of the event is closest to Jones's retelling, which draws upon the Myth of the Flying Africans and stands in most obvious contrast to Ennes's interpretation and conclusions.[13] Following her pattern of repetition and revision (or improvisation), Jones develops the tale of the cliff in stages. The basic tale of the flying Africans—a tale of spiritual transcendence—concerns Africans victimized by New World slavery who take wing and fly back to Africa. Variations of the story include accounts of Africans leaping over the sides of slave ships during the Middle Passage, and tales of a group of Ibos walking back across the Atlantic to Africa.[14]

In one of her trademark techniques, Jones signals her intent to include the same words, while changing their source, tone, and meaning. She writes, for example, "Think about language./ We will make words out/ of words. We will use/ the same words, but they/ will be different" (47).[15] As a first act, she bestows upon Almeyda the name of both the Pernambucan governor who took office at the pivotal historical moment of 1674, D. Pedro de Almeida, and the infantry colonel in the 1694 destroying force, Matias Cardoso de Almeida. This device, or strategy, functions for Jones in several ways. It endows her protagonist with "official" status, changes the meaning (or historical significance) of the name, and repositions a woman victimized by slavery from a marginalized space to a centralized one.[16]

She utilizes a similar approach in naming Almeyda's husband, Anninho. Anninho is pronounced the same as the singular form of "anninjos," which translates literally to "little angels." "Anninjos," in the context of Brazilian slavery, refers to thumbscrews used to punish or torture enslaved persons. Jones modifies the form of the word to signify in a lover's language what Anninho means to Almeyda. As her "little angel," he is associated with the divine in the tender loving care that characterizes his earthly relationship with her. In the present and future moments of the poem, she is in contact with Anninho only in the spiritual sense. Passages in the poem describe Anninho as a powerful, brave, spiritually complex, caring, gentle giant (14). He is a literate man who has never been enslaved, a free African who joined the Palmaristas in order to serve as their spy against the Portuguese. The other aspects of his character counter negative depictions of black men that have long existed and that continue to exist in American culture. In shaping this hero, however, Jones makes him also human by imagining some of his less desirable qualities and by emphasizing some of the rough spots in his relationship with Almeyda. Bestowing the name Anninho on such a multifaceted human being dramatically alters the meaning of the word "anninjos" in the context of New World slavery.

In reimagining the tale of the cliff, Jones first establishes the setting as a naturally beautiful palm grove situated at the bottom of a stone stairway that God created:

> Do you remember the stairway you showed me?
> The one made out of rock
> and you said that no man had formed it
> That it was formed up from the earth
> by God and no man
> It ran up the side of the cliffs.
> You took my arm.
> You called me your woman. (15)

The setting that Jones imagines is a place where the possibility of spiritual union and ascendancy are expressed; the cliffs overlook the site where lovers come together physically and spiritually to commune in a natural setting. Almeyda and Anninho marry there and become "new," invoking the Eden myth with a twist. Almeyda recalls that,

> We walked up the stone steps
> that he said no man had formed
> that only God himself
> had formed,
> and he spread the blanket,
> and we were married there. (19)

She revisits and revises the information in a later passage. As the conjure woman's herbs begin to loosen her memory further, Almeyda again remembers her wedding day. She tells Zibatra that Anninho is her husband, and they have been together every way that "the spirit, the mind and the body can be" (21). She recalls more intimate details of her wedding ceremony, including Anninho's presentation of the protective amulet, the one that a soldier tore away before slicing off her breasts.

Jones develops the idea of the cliff setting through Almeyda's further references to birds and a dream about making feathers. She remembers dreaming about making, not feathers from birds, but "woman-made" feathers (25). All the women of Palmares were in the cliff setting, sitting on blankets "their men had given them," naked to their waists, making feathers (36). At first she does not understand the meaning of the dream, only that she "made the feathers from nothing" (25). In her dream, she comes to believe that making feathers is the right thing to do even though it is not something she does freely (26). In yet another passage, the two lovers share the following exchange:

> It was as if I was going over the edge of a cliff,
> and you flew down and caught me."
> "Flew?"
> "Yes. And scooped me up in your arms,
> like a bird, like a fierce bird." (43)

Birds play an increasingly prominent role in the poem as stand-ins for Almeyda's murdered and dispersed people, and the sounds they make follow the patterns of recitation and improvisation:

> Those birds. It was like they were
> calling each other. No talking.
> One of their voices was lower than
> the other. One would give two
> sounds and then the other three,
> or the first one would give one sound
> and the other three or four. (57)

Their voices become voices of discord, singing a song too painful and too jumbled to bear:

> In a new voice or the old one,
> we must make our love songs.
> Hear the birds.
> They are making a racket, aren't they?
> they are all singing together.
> They are trying to sing in one voice,
> but one discordant voice,
> one voice with many variations.
> It is a difficult song they are singing.
> It hurts my ears to hear them.
> Why are they all trying to sing at once? (62)

And, finally, the discordant voices merge into "one tight, careful voice":

> The birds are back, Anninho.
> yes.
> They are singing in one voice....
> They are singing in one voice, Anninho.
> They are singing in one tight, careful voice. (79)

Representing the transformed and transcendent Palmaristas, the birds sing in one voice. The reason for the woman-made feathers becomes absolutely clear. They were making plans for transcendence in a deliberate, heroic flight of resistance from physical slavery:

> And didn't the war end like that?
> Only cliffs to be jumped from, or surrender?
> ....And our brave Palmaristas,
> jumping from cliffs rather than surrender.
> Oh, if they could have become birds then!...
> Even now, I watch for birds,
> hoping it's some Palmarista!
> We are blessed because we did not just survive

that, but we survived it loving.
We never stopped loving each other. (36)

Again, Almeyda is the blues singer affirming and reaffirming love in the midst of the physical loss that must be endured and transcended. Jones ultimately conveys that for the people of Palmares, the cliff was a very familiar place—a prominent neighborhood feature, and the place where she realized love for Anninho. It follows that going over the cliff was a deliberate act of transcendence, not a thoughtless, scattered, hurried retreat, as Ennes interprets it.

Almeyda completes her spiritual journey, reuniting with Anninho on that plane. During her journey, she provides deeply personal and intimate revelations about her relationship with her husband, and in the process gives us a chronicle of Palmares.

In a larger sense, of course, Almeyda's blues are the blues of a people bound together by a common source of oppression—the Atlantic Slave Trade—and the tale of the flying Africans functions in Jones's poem as a symbol of collective resistance. Indeed, Almeyda declares that "the blood of the whole continent" runs in her veins (12), and she claims the entire earth as her people's history (10). *Song for Anninho* works through the trauma of violent severance, positing Africa as a spiritual home that accompanies its dispersed peoples throughout the world. Almeyda's severed breasts, floating like globes on the water, returned to their source through healing ritual, symbolize this relationship. Jones has taken a basic fact from the historical record and, following in a tradition of black women writers, changed the meaning of the words to render a tale of spiritual transcendence, of resistance and recovery. She places her narrative alongside other interpretations of the facts, and in the process provides a tale that reappropriates the legacy of a people while reconciling Almeyda's past with her present, and future.

Notes

[1] "Palmares" means "palm forest," "palm grove," or an area with palm trees (Dutra and/or Conrad). Rassner discusses both a long oral tradition and the written tradition flowing from the story of Palmares. See also Orser. Nineteenth–century

American novelist–lecturer–poet Frances Ellen Watkins Harper wrote a poem to the memory of Palmares and Zumbi entitled "Death of Zombi, the Chief of the Negro Kingdom in South America." More significantly, however, Jones uses Palmares in her fiction and poetry (*Corregidora*, 1975, *Song for Anninho*, and *Xarque and Other Poems*, 1985) as a symbol of resistance to New World slavery and its legacy. See Rushdy for a scintillating elaboration of Palmares as site and symbol of resistance in Jones's work.

[2] *Quilombo* refers to a community formed by people escaping from slavery. Though scholars often refer to these settlements as *quilombos*, R. K. Kent notes that the term was not in use in seventeenth–century Brazilian vocabulary. The term in use at the time was the word for "hideout," *mocambo* (or *"mukambo"* in Ambundu). See Kent 174–175.

[3] Writing in 1979 Kent noted that "no written document originating in Palmares has come to light. It probably does not exist" (181). Ramos (65) and Rassner (203) made similar assertions. In recent decades, organizations from all over Brazil have joined to create the Zumbi Memorial. Nascimento described the group's first annual pilgrimage to Serra da Barriga in 1980 as "a movingly momentous experience for all involved." The group proclaimed the anniversary of Zumbi's death (November 20) National Black Consciousness Day. Jones published *Song for Anninho* the following year.

[4] See Kent, Klein, and Ramos, in particular.

[5] For example, the image of Margaret Garner, the Cincinnati woman who succeeded in killing one of her children to keep her from being returned to slavery, provided the impetus for Morrison's Sethe (and the narrative about her) in *Beloved* (1987). Later a funeral photograph of a murdered young Harlem woman serves as the basis for the character Dorcas in *Jazz* (1992). In each case, Morrison is left to imagine the woman's life based on the image and whatever information is available. Jones's creative project in *Song for Anninho* is very similar.

[6] As a narrator telling a story of New World slavery, Almeyda becomes the collective subject. Her "I" is representative of a people in much the same way that, for example, Frederick Douglass's "I" is representative of a people in his 1845 *Narrative*. See Rushdy for a discussion of narrative strategies (specifically "intersubjective communion") in narratives about slavery. See Ralph Ellison's definition of "the blues" in "Richard Wright's Blues," and, more broadly, see Baker, Davis, and Henderson.

[7] Sometime around 1676 (sources differ as to the exact date), Zumbi Sueca led a coup against his uncle Ganga Zumba. "Ganga Zumba," according to Conrad, means Great Lord or Great Master—from the hybrid term "Gangasuma" combining the Bunda word "ganga" and the Tupi Indian word "assu" (360).

[8] Rushdy offers some additional information about the governing structure of Palmares and its mirroring of African pluralistic societies.

[9] Bascom notes that Kimbundu folklore tradition contains only folktales and two types of legends: "maka" and "ma–lunda" or "misendu." "Maka" are entertaining and "intended to be instructive." "Ma–lunda" or "mi–sendu" are historical narratives. They are the "chronicles of the tribe and nation, carefully

preserved and transmitted by the head men or elders of each political unit, whose origin, constitution, and vicissitudes they relate" (13).

[10] See, Harris. Harris's critical review provides much more on the structure and movement of the poem. See also Coser, Dubey, and Munoz–Cabrera for discussions of music, tradition, and mythmaking, respectively.

[11] Depending on the source, the date of the event varies.

[12] According to Ennis, the Ovimbundu people of Angola practiced suicide as a mode of vengeance. The suicide's relatives "must avenge the death by action against the person who caused the suicide"; Ennis notes also that "it is believed that the ghost of a suicide will return to haunt and punish those against whom the suicide has been committed" (159).

[13] See, for example, Chesnutt; "All God's Chillen Had Wings," in Bennett; "The Flying Africans," in Courlander; "The People Could Fly," in Hamilton; and "People Who Could Fly," in Lester. Paule Marshall draws upon the legend in *Praisesong for the Widow* (1983), and Morrison invokes it in her fiction, including *Song of Solomon* (1977) and *Beloved* (1987). For critical discussions of flight in literary works, see Hovet and Lounsberry, and Wilentz.

[14] See, Hurston, Mannix and Cowley, and Porter, in Moon.

[15] For further insights on this strategy among black women writers, see Wall.

[16] Poststructuralist analysis describes this device as an appropriation of the colonial name and thus the center space—the "self"—removing the bearer from the status or realm of the subhuman "other." See, for example, Robinson.

Works Cited

Baker, Houston. "A Dream of American Form: Fictive discourse, Black (W)holes, and a Blues Book Most Excellent." *Blues, Ideology, and African American Literature: A Vernacular Theory.* Chicago: University of Chicago Press, 1984. 113–199.

Bascom, William. "The Forms of Folklore: Prose Narratives." *JAF* 78:1 (1965): 3–20.

Bennett, John, ed. *The Doctor to the Dead: Grotesque Legends and Folk Tales of Old Charleston.* New York: Rinehart, 1943. 139–142.

Chesnutt, Charles W. "Sis' Becky's Pickaninny." 1899. *Collected Stories of Charles W. Chesnutt.* Ed. William L. Andrews. New York: Penguin, 1992. 51–62.

Conrad, Robert Edgar. "Glossary." *Children of God's Fire: A Documentary History of Black Slavery in Brazil.* Princeton, NJ: Princeton University Press, 1983.

Coser, Stelamaris. *Bridging the Americas: The Literature of Paule Marshall, Toni Morrison, and Gayl Jones.* Philadelphia: Temple University Press, 1994.

Courlander, Harold, ed. *A Treasury of Afro–American Folklore.* New York: Crown, 1976; reprt. Marlowe and Company, 1996. 285–286.

Davis, Angela Y. "Introduction." *Blues Legacies and Black Feminism: Gertrude "Ma" Rainey, Bessie Smith, and Billie Holiday.* New York: Vintage/Random House, 1998. xi–xx.

Dubey, Madhu. "Gayl Jones and the Matrilineal Metaphor of Tradition." *SIGNS* 20:2 (Winter 1995): 245–267.

Dutra, Frances A. "Glossary." *A Guide to the History of Brazil 1500–1822.* Santa Barbara: ABC–Clio, 1980.

Ellison, Ralph. "Richard Wright's Blues." *Shadow and Act*, 1953. New York: Random House, Quality Paperback Edition, 1994.

Ennes, Ernesto. "The Palmares 'Republic' of Pernambuco." *The Americas.* Washington, DC: Academy of American Francescan History 5:2 (Oct 1948): 200–201.

Ennis, Merlin. *Umbundu: Folktales from Angola.* Boston: Beacon, 1962.

Glassie, Henry. "Tradition." *JAF*, 108:430 (1995): 401.

Hamilton, Virginia, ed. "The People Could Fly," *The People Could Fly: American Black Folktales.* New York: Knopf, 1985. 166–173.

Harper, Frances Ellen Watkins. "Death of Zombi, the Chief of the Negro Kingdom in South America." *A Brighter Coming Day: A Frances Ellen Watkins Harper Reader.* Ed. Frances Smith Foster. New York: Feminist Press, 1990. 172.

Harris, Trudier. "A Spiritual Journey: Gayl Jones's *Song for Anninho*." *Callaloo* 5:3 (Oct 1982): 106–107.

Henderson, Stephen. "The Blues as Black Poetry." *Callaloo* 16, 5:3 (Oct 1982): 22–30.

Hovet, Grace Ann, and Barbara Lounsberry. "Flying as Symbol and Legend in Toni Morrison's *The Bluest Eye, Sula,* and *Song of Solomon.*" *CLA Journal* 27 (1983):119–140.

Hurston, Zora Neale. "The Last Slave Ship," *The American Mercury* 44:243 (1944) 351–358.

Jones, Gayl. *Song for Anninho*. Detroit: Lotus P, 1981.

———. *Liberating Voices: Oral Tradition in African American Literature.* Cambridge, MA: Harvard University Press, 1991.

Kent, R. K. "Palmares: An African State in Brazil." *Maroon Societies.* Ed. Richard Price. Baltimore: Johns Hopkins, 1979. 174–75.

King, Lovalerie. Gayl Jones's *Song for Anninho*: History and Folklore. M.A. Thesis. Emory University, 1996.

Klein, Herbert S. *African Slavery in Latin America and the Caribbean.* New York: Oxford, 1986.

Lester, Julius, ed. *Black Folktales.* New York: Richard W. Baron, 1969. 147–152.

Mannix, Daniel P., and Malcolm Cowley. *Black Cargoes: A History of the Atlantic Slave Trade, 1518–1865.* New York: Viking, 1967. 118.

Marshall, Paule. *Praisesong for the Widow.* New York: G. P. Putnam and Sons, 1983.

Morrison, Toni. "The Site of Memory." *Inventing the Truth: The Art and Craft of Memoir.* Ed. William Zinsser. Boston: Houghton, 1987, rpt 1995. 83–102.

———. *Beloved.* New York: Knopf, 1987.

———. *Song of Solomon.* New York: Knopf, 1977.

Munoz–Cabrera, Patricia. "(Em)Bodying the Flesh: Mythmaking and the Female Body in Gayl Jones' *Song for Anninho* and *Corregidora*. *PALARA* 1 (Fall 1997): 106–116.

Nascimento, Abdias do and Elisa Larkin Nascimento. *Africans in Brazil: A Pan–African Perspective*. Trenton, NJ: Africa World Press, 1992.

Orser, Charles E., Jr. "Toward a Global Historical Archaeology: An Example from Brazil." *Historical Archaeology* 28:1 (1994) 5–22.

Porter, Kenneth. "Blacks and White Mores: The Flying Africans," *Primer for White Folks*. Ed. Bucklin Moon. Garden City, NY: Doubleday, 1945. 171–176.

Ramos, Arthur. "The Negro Republic of Palmares." *The Negro in Brazil*. Transl. Richard Patee. Washington, DC: Associated Publishers, 1939, rpt. 1951.

Rassner, Ronald M. (for Abdias do Nascimento. "Palmares and the Freed Slave in Afro–Brazilian Literature." *Voices from Under: Black Narrative in Latin America and the Caribbean*. Ed. William Luis. Westport, CT: Greenwood Press, 1984.

Robinson, Sally. "We're All Consequences of Something: Cultural Mythologies of Gender and Race in the Novels of Gayl Jones." *Engendering the Subject: Gender and Self–representation in Contemporary Women's Fiction*. Albany: State University of New York Press, 1991.

Rushdy, Ashraf H. A. "'Relate Sexual to Historical': Race, Resistance, and Desire in Gayl Jones's *Corregidora*." *AAR* 34:2 (Summer 2000) 273–297.

Wall, Cheryl. "Taking Positions and Changing Words." *Changing Our Own Words*. New Brunswick, MJ: Rutgers University Press, 1989.

Wilentz, Gay. "If You Surrender to the Air: Folk Legends of Flight and Resistance in African American Literature," *MELUS* 16:1 (1989–90) 21–32.

Afterword:
Voicing Gayl Jones

Gayl Jones has always been a problem for critics. Both she and her work have been resistant to the categorizations so useful and necessary to the academy. Unlike many of her contemporaries, such as Toni Morrison and John Edgar Wideman, she has not made herself available for interviews or other public opportunities to discuss her work or to engage the commentary on it. Her silence on these and other matters is legendary. And the stories about her that have made the news in recent years have only added to the mystery. Her silence has left readers and critics alone with the texts.

And those texts make very strange company. They often depict sexual behavior and sexual violence in ways that do not appear elsewhere in African American writing or in serious writing generally. *Corregidora* tells the story of the latest descendant of a line of women who are compelled to have daughters in order to pass on the story of an abusive slave owner. The short story "Asylum" is told by a woman abused by the mental health system, though it is also clear that she is in fact insane. "White Rat" concerns a black man who hates his own white skin. *Eva's Man* takes the perspective of a woman who believes herself the object of every man's sexual desire and who speaks from a hospital for the criminally insane because she has sexually dismembered her last male lover. Jones's poetry focuses primarily on the experiences of slavery in Brazil and especially the suffering endured by women in that historical reality. Her most recent novels, *The Healing* (1998) and *Mosquito* (1999), while much more upbeat (at least according to reviewers), make use of a disruptive style in which the narrators shift linguistic registers and whose storytelling technique often borders on free association.

Such narratives (including the poetry) resist our usual interpretive efforts and assumptions. They will not fit into an Afrocentric, uplifting, or universalist mold of African American writing. Race clearly plays a role, but that role is constantly shifting before our eyes. Nor do they fit into feminist or womanist categories without strain. While some of them, for example, are stories of victimization, the questionable sanity of the narrators subverts an ideological reading. Nor does the early work (and perhaps the later work as well, though I am taking a minority position here) offer a clear assurance of female triumph over adversity. Relatedly, Jones's narrators are uncomfortable with lesbianism, perhaps even homophobic, and this is a position that is not challenged within the texts. Finally, the voices of the narratives are usually unlike any we have heard. They have been labeled as blues speakers, but it is the blues tinged with paranoia, with surreal cadences, or with a polysyllabic vocabulary juxtaposed to urban slang.

Much of the criticism published before this volume has tried to place Jones's work into the existing critical boxes regardless of the lack of fit. The result has been a distortion of the work even beyond what our enterprise normally does to literature. She *must* be telling us about racism or the male gaze or white male-originated sexual violence or healing traditions or female bonding or *something* we already know about and can process through our critical procedures.

The achievement of the essayists in this collection, as I see it, beyond the specific insights they offer, is that they work more inductively than deductively. That is, rather than starting with a critical method which they plug the texts into, they start with the singularity of Jones's writing and then try to make sense of it using whatever critical tools seem appropriate. The effect of doing this, I would suggest, is that they expand and challenge some of the operating assumptions of those critical methods. They do for criticism what Jones does for our notions of narrative. A few examples will serve to make the point.

LaMonda Horton-Stallings works through the womanist theme of healing in black women's writing. But rather than simply valorize it as a way of understanding subjectivity, she reads *The Healing* as a divination narrative rather than a therapeutic one. The novel is not part of a blues aesthetic, with the emphasis on suffering, but a creative process in which identity is open rather than fixed, in which the quest is for a language that can adequately express a truly independent self that has many names and many possibilities.

Sakira Chandra signifies on genre criticism by placing *Mosquito* in two categories—the neo-slave narrative and the borderland narrative—in order to subvert the categories. In place of a text which focuses on African American slavery, Jones's novel uses the tropes of that genre to discuss the experiences of undocumented workers. The narrative breaks with assumptions about American history and the racialized identity of readers by showing how generic features can cross boundaries by representing other forms of oppression. At the same time, Chandra points out the problematics of celebratory borderland stories. In contrast to Gloria Anzaldúa's claims that the mestiza is the most liberated of subject positions, Jones's borderland world is one where silence is essential for survival and the true self must often be disguised rather than asserted. It is a place not of knowing, but of secrets and subterfuge. In this sense, the muteness that was the sign of oppression and paranoia in the early works, becomes the condition of both persecution and possibility.

Thomas Fahy examines the theme of lesbianism in several works by Jones, in part because criticism generally has been silent about it. This silence, I would suggest, has to do with the clear and repeated expression of homophobia in the narratives. It is hard to claim Ursa Corregidora for feminism, for example, if one has to engage her views of Cat and Jeffy's relationship. What criticism has done is comparable to the treatment of Teacake's abuse of Janie in *Their Eyes Were Watching God*: pretend it is not there. But, of course, Jones refuses to go along with ideological necessity, and Fahy tries to understand why. What he argues for is Jones's insistence that her female characters are caught in a prison-house of masculinist discourse that prohibits any affirming view of lesbianism or, for that matter, for any version of female desire. The only option for Cat is silence; those who speak—Eva, Ursa, and Winnie of "The Women"—do so in the male language of sexual violence. Ursa is the only one who finds an alternative, a blues voice. Thus, Fahy enables the reader to escape the false binary of either ignoring homophobia in the texts or impugning Jones's womanist credentials because of its presence. He asks us instead to see the art of representation in her fiction.

Finally, perhaps the most intriguing piece here returns us to the question of audience and in the process challenges our often elitist assumptions about what constitutes a serious reading. Megan Sweeney employs reader response to describe the experience of incarcerated women reading *Eva's Man*. Their reactions reveal the impact of telling the suppressed story of abuse. Their identification with Eva is complex in that her reaction to abuse exceeds their sense of acceptable boundaries, but in some sense is understandable. Her articulation of her victimization contrasts with their self-silencing and even denial. The descriptions of her treatment both personally and in the psychological and judicial bureaucracies remind them of the refusals to hear their own stories. Sweeney's approach allows us to contemplate new ways of understanding the experiences of women.

What emerges, then, for this reader, is a renewed sense of the importance of Gayl Jones's work. Her silence pushes us back to the texts, where we belong as readers. And the play of silence and speech, of characters that alternately won't speak and won't shut up, reminds us of the great artistry of her language. What she encourages through that language is the potential of our own efforts to exceed what we assumed to be the boundaries of criticism. Our own voices can be restored through listening to hers.

Keith Byerman
Professor of English
Indiana State University

Contributors

Keith Byerman is Professor of English and Women's Studies and Director of University Honors at Indiana State University. He has published several books, including *Seizing the Word: History, Art, and Self in the Work of W. E. B. Du Bois* and *Remembering the Past in Contemporary African American Fiction*. He is coeditor of *Critical Essays on John Edgar Wideman*.

Sarika Chandra is Assistant Professor of English at Wayne State University. She works in the areas of globalization studies and American cultural studies. She is currently working on a book manuscript that examines theories of globalization in relationship to travel and tourist narratives.

Heather Epes is finishing her Ph.D. at the University of North Carolina, Chapel Hill. Her dissertation draws on liberatory and writing center pedagogies to develop relational and student-directed teaching methods. Literary interests include history and cultural influence of American pulp fiction, especially comics, film noir and gothic stylings, and science fiction film and TV. She has published "New Century Coolbooks: Comics as the Font of Immediate Experience" and a review of Maxine Hong Kingston's *The Fifth Book of Peace* in *Paste Magazine*. Her current article project examines layered texts and semiotics in graphic novels.

Thomas Fahy is Assistant Professor of English and Director of the American Studies Program at Long Island University. He has written several books, including *Freak Shows and the Modern American Imagination* (Palgrave Macmillan 2006), a monograph on Gabriel Garcia Marquez (Continuum 2003), and two novels, *The Unspoken* (Simon and Schuster 2007) and *Night Visions* (HarperCollins 2004). He is also the editor of several essay collections on film and contemporary theater—*Considering Alan Ball* (McFarland 2006), *Considering Aaron Sorkin* (McFarland 2005), *Captive Audience* (Routledge 2003), and *Peering Behind the Curtain* (Routledge 2002).

Trudier Harris is J. Carlyle Sitterson Professor of English at the University of North Carolina at Chapel Hill. She has published numerous books, including *Saints, Sinners, Saviors: Strong Black Women in African American Literature* and *Fiction and Folklore: The Novels of Toni Morrison*. Her memoir, *Summer Snow: Reflections from a Black Daughter of the South*, appeared in 2003; it was used to inaugurate the One-Book, One-Community Reading Program in Chapel Hill and Orange County, North Carolina. In 2005, she received the University of North Carolina System Board of Governors' Award for Excellence in Teaching as well as the John Hurt Fisher Award from SAMLA for "distinguished achievement" over the course of her career.

Lovalerie King is Assistant Professor of African American Literature at Penn State-University Park. She has published numerous articles, essays, and reviews on African American literature in such publications as *The Cambridge Companion to the African American Novel*, *MELUS*, *African American Review*, *Callaloo*, *The Oxford Companion to African American Literature*, and others. Her coedited collection, *James Baldwin and Toni Morrison: Comparative Critical and Theoretical Essays* is forthcoming from Palgrave/MacMillan. Her ongoing projects include a book-length study of African American literature's critique of American law (LSU), an introduction to Zora Neale Hurston (Cambridge), and a coedited collection of essays on the African American novel.

Fiona Mills is Assistant Professor of English and Women's Studies at Curry College. Her essays have appeared in *CLA Journal*, *Safundi: Journal of South African and American Comparative Studies* and *Americana: The Institute for the Study of American Popular Culture*. She recently published "Depictions of the U.S. Military – Only 'a few good men' need apply" in *Deceptive Words: The Poetics and Politics of Aaron Sorkin* as well as "Seeing Ethnicity: The Impact of Race and Class on the Critical Reception of Miguel Piñero's *Short Eyes*" in *Captive Audience: Prison and Captivity in Contemporary Theater*.

CONTRIBUTORS

Keith B. Mitchell is Assistant Professor of English and Ethnic Literatures at the University of Massachusetts at Lowell. His main concentration of study is Francophone and Anglophone Caribbean literature and African American literature. He has published "Naming That Which Dare Not Speak: Homosexual Desire in Joseph Zobel's *La rue cases nègres*" in *Rhetoric of the Other* (2002) and entries on Paule Marshall in *The Oxford Companion to African American Literature* (1997). Articles to be published in 2006 include: "All Our Yesterdays" in *Changing Currents: Anglophone, Francophone, and Hispaniophone Literary and Cultural Criticism*, and "Femininity, Abjection, and (Black) Masculinity in James Baldwin's *Giovanni's Room* and Toni Morrison's *Beloved*" in *James Baldwin and Toni Morrison: Comparative Critical and Theoretical Essays*. He is currently completing an essay entitled "Multiculturalism and the Cultural Mulatto in Andrea Lee's *Sarah Phillips*."

Howard Rambsy's most recent achievement—that of curator of *Visualizing Black Writers: An Extra-literary Exhibit from the Eugene B. Redmond Collection*—reflects his combined interests in African American literature and mixed media art. Currently, he teaches literature and composition at Southern Illinois University-Edwardsville, and is completing a project on canon formation and black arts poetry.

L.H. Stallings is Assistant Professor of English at the University of Florida in Gainesville. Her areas of research and teaching are African American literature and folklore, black cultural studies, and gender and sexuality studies.

Megan Sweeney is Assistant Professor of English at the Center for AfroAmerican and African Studies at the University of Michigan. She has recently published essays in *Modern Fiction Studies*; *Feminist Studies*; *Meridians: Feminism, Race, Transnationalism*; *Genre: Forms of Discourse and Culture*; and *Discourse: Journal for Theoretical Studies in Media and Culture*. Megan's book project weaves together ethnographic and literary analysis in exploring cultures of reading in women's prisons.

Jill Terry is Head of English and Cultural Studies at University College Worcester, UK. Her Ph.D. thesis examined Gayl Jones's writing as one of its case studies. Her main research interest is the relationship between orality and literature, especially in relation to music. She has published work on Alice Walker in *Critical Survey* and has contributed a chapter on Oral Culture and Literature in the *Blackwell's Companion to the Literature and Culture of the American South.*

Shubha Venugopal is Assistant Professor at Kutztown University of Pennsylvania. She completed her dissertation at the University of Michigan on African American women writers. She continues to pursue her work on the complex interactions between black women and their communities and on the nature of female friendships as represented in black women's novels. Her areas of interest include African American literature, postcolonial literature, ethnic American literature, and creative writing.

AFRICAN AMERICAN LITERATURE AND CULTURE

EXPANDING AND EXPLODING THE BOUNDARIES

General Editor
Carlyle V. Thompson

The purpose of this series is to present innovative, in-depth, and provocatively critical literary and cultural investigations of critical issues in African American literature and life. We welcome critiques of fiction, poetry, drama, film, sports, and popular culture. Of particular interest are literary and cultural analyses that involve contemporary psychoanalytical criticism, new historicism, deconstructionism, critical race theory, critical legal theory, and critical gender theory.

For additional information about this series or for the submission of manuscripts, please contact:

Peter Lang Publishing, Inc.
Acquisitions Department
275 Seventh Avenue, 28th floor
New York, New York 10001

To order other books in this series, please contact our Customer Service Department:

(800) 770-LANG (within the U.S.)
(212) 647-7706 (outside the U.S.)
(212) 647-7707 FAX

Or browse online by series:

www.peterlangusa.com

www.ingramcontent.com/pod-product-compliance
Lightning Source LLC
Chambersburg PA
CBHW050121020526
44112CB00035B/2240